Guiltless Catholic Parenting From A to Y*

Also by Bert Ghezzi

50 Ways to Tap the Power of the Sacraments

Keeping Your Kids Catholic

The Angry Christian

Facing Your Feelings

Sharing Your Faith

Becoming More Like Jesus

Transforming Problems

Getting Free

Build With the Lord

Guiltless Catholic Parenting from A to Y*

**Nobody Knows Everything There Is to Know, But Here's Wisdom to Help You Do It Well*

Bert Ghezzi

Servant Publications
Ann Arbor, Michigan

Charis Books is an imprint of Servant Publications especially designed to serve Roman Catholics.

The editor and authors have made every effort to protect the privacy of individuals whose stories are told in this book. Some accounts have been fictionalized by combining facts and persons from actual events, and when necessary names have been changed so that subjects cannot be identified.

Published by Servant Publications
P.O. Box 8617
Ann Arbor, Michigan 48107

Cover design by Gerald Gawronski

99 10 9 8 7 6 5 4

Printed in the United States of America
ISBN 0-89283-892-2

Library of Congress Cataloging-in-Publication Data

Guiltless Catholic parenting from A to Y / [edited by] Bert Ghezzi.
p. cm.
Includes bibliographical references
ISBN 0-89283-892-2
1. Parenting—Religious aspects—Catholic Church. 2. Christian education of children. I. Ghezzi, Bert.
BX2352.G85 1995
248.8'45'08822—dc20 95-9337
CIP

Contents

THREE / TALKING TO GOD

Praying with children and for them not only makes family life go much better. It makes it last forever because it prepares us for eternal life.

FOUR / MEET JESUS IN THE SACRAMENTS

Parents must show their children that worship does not end on Sunday morning but extends into daily Christian living.

FIVE / COMPASSION BEGINS AT HOME

The more the members of a Christian family reach out to serve others, the more is love multiplied among them.

Acknowledgments

My wife and children feign disinterest in the stories I tell about them to illustrate our family successes and failures. But now and then I catch one of them scanning pages to find where he or she is mentioned. As a writer I appreciate the perspective their pretended distance creates and the support of their affectionate curiosity. Their love makes my life worthwhile.

Thanks to the librarians of Barry University, Miami Shores, Florida, who helped me mine magazines and books to find some of the jewels I share here.

I am grateful to my editors—Heidi Hess and Louise Bourassa Perrotta—who rooted out every error they found. Any mistakes that are left are mine alone.

My cap is off to Diane Bareis, who gave the book a handsome design. I also salute Gerry Gawronski, my gifted friend, who created the covers for this book and its predecessor, *Keeping Your Kids Catholic.*

And a special word of gratitude to my friends Juli Godeen, Mary Graulich, Peg VandeVoorde and Sharon Zielinski, who carefully put all the words you will read into type.

Contributors

Thanks to the following writers whose honest sharing and good counsel give us hope for our families. I suspect if we pool their wisdom we may even find the *Z* of no-guilt Catholic parenting.

Janet Alampi has seven years' teaching experience in a Catholic high school and was principal for five years in a Catholic all-girls' school. She is currently managing editor of *The Catholic Transcript*, Hartford, Connecticut. She and her husband, Frank, have two small children.

Mark Berchem is executive director of NET Ministries, Inc. National Evangelization Teams trains and sends young Catholic men and women to evangelize teens in parishes and dioceses throughout the world.

Therese Boucher is a religious educator and author. She is a consultant for CHARISM, an institute for spirituality and ministry in the Diocese of Rockville Centre, New York. She and her husband, John, are the parents of five children.

Fr. Edward Buelt is vice-chancellor of the Archdiocese of Denver, Colorado.

Ann Carey is a widely published, award-winning writer and a teacher. She and her husband live in Indiana and are parents of three children.

Dolores Curran has written on family and parenting issues for many years. She is a syndicated columnist and author of many books. She won the Christopher Award for *Traits of a Healthy Family* (Harper & Row).

Sr. Thérèse Del Genio, a Sister of Notre Dame de Namur, is a certified senior addiction counselor for Illinois. She has served as director of field placement and as an adjunct faculty member for The Catholic Theological Union of Chicago.

Bill Dodds is an author of many books for both adults and children, including *Dads, Catholic Style* (Servant) and *Bedtime Parables* (Our Sunday Visitor). With his wife, Monica, he writes a family column for *Columbia* magazine. Together they wrote *The Joy of Marriage* (Meadowbrook Press), and they present seminars on marriage, family life and caring for aging parents.

Richard F. Easton is professor of English at Washington and Jefferson College, Washington, Pennsylvania. He and his wife, Patricia, have three children.

Kathy and Mitch Finley have three sons. Together they served for five years as directors of the Family Life Office of the Diocese of Spokane. The Finleys have written many books, including *Christian Families in the Real World* (Thomas More Press).

Keith Fournier is executive director of The American Center for Law and Justice and is the founder and president of Liberty, Life and Family. He is the author of numerous books, including *A House United?* (NavPress) and *Bringing Christ's Presence into Your Home* (Thomas Nelson).

Mary Bahr Fritts is the author of humorous articles and several childrens' books, including *The Memory Box*. She and her husband, Bill, have six sons and an outstanding sense of humor.

Patricia L. Fry has written many books and articles and teaches others to write well. She has three daughters and six grandchildren.

Fr. Dale J. Fushek is pastor of St. Timothy's Church, Mesa, Arizona. He is the founder of LIFE TEEN, an evangelistic program for teens that is centered around the Eucharist. LIFE TEEN is now in three hundred parishes across the country, and growing.

Fr. Fred Gaglia, Ph.D., is pastor of Sacred Heart Church in Etiwanda, California, where he sponsors a flourishing LIFE TEEN program.

Fr. Benedict Groeschel, C.F.R., is director of spiritual development for the Archdiocese of New York and a frequent host of series on Eternal Word Television Network. His many books include *Heaven in Our Hands, Spiritual Passages* and *A Still Small Voice.*

Ray Guarendi, Ph.D., is a clinical psychologist who specializes in parenting and family issues. Nationally known as a speaker and syndicated columnist, he is the author of *Back to the Family* (Villard Books) and *You're a Better Parent Than You Think!* (Fireside).

Peter Herbeck and his wife, Debbie, have four children and have worked in youth ministry for the past ten years. Peter is the missions director for Renewal Ministries.

Angela Elwell Hunt is a popular author of adult and youth fiction who lives in Seminole, Florida. She and her husband work in teen youth ministry. Her fiction series include *The Theyn Chronicles* for adults and *The Colonial Captives* for young people.

Neta Jackson is a free-lance writer. She and her husband, Dave, share their Chicago home with two teenage daughters, assorted pets and numerous teenage friends.

Ron Keller is a Ph.D. in Christian counseling and psychology. He is the author of ten books, including *Twelve Steps to a New Day* (Thomas Nelson). Ron is married in a blended family with five children.

Molly Kelly is a Philadelphia homemaker, single parent, author and lecturer. She speaks to more than fifty thousand teens annually throughout the United States and Canada, inviting them to choose chastity as the way to health and happiness. She has raised six sons and two daughters and has provided a home to five pregnant teens.

Mary Ann Kuharski is a free-lance writer, homemaker and mother of thirteen children, ages five to twenty-five, six of whom are adopted and of mixed races. She is the author of *Raising Catholic Children* and *Parenting With Prayer* (Our Sunday Visitor).

Wendy Leifeld and Martin, her husband, have four children. She is a regular columnist in *Catholic Parent* magazine and author of *Mothers of the Saints* (Servant).

Paul R. Leingang and Jane, his wife, are presidents of the Christian Family Movement. They have two college-age sons. Paul is editor of *The Message* and director of communications for the Diocese of Evansville, Indiana. His column, *Taking the Time to Make a Difference,* is syndicated in the Catholic press.

Patricia Lorenz is a single parent, mother of four children. She is an acclaimed free-lance writer of more than three hundred articles, many of which have appeared in *Guideposts* and *Reader's Digest.*

Patti Gallagher Mansfield and Al, her husband, are internationally recognized leaders in the Catholic charismatic renewal. They have four children. Patti's most recent book is *As By a New Pentecost* (Franciscan University Press).

Eileen C. Marx is a syndicated columnist who lives in Maryland with her husband and two small children.

Elizabeth McNamer teaches religious studies at Rocky Mountain College in Billings, Montana. She is a free-lance writer and lecturer and has several videos in national circulation. She and her husband of thirty-three years have five grown children, all of whom are practicing Catholics.

Michael Medved is cohost of the weekly PBS series, *Sneak Previews,* and the author of seven books, including the recent best-seller, *Hollywood vs. America* (Harper Collins).

Catherine M. Odell has been a writer in the Catholic press for eighteen years. Her many books include *The First Human Right* and *Those Who Saw Her: The Apparitions of Mary* (Our Sunday Visitor).

Leslie Payne is a homeschooling single parent, free-lance writer and editor of *The Catholic Home Educator,* the magazine of the National Association of Catholic Home Educators.

Meg Raul is the mother of ten children and a free-lance writer.

Sr. Ann Regan is principal of the Academy of the Holy Names in Tampa, Florida.

Ann Shields is an evangelist, author and popular conference speaker. She has worked many years in youth ministry. Currently she serves as a speaker and writer with Renewal Ministries.

Paul Thigpen and Leisa, his wife, have two children. They are also coauthors of *52 Simple Ways to Build Family Traditions* (Oliver Nelson).

Lisa and Steve Walker are the parents of two children. They are nationally recognized youth ministers who speak frequently at conferences and consult with parishes and dioceses. Steve and Lisa are founders of the Catholic Work Camps and coauthors of *Are We Having Fun Yet?* (TEL Publishers, Ltd.). Lisa's most recent book is *Women in Youth Ministry* (Don Bosco Multimedia)

ONE

No-Guilt Catholic Parenting

No, this is not an oxymoron. Catholic parents can raise kids in the faith without feeling guilty, if they faithfully do a few things that are important but easy to accomplish.

Catholic Parenting Without Guilt—*Oh, Really?!*

How to get the most out of this book

Bert Ghezzi

"Now, sisters and brothers, let's welcome our little candidates," said Father Joe. He signalled the young couple to bring their children forward to the baptismal font.

Mary and Bob had just recently returned to the Catholic church after several years of inactivity. Today their two children, two-month-old Carla and two-year-old Scott, were to be baptized during mass. Bob and Mary were sitting in the back pew because they thought the children might be fussy.

At the priest's invitation, they swept the little ones into their arms and started down the center aisle. But young Scott began to squirm, vigorously resisting the move. To calm him Mary whispered words of comfort in his ear.

"It's all right, Scottie," she said. "Father Joe's going to bless you and you are going to become a Catholic." It didn't work.

All the way to the front, Scott screamed, "But I don't want to be a *Cath-o-lic!* I don't want to be a *Cath-o-lic!*"

A lot of our kids are like Scott. Many resist our efforts to raise them Catholic. Some come into the church kicking and screaming. Others don't make it. Like Bob and Mary, they drift away for one reason or another.

And we, the battle-scarred, war-weary parents—how do we feel? Tired. Worn down. Discouraged. Guilty.

Especially *guilty*. All the while we are raising our kids, we feel like we could be doing more to introduce them to the faith. We think maybe we should be doing something differently. We compare ourselves to parents who seem to be doing better. We look back and recriminate. "Maybe," we think, "we should have taken a second mortgage and sent Tom to a Catholic college."

We Catholics are famous for our guilt. We're good at it. That's why the idea of *guiltless* Catholic parenting may strike us as strange. But no-guilt Catholic parenting is not an oxymoron, an impossible combination of contradictions like "jumbo shrimp."

Quite the contrary! *Guiltless* Catholic parenting is the way it should be. Here are two reasons that I'll explain more fully in articles below:

- God does not hold parents accountable for their kids' decisions. He gave our children free wills so that they could make their own faith choices. All he expects parents to do is our best job of pointing the way to faith. We're just supposed to prepare our children to choose rightly, not choose for them. If we do what we can as best we can, there's no guilt and thus no reason to feel guilty.

- To do a good job of raising our kids Catholic, we don't need to do a lot of things. We don't need, for example, to control every detail of our kids' lives. We only need to do a few things faithfully to form them as Catholics. Like introducing them to Catholic practices, teaching them to pray, talking to them about our experience of God and other actions we'll discuss in this book. We don't even need to be exemplary religious educators, let alone saints, to perform the task well. All the Lord wants is our best effort.

Aiming to do only the important things will give your family a Catholic shape. It works like aiming an arrow at a target. Focusing on the bull's-eye gives the arrow a certain arc. As the arrow moves through the air it carves out a shape called a *trajectory*. When we focus on our "bull's-eye"—doing the important things—we give our family a certain shape. That "trajectory" is a Catholic way of living that will communicate the faith to our children.

You can hang on to your guilt, if you like. But my wife and I put ours down a long time ago. Mary Lou and I gave ourselves permission to be guilt-free Catholic parents. Here are some truths we discovered that helped us:

- *Family life is messy.* So don't expect your religious education efforts to be flawless. They will be messy too.
- *To raise kids Catholic you don't have to do everything perfectly.* Just do some things consistently as well as you can.
- *When circumstances foul up your well-laid plans, laugh a little.* A good sense of humor fosters a family's growth in faith.
- *It's OK to start over as many times as you need to.* No one is counting failed efforts except you. When something doesn't work, try something new or take a different approach.
- *Let the Holy Spirit carry his part of the load.* His is a big piece of the effort and he wants to do it. Don't try to do God's work for him. He can handle it. Mary Lou and I want to hand on the faith to our four sons and three daughters. We struggle along, doing what we can to nudge them in the right direction. But we do it guiltlessly.

Now, here's a problem. This book, which I intended to free parents of guilt, could cause you to feel more guilty. I hate books that do that to me. You could let the sheer volume of good suggestions contained here overwhelm you. Or you could get the mistaken notion that I and the other writers are the *perfect* Catholic parents that you could never measure up to. This manual that was supposed to defuse your guilt *could* make you feel worse.

So I took some steps to prevent this. First, as you read this you won't bump into any "experts" who offer theories that are guaranteed to work. I did not invite any *perfect Catholic parents* to write articles. The only parents who contributed to this book are normal moms and dads who can share practical wisdom learned from successes *and failures.*

I have also designed the book so that you won't feel as though you need to implement all the ideas that strike you. You couldn't accomplish them all in this lifetime anyway. And you don't need to. Remember, you can raise your kids Catholic guiltlessly by consistently doing a few important things.

A word of encouragement to my single-parent readers. Single parents seem more susceptible to feeling guilty than couples. Your job is twice as hard because you wear two hats. So it's very easy for you to feel like you're not doing very well at raising your kids Catholic. But you can successfully take the approach suggested here. Just select a few important things and keep on doing them. It should bring you hope.

The secret that makes guiltless Catholic parenting possible is the Holy Spirit. We parents just raise the sails. The breath of the Spirit wafts our families home to the Lord and his church.

Suggestions for Using This Book

You can read *Guiltless Catholic Parenting from A to Y** on your own. Or couples can read it together. A single parent can read it alone or with another single parent or friend. The book is tailored both for personal and for group use.

For Personal Use

1. You can turn directly to topics important to you. Or you can work through the book systematically from cover to cover.

2. Use the questions *For Discussion* and *For Reflection* at the end of each article. They will help you assess your personal and family situations. They will also give you action ideas for steps you can consider implementing in your family.
3. As you read through the articles, keep track of ideas that catch your attention. You can record them on the Action Idea Lists that appear in *Think, Pray & Act* at the end of each chapter. Or write them in your journal or a notebook.
4. Be determined to choose only one idea at a time. The action you select should meet these two criteria. The idea must be:
    a. important to you and to your family
    b. easy to accomplish
5. At any point you may bump into an idea that "fits" and decide to do it. Or you may decide to keep track of all the suggestions that appeal to you, then use the *Action Idea List* and *Decision Grid* to sort through your possibilities. (Instructions for using the *Action Idea List* and the *Decision Grid* are at the end of this chapter, beginning on page 36.)
6. Members of two-parent teams must discuss action ideas with their spouses. Single parents will find it helpful to talk over their ideas with another single parent or a friend. If for some reason your spouse is not involved in raising your children Catholic, you may find some useful advice in the article, "When Daddy (or Mommy) Doesn't Go to Church," page 59.
7. You may use the Action Plans to ensure that you cover all the bases when you plan to implement an idea. These forms are located in *Think, Pray & Act* on pages 41-43.
8. Don't forget that the Holy Spirit is your partner in the enterprise of educating your kids in the faith. Be sure to ask his guidance in selecting an appropriate action. Pray for his direction and support in making it happen.
9. Once you have accomplished your goal and implemented the

idea, you can start over. Choose another easy-to-accomplish action that's important to you and do it.

10. Doing a few important things one at a time will make you successful, give you hope and keep you free of guilt.

For Group Use

11. *Guiltless Catholic Parenting from A to Y** is also designed for groups. It is ideal for adult education programs or for Catholic family groups.
12. Questions *For Discussion* and *For Reflection* follow every article, except those that are lists of action ideas. Groups or classes can read articles before meeting and use these questions to stimulate discussion.
13. See the article, "A Pattern for a Catholic Family Group," page 250, for ideas on parents' meetings. Participants will find regular sharing with other parents very encouraging. We're all strugglers and need the support of friends.
14. Most Catholic family groups combine prayer and study with sharing about family life and fellowship. Group members will gradually become more comfortable with each other and develop some mutual commitment. As that happens members may consider making themselves accountable to the group for implementing their action ideas.

Bert Ghezzi

God Has No Grandkids

God himself has taken the guilt out of Catholic parenting by giving our children the freedom to choose him, or not.

Bert Ghezzi

The proof of the pudding, they say, is in the eating. In most cases that's true. When we are making anything, the test of our effort is the final product. Mary Lou's "orange-juice rolls" are a family breakfast favorite. But if they don't come out just right, she gets questions like, "Did you put in too much applesauce?" or "Was the oven set too high?" When the ingredients are right and the recipe is followed exactly, we expect the results to be perfect.

> Mary Lou Ghezzi's
> Orange Juice Rolls
>
> 1 c. canned applesauce
> 1 tbls. grated orange rind
> 2 tbls. orange juice concentrate
> 1/2 c. butter or margarine
> 1/2 c. brown sugar
> 1 tube of 10-12 brown & serve biscuits
>
> Mix the first five ingredients. Pour into a buttered 9 x 12-inch baking dish. Top with brown and serve biscuits. Bake according to instructions on package.

But this rule does not hold in the matter of handing on the faith to children. Parents can follow their "recipe" exactly and still have mixed results. One family I know has four adult children. At present, one is an active Catholic, one an inactive Catholic, one a member of a non-denominational fellowship and one an atheist in jail on drug charges. The mom and dad worked hard to raise their children Catholic. All the right ingredients, all the right steps, but somehow things didn't turn out the way they were supposed to.

Looking at these "products" does not provide a fair basis for judging the parents' efforts. The children's faith is not the proof of the parenting. The factor that disproves the rule is human freedom. Parents can do everything to influence their children. Pray. Teach. Exhort. Nudge. Pressure. Punish. But in the end the children must make their own faith choices. We can lead our kids to the water of life, but we cannot make them drink.

> **Mary Lou and Bert Ghezzi's Recipe for Raising Children Catholic**
>
> - Do everything possible to introduce the child to the Lord.
> - Form the child in Catholic faith and culture.
> - Build a resilient family relationship based on love and forgiveness.
> - Rely on the Catholic community for help.
> - Pray fervently, expecting the Lord to act.
>
> Taking these steps will prepare a child to make the right faith choices. The rest is up to the child and to God.

It would be nice, wouldn't it, if we could hand on the faith to our kids like we do physical traits? Wouldn't it have been reasonable for God to arrange for all the offspring of faithful Catholics to follow suit? Maybe, but that's not how the Lord has set things up. God has no grandchildren, as David duPlessis, the great Pentecostal evangelist, used to say. God relates to every one of his creatures personally, inviting them one by one into his family. That free choice to follow him and to belong to his church is what God wants. So the Lord has only sons and daughters. No grandkids.

I know some Catholic parents who cultivate guilt feelings because a child has left the church. They second-guess all their good efforts. "Maybe I wasn't a good enough example," they might say. Or, "Maybe we should have used our savings to send her to a Catholic college." When they learn that "God has no grandchildren," they should feel grace pouring all over them.

The Lord is not going to judge parents by the choices their children make. He will judge our children on their choices. He will judge parents only on how well we prepared them to make the right choices.

What the Lord wants is that we do the best we know how and let him do the rest. We should work as though raising our kids Catholic depends entirely on us and pray as though it depends entirely on God. Because it does. The proof of our parenting is in the praying.

For Discussion

1. What does it mean to say that "God has no grandkids?"
2. What are parents responsible for in handing on the faith to children?

For Reflection

1. Do I tend to judge how well I have done as a Catholic parent by the choices my kids make?
2. Do I feel guilty about any of the choices I have made in preparing my kids for faith?
3. When the Lord judges me as a parent, what do I think he will be looking for?

On-Purpose Parents

If we want our children to grow up as disciples of Christ, we must act deliberately to introduce them to the Lord and the church.

Bert Ghezzi

My mother made great sacrifices to raise her kids Catholic. She was a single parent who did without many things so she could send four of us to Catholic schools. She was generous, and her life was hard. Her strategy for handing on the faith to us was simple—she let the parish do it. We had a very wholesome family life. But my mom did not have to do much at home to ensure our Catholic formation. She got us to school early so that we could be at daily mass, and we never missed Sunday worship. She let the parish do the rest.

In the 1950s hers was a reasonably good approach. Back then parishes seemed to transform little pagans into little Catholics almost automatically. We were members of St. Anne Church in Castle Shannon, Pennsylvania, a fast-growing suburban parish south of Pittsburgh. My mom entrusted us to the care of a dozen Sisters of Divine Providence and a team of three priests. The parish culture did its job. It gave me a good Catholic education and a peer group of Catholic friends.

My mom's strategy won't work for Catholic parents in the 1990s. Society has changed and so has the church. When I was a kid, society was stable. For a quarter of a century our family lived in the same house, surrounded by Catholic relatives and friends. That secure social environment let the parish system work relatively well.

Today things are much different. Our highly mobile society makes it much harder to raise our kids Catholic. For example, over the past thirty years my family has lived in seven different houses in four cities. We now belong to a parish of nearly ten thousand members that has a 30 percent annual turnover.

This social mobility and other forces have radically changed our parishes. Present day Catholic culture no longer "automatically" keeps kids Catholic. Statistics show that of the many young people who left the church in the 1980s, 91 percent attended Sunday mass regularly when they were growing up, and 75 percent spent at least five years in Catholic schools. That's not an indictment of parishes or Catholic schools. It's an indication that something more is needed today. That something is the leadership of parents in the home.

If we don't introduce our kids to the Lord and the church at home, very likely they will not grow up to be adult Catholic Christians. We must faithfully attend to a few things that will introduce our families to Catholic ways and instruct them in Catholic truths. Things like telling kids about our own relation to God, having family prayer times, creating customs that celebrate the liturgical year, studying the Bible and lives of the saints, interesting kids in the sacraments and involving them in Christian service.

Raising kids Catholic requires that we be deliberate about it. Or it won't happen. We must be *on-purpose* parents. Kevin McCarthy's helpful book, *The On-Purpose Person* (Piñon Press), focused me on the task. Sometimes I feel immobilized by the gigantic responsibility of handing on the faith. I get overwhelmed by the apparent multitude of actions required to keep my kids Catholic. I am tempted to feel guilty about not doing enough. But Kevin taught me to prioritize my actions, to select the most important one, and to do it repeatedly until it becomes a habit. Limiting myself to attempting only what's both important and possible helps me succeed and nips guilt in the bud.

Now I regularly make long lists of possible actions. From them I choose the one that will make the biggest contribution to my family's Catholic life. Right now my list includes these hot items: renewing family prayer time, teaching spontaneous prayer, explaining the meaning of the mass, increasing use of the sacrament of reconciliation and encouraging Bible study. I think I am going to work on the family prayer time first. That will give me a captive audience for tackling my other concerns.

For Discussion

1. Why is it not possible for parents to leave forming their kids Catholic to the parish?
2. What does it mean to be an *on-purpose* parent?

For Reflection

1. Do I take a deliberate approach to handing on the faith to my children?

2. What purposeful steps am I taking now?
3. Am I trying too much or too little? What can I do differently?

What Do Catholic Kids Need?

Nine needs that parents can meet, even if they're busy

Ron Keller

How can we parents give kids our best when we have so many other commitments?

Many young people in America are in great pain. Worse still, they medicate this pain with television, videos, electronic games and other "things." But they do know that things alone are not enough. They know that human relationships, too, are important. And they feel cheated if they don't have them—especially with their parents.

I'm the father of five children, four of them teenagers. Both my wife and I work full time. We know our kids deserve to have good relationships with us, that we need to make them the top priority in our lives.

It's a tough balancing act. But by spending just a few minutes each day, we've discovered that we can meet our kids' basic needs. Though we will never be perfect parents, we can give our kids what they deserve.

By using the acronym **C-A-T-H-O-L-I-C-S**, I have identified nine simple things I believe children deserve. And we *can* give these things to our kids, even when we are busy.

C = Caring

Our kids deserve to have their physical needs cared for. Providing meals, laying out their clothes, making sure they've showered, and helping them with their homework are just a few ways that we can care for our kids. If we are too busy to do these simple things, we are too busy. Perhaps God is trying to speak to us about the need for better scheduling and anticipating, or for a change in our lifestyle.

A = Attention

Every kid longs for and needs attention. If parents don't provide it, kids will find it elsewhere—sometimes in unacceptable ways. From early on, kids are good at letting us know about this need. So if we pay attention, we will know when it is important to stop what we're doing and find out what's happening with them.

Our kids are pleading for us to ask them, "What is life really like for you today?" They want to answer that question, but they won't until they know they have our undivided attention.

T = Teaching

Most kids can tell you more about most baseball players than they can about apostles or saints. In many cases, though, that's not their fault.

Kids need to know that Christ is the way, the truth, and the life. Early on and all the way through their lives, they need to be taught about God and the Scriptures. And, in cooperation with the church, parents have the joyous assignment of accomplishing this part of their children's education.

This does not take much time or skill. A few minutes each day devoted to conversational prayer or Scripture around the table is all it takes for kids to get the message that faith in God is important.

H = Hugs

Our kids deserve our admiration, affirmation and affection. All kids deserve to be held and hugged each day—not just because they have ***done*** something special, but because they ***are*** something special.

O = Oasis

Home for kids should be a safe place where they will be accepted for what they are and encouraged to be who they are.

Life can be difficult for kids. Home needs to be the place they can return to for assurance that they are OK, the place where they are protected from unhealthy and threatening behaviors and ideas. Parents help kids feel safe, not only physically but psychologically and spiritually, by providing boundaries and rules.

Another important part of this, I believe, is the need for daily prayer for our family and each of our children.

L = Love

Have you ever met a kid who's been loved too much? Kids need clear verbal, written and physical expressions of love. Say it over and over in different ways. Ask your kids if they are convinced. Joke about it with them. But be sure that their young hearts are saturated with love.

I = Individual Time

This could be the remedy to most family problems. A regular fifteen-minute private time with your kid could change his or her life. This time lets kids know they are important, that you care about every dimension of their lives.

Invest time with your kids, individually, just as you do with your adult friends. Life is relationship. When relationships are good, life is good. Individual time will give kids the platform to share feelings with us, and our relationships will grow deeper and stronger.

C = Corrections

Kids need parents who care enough to appropriately discipline them. *No* can be the best word some kids could hear.

Kids need help in learning to discern right from wrong. Catholic parents, especially, will need to correct some incorrect teaching our kids have received at school or from friends. We can also encourage our kids to evaluate what they see on television, in movies and in life, in the light of their faith.

S = Service

Like Jesus, parents must be servants. Not doormats, but servants. There is a difference.

A servant has willingly given his or her life to Christ and allows the Holy Spirit to guide every aspect of daily parenting. This person knows how to help kids appropriately with things that they cannot do on their own.

A servant prays for his or her children through the day, seeking

God's protection and guidance. When kids see Jesus at work in and through us, they see a model for their own lives. Kids deserve our best. They deserve to see God at work in their lives. Kids deserve parents who are *Catholics.*

For Discussion

What do you think children need most to help them embrace faith in God? Why?

For Reflection

1. Which of the kids' needs listed here do I think I meet the best?
2. Which one do I think I meet the least? What one thing might I do to improve in this area?

Parents' Time-Out to Talk

A brief weekly conversation helps parents stay on top of their job, and it takes the pressure off, too, by helping us focus on doing a few things well.

Bert Ghezzi

I suggest that Catholic parents consider taking a weekly break from life's busy round of activities. No, not a vacation (that's another issue!) but a fifteen-minute time-out to assess the family's spiritual life. For Mary Lou and me, this has turned out to be a key element in adopting a purposeful approach to passing on the faith.

Of course, there are different approaches to raising kids Catholic. Some parents let things drift, hoping that their good Catholic example rubs off on the children. This strategy leaves plenty of room for grace, but it also gives leeway to influences that undermine the effort. At the other extreme, some parents work at controlling everything in the family's life in order to give it a Catholic shape.

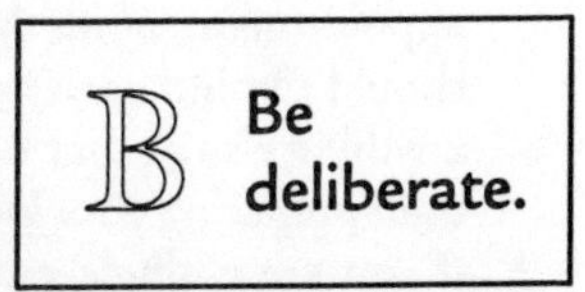

Attention to detail has the advantage of being an active approach. But maintaining strict overall control soon becomes a burden both to parents and children.

My preferred approach combines grace and purposeful action, the best elements of drifting and controlling. I think we should concentrate on a few important things that move the family in a Catholic direction and draw everything else along. Worshiping together at mass, family prayer time, discerning the media, informal instruction in the faith and conversations about the Lord are the kinds of activities I have in mind. They combine our effort with the Lord's to build a family culture that gives kids a Catholic formation.

We don't need to make all these things happen at once. We

Finding Time to Talk

Parents need to make time in their busy schedules for regular conversations about their family's spiritual condition. Investing just a few minutes each week will keep you focused on the goal of raising your kids Catholic. Here are some tips that will help you find a time that's right for you:

- **Pick a day and time that works every week. Having a regular time slot makes it easier to be faithful to meeting.**
- **Look for a time and place that will allow you to talk without interruption.**
- **If your kids are younger, you could get together one evening just after putting them to bed. Or have older children watch younger ones in order to give you a chance for a conversation.**
- **Treat your conversation time as you would any other appointment. Write the day and time on your calendar. Parents should remind each other about it and decide not to schedule anything else at that time. Nothing else in life is more important than preparing your kids for their eternal lives.**
- **If you are a single parent, set up a regular meeting time with another Catholic single parent or a friend and review with him or her what you are doing to raise your kids Catholic.**

Bert Ghezzi

can start with things we feel strongest about and make them happen one at a time. But to ensure success we must be deliberate about it.

Taking this purposeful approach requires that we take some time to discuss how things are going. Moms and dads—married couples and single parents—need to be talking regularly about what they're doing to raise their kids Catholic. Couples can often squeeze valuable conversations between hectic events. Single parents should team up with another Catholic single parent or with a friend or support group and talk things over regularly. Whatever our situation, we really need to set aside some time devoted exclusively to discussing what we're doing to create a Catholic family. We need a parents' "time-out," a break in the action that gives us a chance to regroup. Taking just fifteen minutes a week to review the family's spiritual life will help keep it on track.

A quarter hour a week can make the remaining 167-3/4 hours go much better. It is an opportunity for a variety of important discussions and decisions. We can take up different topics each week. We can use the fifteen minutes to:

- Evaluate how family members are doing in their relationship with God and with each other and decide what we can do to help them.
- Tackle problems and figure out how we are going to resolve them.
- Make plans to start activities that will form kids in the faith, like a family prayer time.
- Determine boundaries that support our kids' Christian lives, like limiting their access to the media.
- Encourage each other in our roles as parents.

We should also remember to include a Third Person in our weekly conversations. We can open and close our fifteen minutes with prayer to the Holy Spirit, who has a lot to say to us about our families.

For Discussion

Why do parents need to take time to talk about the family?

For Reflection

1. (Couples) Do we have regular conversations about our family?
2. (Single parents) Am I talking regularly with someone about my family?

How to Use Action Idea Lists, Decision Grids and Action Plans

In your effort to raise your kids Catholic, you should attempt only one new action or renewed activity at a time. You may want to choose that idea while you are reading through a chapter. Be sure that the action you select is both *important* to you and your family and also *easy to accomplish*. These criteria make success more likely and, thus, galvanize you against guilt.

But you may decide to accumulate many ideas while you are reading and choose your action item from among many good possibilities. If you find this approach appealing, consider using an *Action Idea List*, a *Decision Grid* and *Action Plan* described below. The *Think, Pray & Act* section at the end of each chapter reminds you to choose an action and suggests using these tools. It also includes resources for additional consultation.

In order to utilize the *Action Idea List*, *Decision Grid* and *Action Plan*, you will need either to make photocopies from the samples at the end of this chapter, or draw your own versions of these forms. You may want to keep a notebook or journal to help you track and sort your action ideas. If you like, you could incorporate these tools with your journal notes.

Action Idea Lists. The *Action Idea List* is a convenient form you can use to record all the ideas that seem promising for your family. When a good idea strikes you, write it in the center

Action Idea List

Importance High, Medium, Low	Action	Accomplishment Hard, Medium, Easy
low	1. weeknight Bible study	medium
high	2. kids in Catholic school	hard
high	3. bi-weekly family night	medium
low	4. Habitat for Humanity	hard
medium	5. send Joe to Summer Camp	easy
high	6. teach traditional prayers	easy
medium	7. start Catholic parents group	hard
	8.	
	9.	

column on the *Action Idea List.* (See sample above). There are blanks for twenty-five actions.

When you are ready to choose your action, use the *Action Idea List* to help you choose from among the possibilities on your list. In the left hand column, rate potential actions in terms of their importance to you and your family. How big an impact will the action have on your family's life? High? Medium? Low? Record your rating for each possible action in the blank provided.

Now turn to the right hand column and repeat the process. Rate each potential action in terms of its ease of accomplishment. Will it be hard to do? Medium? Easy? Record your rating for each item in the blank provided.

Now you are ready to use the *Decision Grid.*

Decision Grid. The *Decision Grid* will help you identify the best possible action for you to take. On the *Decision Grid,* plot each item you have written on the *Action Idea List.* Record the item's number in the box that matches its two characteristics.

Decision Grid

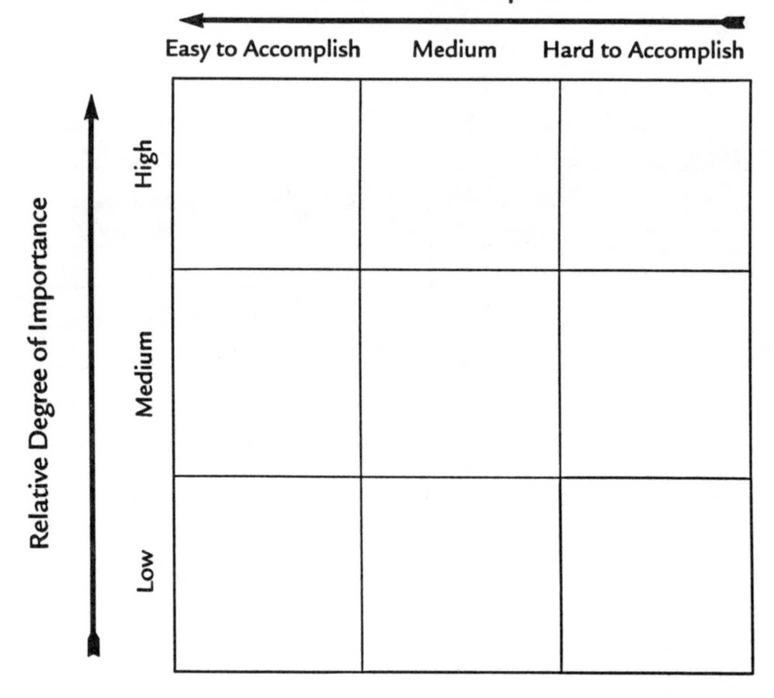

(See sample above). For example, Item 4 in the sample "Work with Habitat for Humanity," was rated low in importance and hard to accomplish. So it appears in the bottom right square on the grid, which is "hard" and "low." Item 2 shows up in the upper right hand square on the sample grid because it was rated "hard" and "high."

The item that you are looking for will appear in the upper left hand square. It identifies the possibility that is both important and easy to accomplish. Item 6 in the sample, "Teach traditional prayers," is the action of choice. If in your sorting you find no action that is both easy and important, I suggest you choose an item that is of medium importance, but easy to do. In our sample, if nothing had appeared in the upper left square, the parents would have chosen Item 5, "Send Joe to summer work camp." Of course, you may occasionally decide that an important item that is hard or medium to accomplish is worth making the effort, and do it.

Once you have decided on the right action, you should develop a little plan to make it happen. If you like, you can use the *Action Plan* form.

Action Plan. The *Action Plan* form (see page 43) ensures that you think through the action carefully before you attempt it. Nothing novel here—just five *Ws* and an *H:* What? Why? Who? When? Where? and How? Don't neglect the *Why*. Figuring out the reason for the action will help you explain it to your children. Teaching them about what you are doing is as important as doing it.

Resources. Each *Think, Pray & Act* concludes with a list of books, magazines, organizations or resources that you may consult for additional information or for assistance.

Think, Pray & Act

No More Guilt

What good ideas have you had about raising your kids Catholic? Have you had some thoughts about how you can do it without feeling guilty? What one thing can you do differently? Use the tools described above to help you choose just the right course of action. Refer to the questions *For Discussion* and *For Reflection* at the end of articles. They will help you take stock of the situation in your family. Remember to invite the Holy Spirit to guide your thoughts and actions. He is even more interested than you in your children's Christian formation.

Resources

- *Catholic Parent* is a practical magazine written by parents for parents (800-348-2440).

- *Follow the Way of Love,* a pastoral message of the U.S. Catholic bishops to families (U.S.C.C. Office for Publishing and Promotion: 800-235-USCC).
- Bert Ghezzi, *Keeping Your Kids Catholic* (Servant Book Express: 313-677-6490). This book is a companion to *Guiltless Catholic Parenting from A to Y**.
- Kevin McCarthy, *The On-Purpose Person: Making Your Life Make Sense* (Piñon Press: 407-657-6000).

Action Idea List

Importance High, Medium, Low	Action	Accomplishment Hard, Medium, Easy
______	1. ______	______
______	2. ______	______
______	3. ______	______
______	4. ______	______
______	5. ______	______
______	6. ______	______
______	7. ______	______
______	8. ______	______
______	9. ______	______
______	10. ______	______
______	11. ______	______
______	12. ______	______
______	13. ______	______
______	14. ______	______
______	15. ______	______
______	16. ______	______
______	17. ______	______
______	18. ______	______
______	19. ______	______
______	20. ______	______
______	21. ______	______
______	22. ______	______
______	23. ______	______
______	24. ______	______
______	25. ______	______

Decision Grid

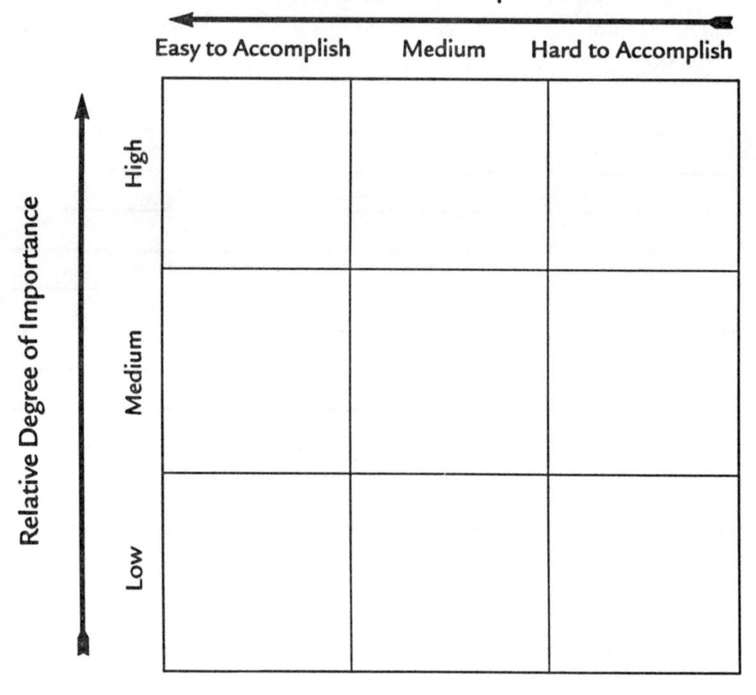

Action Plan

What? ____________________

Why? ____________________

Who? ____________________

How? ____________________

When? ____________________

Where? ____________________

TWO

Talking with Kids

Maintaining good family communications creates frequent occasions of grace for both parents and kids.

Show *and* Tell

The most important gift parents can give children is speaking openly about their relationship with the Lord.

Bert Ghezzi

I'll tell you a secret if you promise not to share it with my kids. Here it is: My wife and I are a big influence in our childrens' lives. Even Paul, my second oldest son, who has worked hard for twenty-eight years to be different, becomes more like me every day. Ah, how sweet it is! Even though all evidence may seem to be to the contrary, you are also significantly influencing your kids.

That's good because we can use this natural influence to nudge our children toward the Lord. Doing everything we can to help them meet God is our most important parental duty. Experience has taught me that this business of introducing kids to the Lord is a matter of both show *and* tell.

My mother was an exemplary Catholic Christian. Though she was a single parent of four kids, she got us to mass every Sunday and often daily, prayed for us nightly on her knees and made great sacrifices to send us to Catholic schools. However, in the twenty-three years I lived at home, I cannot remember her ever talking to me about her own relationship with the Lord, although I know now it had to have been intimate. My mom was good at "show," but not so good at "tell." Perhaps, like many of us, she felt that faith was too private a topic to discuss, even with her kids.

No one told me about the possibility of a personal relationship with God until I was twenty years old. One evening early in Lent of my junior year at college, a professor friend engaged me in a conversation about prayer. He talked to me frankly about his experience of God's love for him and his own love for God.

Excited by the possibility of knowing God directly, I determined not to wait another day. Late that night I knelt in the quiet darkness of my room and told the Lord that I wanted to know him just like my friend did. As I began to pray, the Lord made his presence known to me in an extraordinary way. God's reaching out to me in love that night drew me to serve him all these years. My friend's decision to "show and tell" me about his divine relationship helped shape my life.

"Show" without "tell" will not be enough for our children. They need to hear us speak openly about our relationship with God. All that matters most in their lives depends on it. Our good example is important, but unless we talk to our kids about our friendship with the Lord they are apt to misinterpret our behavior as an empty show. Worse, they may never discover the possibility of personally knowing and loving God.

Parents must take a deliberate approach to talking to their kids about God, deciding both to take every chance that comes up in daily conversation and to create more formal opportunities. For example, when our kids get sick or face a challenge at school, Mary Lou and I pray aloud with them and we urge them to pray in their own words. Informal prayer shows kids plainly that God is a person who is present and takes an interest in us. Parents can use these moments of spontaneous family prayer as occasions to say some things about their relationship with God.

When our children reach milestones, like confirmation or marriage, Mary Lou and I have written them letters explaining our faith. Recently our teenage daughter Clare made a parish retreat and the whole family sent her letters. In my letter I told my daughter how much I want her to come to know God. "Dear Clare," I wrote, "every morning I ask the Lord to reveal himself to you...."

For Discussion

1. Why is a parent's good example not enough to lead children to Christ and the church?
2. Why do you think parents must take a deliberate approach to talking to their children about the faith?

For Reflection

1. Do I speak regularly to my children about my relationship to God and the church?
2. How can I increase my communication about faith to my family?

The Family That Dines Together, Binds Together

Don't underestimate the importance of eating together as an opportunity for developing family communications.

Paul Thigpen

It was the worst mistake our family ever made. After renting a home for twenty-three years, my parents were finally building their own. Our family excitedly searched till at last we found a house plan that fit our needs perfectly. Or so we thought. But years later we found ourselves wishing we had never allowed one particular element in the design.

We combined an eat-in kitchen with the den—and our television was in the den.

Some friends gave us TV trays as a house-warming gift, and the rest was inevitable. Soon, gone were the smiles across the dinner table, the lively banter, the courteous exchange of *please* and *thank you* while we passed the butter. Instead, most of our family meals for years afterward were served from the stove and eaten around the tube, whose relentless noise hindered and finally silenced our conversation.

Before long, the dinner hour found us scattered across town—working, shopping, attending meetings, visiting friends. Mom left the food on the stove for self-service throughout the evening. And without quite realizing it, we had lost something precious.

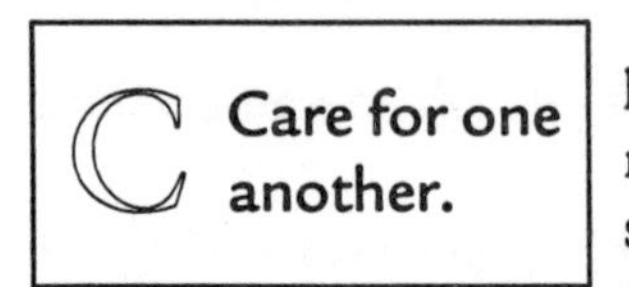

I sometimes wonder how many households have made the same mistake we did. Not just those who sacrifice family fellowship on the altar of the TV. I mean all those who have allowed any obstacle—business or pleasure, hectic schedules or skewed priorities—to rob them of shared mealtimes. Though they may not realize it, they've given up a valuable source of family strength.

Why is it so important for a family to come together regularly to eat? First of all, mealtime is an ideal time to build a sense of *family identity, belonging and commitment.* Have you ever noticed how attached family members can get to a particular seat at the dinner table? That's because family meals together make them feel they have a place of their own—a place where they belong, where they know who they are and where they fit in.

By sitting down around the table, we're proclaiming ourselves to be a small but unique community. For a brief time, we've withdrawn from all our wider associations so we can declare our allegiance to the family circle. When we're willing to forego work, entertainment or social events for the sake of this time together, we're making a powerful statement to the rest of the household: We are a family, we belong to one another and we are committed to one another.

A second reason why families need to break bread together daily is so they can *share their lives as they share the food.* Once upon a time, the great majority of families spent most of their days together. Both the parents' work and the children's school were at home. But now the generations tend to go their separate ways soon after breakfast. So it's critical that they come back together each day to get reacquainted. Mealtimes provide a natural occasion for staying in touch.

The dining room also provides a training ground where family members learn to *respect, serve and cooperate with one another*—a third reason for coming together around the table. That's why the ancient Greeks included table etiquette in their study of ethics. They realized that good manners are simply one way to show concern for the welfare of others. When we practice small courtesies around the table—serving someone's plate, passing a dish, complimenting the cook—we're affirming one another as cherished family members.

These small lessons in kindness are extended to a wider circle whenever we open our table to guests. Thus, *hospitality*—an important Christian virtue—becomes yet another reason for a regular family mealtime. Before taverns were common, providing food for hungry travelers was considered a moral obligation. In

How to Stimulate Mealtime Conversations

If the traditional "How was your day?" falls flat at your dinner table, try these ideas for a thought-provoking exchange:

- Announce one night that the next evening every family member is expected to bring to the table at least one funny story, joke or riddle to share. Laughter aids digestion!
- Choose a compelling item from the news headlines or a topic of special interest to your family. Have someone give a brief oral report on it at dinner the following evening. Be prepared with lots of questions.
- Give each person a paper place mat with three thought-provoking questions written on it. Then take turns answering them. Think of questions that require concrete, specific answers with revealing implications: If you could spend a day with anyone in the world, who would it be and what would you do together? Which Bible character or saint do you identify with the most, and why? If you could be president for a day, what would you do?
- Keep the talk positive. This isn't the time for correcting, arguing or complaining; those table habits kill conversation and cause indigestion. Focus instead on how you can affirm, encourage and get to know your family.

Paul Thigpen

the ancient Near East, even an enemy might expect to be shown hospitality under certain circumstances. That act of charity would then oblige him to lay down his sword; he couldn't honorably fight those who had shared their bread with him.

With that in mind, one family I know regularly invites dinner guests of different backgrounds. In this way they bring together young and old, rich and poor—folks who otherwise might never have had a chance to get acquainted, who might even have been inclined to misunderstand one another before they broke bread together under the same roof. Think how much good that family has done simply by practicing hospitality!

Finally, and most importantly, the meal table can become a kind of *family altar*, a place where we meet God to thank him for being faithful to provide our daily bread. If mealtimes are set apart with sincere prayers of blessing and thanks, we can use the occasion to turn our family's attention to the Lord daily—and to cultivate a sense of gratitude for all his good gifts.

For Discussion

Why do you think it's important for families to eat meals together?

For Reflection

1. Do we eat at least one meal a day together?
2. What could we do to encourage or improve communication at our mealtimes?

The Fish Story—The Grace of Humor

A sense of humor can enhance family communications.

Mary Bahr Fritts

Comedian Bill Dana, better known as Jose Jimenez, once said, "Nothing breeds humor like adversity." The wisdom of these words escaped me until my husband, our four sons and I discovered it accidentally, with the Fish Story.

Our adversity? The abyss of financial stress. Through job transfers, office closings, a company bankruptcy and the inability to sell a house in a failing economy, our financial security twice took a nosedive.

Depression and *Stress* moved into our home. *Joy* and *Laughter* moved out. We didn't realize what was missing until one night, at the dinner table, we rediscovered it: laughter and its magical powers.

I had juggled the budget all afternoon until it was time to pull out the pasta pot for dinner. It's one of life's little ironies that in those times when we most need to celebrate, we can least afford it. I bemoaned the fact that we were a steak and potatoes family struggling to survive a spaghetti economy. I was stirring the Italian sauce when Bill came home from work.

"Budget night already?" He eyed the pasta.

I nodded glumly.

"It'll get better." He soothed me with intense blue eyes.

"Tonight's the night, don't you think?" I asked. Surely the boys could sense something was wrong. Our finances were wearing us both down. We had little patience and no sense of fun anymore. They needed reassurance that finances were causing our gloom and not an impending divorce, as had happened in too many of their classmates' families.

"It'll help," Bill had said, "if we let them choose some of the cut-back decisions."

After we finished dinner, I sensed Bill was preparing a speech. Actually, it looked more like a presentation for a board of directors was coming.

"We have some decisions to make," he began. The boys looked at us eagerly, as children do when they believe that parents have nothing but answers and surprises. And we looked back into those trusting faces, hoping that we wouldn't disappoint them.

"The time has come, the walrus said, to think of many things. We've got a pile of bills to pay but not the gold of kings." He sounded like the greeting cards he creates for me every year when, late in the afternoon of my birthday, it occurs to him that he forgot.

The room was quiet, not a common atmosphere in our household. The solemnity neared absurdity as I watched a movie play on Bill's face. Somewhere between the salad and the dessert those cherubic little faces had gotten to him; he didn't have the guts to tell them we couldn't afford a vacation this year.

Bill comes from a school of thought that stands by the old Vermont proverb, "Never speak unless you can improve the silence." He's got one uncle who never has. On the other hand, his aunt is a firm believer in O. Henry's adage, "Inject a few raisins of conversation into the tasteless dough of existence." Coming from stock like this, Bill measures his words carefully, with his nose acting as the barometer. When his nostrils flare and his nose sends a glare, I know he's about to "inject a few raisins" with style.

And so began the original Fish Story.

Bill: "Seriously, folks. We can't afford two houses. Can't even afford one. Whaddya think? Sell them both and buy a houseboat?"

Three-year-old Jeremy scraped a noodle off his tray and threw it, moving the story right along. The rest of us sat silently until our nine-year-old reacted to the blarney.

Jordan: "But I like my friends. I don't wanna move again. Ever!"

Bill: "Well, if we had a houseboat you'd be one popular kid at school. You'd have friends standing in line, waiting to fish out your window."

If ever I toyed with the idea of stopping him, that last line nixed it. How was Bill going to get out of this one?

Jordan: "Out my window? Fish out my window?"

Jason (our fourteen-year-old resident pessimist): "Yeah. They land on your bed and watch Mom make *you* wash the sheets."

Joshua (eleven years old; sports sense yes, imagination no): "But I can't see the bobber from my window."

Bill: "You won't have to. You'll know when to reel those fish in. You can hear them humming."

Joshua: "Hear them coming?"

Bill: "No, *humming*. Remember Grandpa Larson's story?" (Now he brings my family into this...) "The one about Swedish walleye? They hum. Just one tune, though."

Jason (who finally had a grasp of the situation): "Are those the same fish that fly, Dad?"

Bill: "Sure are, son. And if you hum the right tune, they fly right into your lap."

Whether or not the boys realized that Dad was telling them a Fish Story didn't matter. What mattered was how they kept the story going. And as the story grew, we all got sillier. And laughter reigned that night, in a house that had not the gold of kings.

After that, when gloom descended at bill-paying time—no pizza because the price of two large deep-dish will pay the vet bill for five gerbils, two cats and a rabbit; no new sofa without lumps because our orthodontist is adding a wing onto his house; and no first-run movies because thirteen bath towels in one day's laundry basket escalates the electric bill high enough to challenge the budget of a small country—we salvage our sagging spirits with the Fish Story.

Usually served once a month, its predictability depends upon whether the bills we just paid were due on that fifteenth or some other long-ago fifteenth. As we grump around the table, I can see it coming. So I serve the food, we thank the Lord, and I sit back and watch the fun.

Jordan (now thirteen): "Ah, Mom, spaghetti again? Can't we ever order pizza?"

Bill (ignoring the complaint): "Did you know it's a scientific fact that noodles act like mini roto-rooters? They clean out the cobwebs in your veins."

Joshua (now fifteen, plays along for the benefit of his little brother, plus the fact that he's into science and Dad may be telling the truth this time): "And how do the cobwebs get there in the first place?"

Bill: "The spiders crawl in when you snore with your mouth open."

Jeremy (who believes all of this): "You got spiders in ya,' Dad?"

Bill: "No, I don't. Because I don't snore." His nose gets rosy.

Jason (who has a room right next to ours): "Uh-*huuuuuuh.*"

Bill: "No, I whistle. Truly. Spiders hate whistling. It pops their eardrums."

At this point, Bill's nose is neon. Jeremy checks my face for a signal and we all explode with laughter. We're OK once more, because we're all in this together—and lies and love and laughter are better than a dinner out on the town any day. Well, maybe not according to Jordan. He really does hate spaghetti....

After a few sessions of the Fish Story, I noticed a change in attitude. Grouching, fighting and tears became less frequent, while laughter and playfulness increased. It brought to mind a line from Paul Pearsall's *Super Joy:* "We come to feel as we behave." Reworded, it sounds like something from Mary Poppins: "A spoonful of sugar makes the medicine go down."

I had no idea, however, that we were in such great shape until our wee one came home milking a grump session. He'd just lost a wrestling tournament. "I woulda won if he wasn't so mean." He slammed the front door. "I woulda won if he wasn't so big." He slammed the back door. "I woulda won if..."

"Get Grumpy into the bathtub," I suggested to Jordan, who had bath-duty. Jordan, whose sense of humor has surpassed our wildest dreams, lured Jeremy into the tub. I forgot all about the little grouch until I was suddenly overwhelmed by the silence coming from the bathroom. In a house full of boys, silence is a dangerous sound. So I did what any mother of sons does. I eavesdropped. Bill heard the silence, too, and joined me in the hallway.

"What's going on?"

"I'm not sure," I whispered as we plastered our ears to the door.

Jeremy: "I shoulda won but he pinched me."
Jordan: "Bit you! He bit you?"
Jeremy: "No, pinched!"
Jordan: "What did he bite off?"
Jeremy (who's trying to grumble, but gives in to little snickers of delight): "No, *pinched.*"
Jordan: "An inch? He bit off an inch? Where?"
Jeremy (who's beginning to enjoy this in spite of himself): "Off my nose," he giggled.
Jordan: "Well, then we've got to use this super-globbity glue" (he probably held a handful of soap-suds) "to glue it right back on. Or you won't be able to smell when you need a bath."

We stood in the hallway, Bill and I, listening to squeals and splashing water. And we didn't yell at them for ruining the floor tile, because we were feeling too smug. Smug because they were using the Fish Story to heal life's little hurts.

Today, we still have more bills than money. We still wonder how we'll make it. But somehow we do. And we firmly believe that the "somehow" is the Fish Story. It brings out the child in us. And for a child, laughter comes easily. And with laughter comes hope. And with hope, we live well.

For Discussion
Why do you think humor is important for healthy family communications?

For Reflection
1. In our family do we approach adversity with a sense of humor?
2. What could we do to introduce a sense of fun into our family relationships?

Is Your Home Teenager-Friendly?

We can improve relationships with our teenagers by welcoming their friends into our home.

Neta Jackson

I was going to title this, "Be Friends with Your Teen's Friends"—but your teenager might see it and wail, "My friends are MY friends! Pick on someone your own age."

This was definitely my foster daughter's attitude when I asked

Welcoming the Unwelcome

Jesus' words about hospitality were sorely tested for me when one of my daughters made friends with a "questionable" young man who was several years older than she. I didn't even want them to be friends, much less risk a romantic involvement. Every time this young man—I'll call him Zed—came around, I literally stiffened up. I didn't want him to feel welcomed at my house. I just wanted him to go away.

But the friendship blossomed, and they wanted to date. Our gut reaction was to forbid it ("Lock her in her room! We'll move out of the state!"), but for some reason the Holy Spirit seemed to nudge both me and my husband: "Treat this young man like a real person."

We decided to accept the relationship and went on the offensive: We invited Zed to dinner, encouraged him to spend time at our house, even shared our Christmas Eve family celebration with him, including some simple gifts. At first he was afraid of us (after all, we'd been giving him the cold shoulder for six months), but he soon warmed up to the hospitality and even began going to church with us.

After a few months of not having to fight us about him, our daughter decided to break off the relationship, but not before my husband had a chance to talk to Zed about Jesus. Eventually, he was baptized.

We are still astounded at this turn of events, but it has helped remind us that each time we extend our friendship to one of our teenager's friends, we may be building a bridge of acceptance that has eternal significance.

Neta Jackson

her how she thought parents should relate to their kids' friends. "Don't hang around too much and don't ask too many questions," she said, referring, no doubt, to our rule that we have to meet any boy who wants to take her out.

But it was that same foster daughter who was feeling rejected recently by her girlfriend Katie's parents. "They don't want me over there," she complained.

"They seemed glad to have you when I asked if you could stay that weekend we were out of town," I said.

"That's because Katie's mom was talking to *you*. But when she talks to *me*, it's like 'Oh. Hi.'" The tone of voice she mimicked was oh-it's-YOU-again. "And if Katie asks me to sleep over, her mom gives a big sigh and says, 'I guess.'"

The wounds of a teenager who had experienced a lot of rejection in her life were obviously still tender. But kids quickly sense who likes them and who doesn't.

How many times has my tone of voice communicated rejection instead of welcome? I wondered. I have to admit I don't always feel welcoming toward my teenagers' friends. Copious amounts of food disappear at an alarming rate. Strange boys show up at the door asking for one of my daughters (I sometimes sic my six-foot-two-inch husband on 'em). Or the Friday night crowd wants to watch a video at *our* house (which means my husband and I are relegated to the kitchen or bedroom).

But just when I'm grumbling because four teenagers are in the kitchen having a "snack" that resembles a four-course meal, I remember something Jesus said. "If, as my representatives, you give even a cup of cold water to a little child, you will certainly be rewarded" (Matthew 10:42). And once, when Jesus' disciples were arguing about who—and what—was really important, he said, "Whoever welcomes one of these little children in my name welcomes me" (Mark 9:37). I must remember, too, that sometimes "little ones" come in giant, adolescent sizes.

Our teenagers don't want us to be "buddies" with their friends—but whether they admit it or not, they care if you and your home say "Welcome." Some of the following can make a big difference:

- ***Know your teenager's friends by name.*** Sounds obvious but gets difficult as the circle of friends enlarges. It's hard to be friendly if you don't have a clue if this is Phil, Steve or Jacob.
- ***Watch your tone of voice.*** Your words may be saying "Welcome," but your tone of voice can convey irritation or disinterest. A few genuinely friendly words go a long way.
- ***Budget for snack food.*** If you've been fighting your teenager over feeding the five thousand, consider stocking a shelf or agreeing to certain snack foods that are free to use. It's a small price to pay for a home that says, "You're welcome here."
- ***Be clear about rules.*** At our house, an adult must be home for parties and visits from the opposite sex, boys can't be in girls' bedrooms (and vice versa), no R-rated videos are allowed, snack dishes must be cleared out of the living room, and so on. If the rules have been communicated ahead of time, then you can deal with situations that arise in a matter-of-fact way rather than getting upset.
- ***Respond to requests genuinely.*** Before the kids got their driver's licenses, I would often get pressed into shuttle service. Sometimes my mouth would say "yes," but I'd act angry or frustrated. One day my daughter said, "Mom, if you don't want to drive me and my friends, just say so. I'd rather you say 'no' than make me feel guilty for asking." Ouch. A good reminder that saying "yes" to a request is a matter of attitude as well as words. And NO is a viable choice.
- ***Don't embarrass your teenager*** in front of his or her friends. If a problem arises, call your teenager aside, say what needs to happen and let your teenager communicate to his or her friends.
- ***Invite your teenager's friends for supper.*** Breaking bread together has always been a symbol of friendship and hospitality. Sitting around a dinner table is a good way to get to know your teenager's friends beyond the superficial level. It's also a way to share your life and family values with teenagers who may not have "family dinner" at home.
- ***Value teenagers' thoughts and opinions.*** If you have a chance to talk—that family dinner, for instance—ask what they think

about social issues, the latest movies, politics. And respect their opinions, even if you disagree.

- ***If possible, set aside some space*** in the house for teenagers to hang out. Or (as we have had to do, since we have no family room) agree with your teenager on certain nights when friends can be over, and certain nights when *you* can have the living room.
- ***Make a point to remember personal things*** about different friends and inquire about them, "How was your trip to Washington, D.C.?" "How's the job hunt going?" These conversations don't have to be long, but they communicate care and concern.

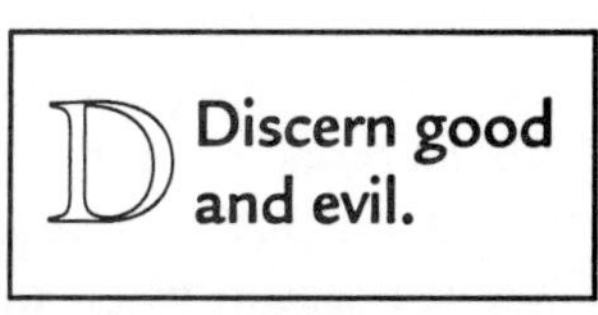

- ***Pray for your teenager's friends.*** If you have a family prayer time, pray with your teenagers for their friends. As you pray for these kids—even the ones who aren't so likable—you will develop a genuine care and concern.

For Discussion

How can welcoming teens' friends affect family communications?

For Reflection

1. Is our home teenager-friendly?
2. How could we be more welcoming to our children's friends?

When Daddy (or Mommy) Doesn't Go to Church

Even if your spouse doesn't share your commitment, you can do many things to plant the seeds of faith in your children.

Bert Ghezzi

When I present a workshop on raising kids Catholic, someone asks me this question: How can I bring up my child Catholic if my husband (wife) does not share my commitment?

Many Catholics are married but feel alone as Christians. That may work OK, or at least be tolerable, in a family of two. But when children arrive, the situation gets complicated, sometimes painfully. An actively Catholic mom, for example, and a disinterested dad give mixed signals to the kids. "Why do I have to go to mass?" asks your eight-year-old. "Daddy doesn't go." What do you say to this child? You might explain, "Daddy worships God in his own way." But you can expect the child to say, "So why can't I stay home and worship his way." There's no easy answer for that one.

A parent in these circumstances also finds it difficult to create a Catholic home environment. How do you have a family prayer time when one parent is absent? How do you celebrate a Christian season when one parent doesn't seem to care? No simple solutions here, either.

But if you find yourself in this situation you are not hopelessly stuck. There are many things you can do. Consider the following suggestions and make your own plan of action:

Do everything you can that doesn't require your spouse's involvement. Consider the many chances you have daily to influence your children.

- You can speak to them one-on-one about the Lord and the Christian community. Telling about our own experience of God is perhaps the most important thing a parent can do for children. Our witness prepares them for faith. So seize every opportunity. A son shows you a tree frog; you say something about the Creator. A daughter comes in drenched from the rain; you remind her about baptism.
- You can read the Bible and Christian stories to them. All children seem to enjoy listening to a parent read aloud. Take advantage of it.
- You can pray with them privately and show them how to pray. Teach them the Our Father, the Hail Mary, the Apostles' Creed and other traditional prayers. Make it a custom to say these prayers when you tuck them in at night. You can also pray with them informally when you are driving them to school or to a sports event. When they are sick, place your hand on them and ask the Lord to make them well.

- You can set an example. Your faithfulness, love and hope will rub off on your children. But, of course, they might not let you know it until they become adults.

Don'ts and Do's

✗ Don't attempt things your spouse opposes.

✗ Don't speak negatively about your spouse.

✗ Don't nag your spouse.

✗ Don't try to change your spouse.

✔ Do pray for your spouse and your children.

✔ Do everything you can do one-on-one with your kids.

✔ Do look for activities your spouse can support.

✔ Do get all the help you can.

Bert Ghezzi

Ask your spouse to cooperate as much as possible. Sometimes a noninvolved spouse is willing to support, or at least not to oppose, efforts to raise children in the faith. If so, you may be able to get your partner's agreement on some things like family customs. He or she may be willing to let you have a family prayer time. Or have seasonal devotions during Advent or Lent. Consider asking your spouse to encourage the children. "I want you to go to church with your mom," he might say. "I am not going with you for my own reasons. Someday when you're older you'll understand." Your spouse may even be interested in joining the family in some service to others. Perhaps the whole family might serve once or twice a year at a local soup kitchen.

Get as much help as you can. Involve yourself in the local Catholic community. You need the fellowship of others who face challenges like yours. And your kids need the community, too. Encourage them to spend time with other Catholic youth. Often a parish youth ministry provides a Catholic peer group for them.

If your spouse is hostile and opposes you, you may need the advice of your pastor or of a professional counselor. Don't be too proud or embarrassed to ask.

Stop thinking that you are alone. The Holy Spirit is your partner for handing on the faith to your kids. You can count on him to guide you. He will prompt you with the right words to teach your kids. He will give you answers to their hard questions. He will show you what to do to lead them to Christ and the church. Your job is only to plant the seeds of faith. His job is to bring them to fruition. So start every day by asking your Partner for help.

For Discussion

1. What difficulties in raising children in the faith may face a Catholic whose spouse is not involved?
2. What can a parent whose spouse is not involved do to raise the children Catholic?

For Reflection

1. Does your spouse share your Christian commitment?
2. (If not) What can you do to raise your children in the faith?

25 Ways to Strengthen Family Ties

Pause your busyness and spend time with your children.

Patricia L. Fry

Most of us feel that we can count on the family to be there when our other activities end. When you're maintaining a frantic pace, your family may be the only constant. Most outside obligations have a sense of urgency about them, while the family remains day in and day out. You trust that the family will wait until your business deal is closed, the church rummage sale is over or your ceramic class ends.

Don't wait. You can choose to spend quality time with your family even when you're at your busiest. I offer twenty-five family togetherness activities to adapt to any schedule, any energy level and any area of interest. Some, I suspect, could become cherished family traditions.

10-Minute Family Breaks. These suggestions are impromptu feel-good ideas that take no advance preparation and less than ten minutes to accomplish.

1. Walk around the yard or sit in private with a family member for a few minutes after work and talk about whatever seems important at the time.
2. Set aside time each day for family prayer. If the entire family rarely dines together, try gathering in the entry hall or on the front porch in the morning as everyone is leaving the house. Or pray together in the evening at bedtime.
3. Stop to give (and receive) a warm hug from a family member who is handiest at the moment.
4. Write a personal note to a child, husband, wife, sister or brother from time to time letting them know you are proud of them and love them. Leave the note on the bathroom mirror, with their school books or briefcase or tuck it in with their lunch.
5. Call one of the children or your spouse from work for no other reason than to say, "I love you."
6. Lie on the grass together and discuss cloud formations.
7. Pick or buy a bouquet of flowers for a family member who has been extra patient, helpful, sad, brave or responsible.
8. Gather in front of the fireplace (in winter) or on the porch (in summer) to share funny stories, poetry, ideas on a problem someone wants to air, or concerns about a current community or world event.
9. Spend the evening in a different room than you're used to, preferably one without a television set. It could be one of the children's rooms, your office, your bedroom or even the kitchen. Just be. It may surprise you how a change in environment can encourage new topics of conversation.
10. Eat a meal in a different place from time to time: patio, family room, on a blanket in the backyard or in the dining room (as opposed to the kitchen) for a change in atmosphere and mood.

11. Play a game such as charades, Pictionary, Taboo or sardines (It's like hide-and-seek, but only one person hides. When the others find that person, they join the hidden person in that hiding place). There's no need for elaborate planning or lengthy time commitments. These play sessions can be impromptu and brief.

Minimal Planning Reaps Major Dividends. The following may take some effort on someone's part to prepare. Put the children in charge or work on the project as a family during evenings in front of the television. Once the groundwork is laid, the family will be free to enjoy the results with little effort.

12. Write down ten or twenty ideas for spending a family evening or weekend. Put them in a basket to be drawn when the time becomes available. Some typical ideas might be putting together a puzzle, making banana splits, designing clothes for paper dolls, playing marbles, having a lip-sync contest, or putting on a family talent show.
13. Design cards with inspirational messages that are particularly meaningful to your family. Keep them in a container for each family member to draw from every morning. Some I've placed in our box are: "Laughter is the best medicine." "Forgive and find peace." "Love is all there is. God is love." "Promote happiness. Smile!" "Give and you shall receive."
14. Encourage everyone to help in meal preparation one night a week. This will bring everyone together working toward one common goal.
15. Delegate chores to allow more time together. Even the smallest family members can participate in household tasks. Not only is it good for the children to know what goes into running the household, but this also encourages time together.
16. Take the children with you to the tennis court or the biking, walking or hiking trail. Young children can chase tennis balls and be toted or strollered along a trail.

17. Participate as a family in activities the children enjoy. Take your pick of basketball, baseball, soccer, horseback riding or model-airplane flying.
18. When you have to work weekends or holidays, if possible, take one of the children with you to the office. They can bring school work or a good book to keep them busy. Or they can help you by making copies, putting stamps on envelopes, filing, or organizing merchandise. If you bring work home from the office, include something with which the children can help.

Simple Plans, Happy Memories. The following suggestions take only a little more time and effort, and they are wonderful ways of nurturing and enjoying family togetherness.

19. Encourage everyone to participate in planting and caring for a small herb, flower or vegetable garden. Creating and nurturing something that grows and changes is an extremely gratifying activity, made even more so when shared. Yard work is a favorite activity for many families.
20. Get up an hour earlier than usual and take a walk or bike ride as a family.
21. Encourage each family member to give something of themselves to another from time to time. If one or more members of your family have trouble deciding what to do, create a "Giving Basket" that contains slips of paper with task ideas to do for each member of the family.

Plan Ahead to Multiply Times to Treasure. Then there are those items for which you will have to go a little out of your way and, perhaps, make some compromises.

22. During your lunch hour meet a family member for a sack lunch in a local park, at the beach or in a country setting. Or take a child to lunch at a restaurant.
23. Celebrate special accomplishments with dinner out. Such achievements could be a project completed, good grade,

weight loss, new record at the gym, tennis victory, a small child remembering to brush his teeth or a day without bickering among the children.

24. Visit someone who is lonely. Prepare a meal for someone who is ill or has experienced a recent loss.
25. Participate in community and church activities that can include the whole family. What a joyful learning experience for a child to work side by side with the family—for example, preparing and serving meals to the homeless on Thanksgiving Day or collecting, wrapping and delivering food and gifts for the poor at Christmas.

Think, Pray & Act

Keep Talking

Talking to our kids is a main way we introduce them to Christ and the church. Thus, we must maintain good family communications. We want to keep everyone talking to each other. Use the questions *For Discussion* and *For Reflection* to assess your family's communications. Have you thought of one thing you might do to improve them? If you prefer, use the tools on pages 41 to 43 to help you select an action that will work for your family. Expect the Holy Spirit to guide your decision.

Resources

- *How to Talk to Your Child About...* (booklets on various topics); or the book, *Talking to Your Child About Being Catholic* (Our Sunday Visitor: 800-348-2440).
- Bert Ghezzi, *Sharing Your Faith: A User's Guide to Evangelization* (Our Sunday Visitor: 800-348-2440).
- William J. O'Malley, S.J., *Converting the Baptized* (Tabor Publishing: 214-390-6300).

THREE

Talking to God

Praying with children and for them not only makes family life go much better. It makes it last forever because it prepares us for eternal life.

Family Prayer... Just Do It!

The perfect circumstances for starting family prayer don't exist, so plunge in and do the best you can.

Patti Gallagher Mansfield

"Honey, someone wants you to write an article about how our family prays," Al chuckled. *That will be a short article,* I thought.

How does our family pray? *Poorly!* Gone are the days when I would glibly give any advice on parenting. With three teenagers and an eight-year-old to keep us humble, Al and I have learned to say, "We're just doing our best and trusting God—a lot." Like you, we're Catholic parents trying to raise Catholic kids in today's anything-but-Catholic world.

Family prayer. How do you begin? Just begin! How do you do it? Just do it! I'm not being facetious or naive. Make up your mind, then do it. Sometimes we're waiting for optimum conditions: once the baby's older, when football season ends, after taxes. But there's never going to be a perfect time, free from stress, illness or an impossible schedule. "Anything worth doing is worth doing poorly," said Chesterton. So, let's quit making excuses and begin praying. Poorly, if necessary!

We pray liturgically. Every Sunday the Mansfields attend mass in two shifts. We got into this habit when the children were very young and my husband found them too distracting. I came to enjoy my hour of quiet prayer without a baby in tow. Other Catholic families insist on celebrating mass together. I remember rushing into mass late one Sunday after our third child was born. Sitting in the front pew was another mom who had just given birth to her fifth. The baby was sleeping quietly in his carrier, the other children were lined up like little angels next to her husband and *she* looked disgustingly thin and well-rested. Some people can do that, I thought. Not us.

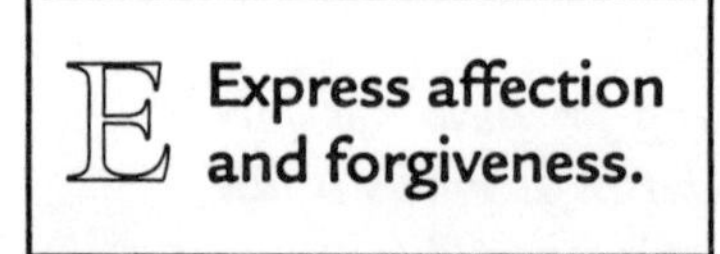

Al has been very strong in encouraging the children to follow along in their missalettes, join in the responses and dress appropriately. "Worship the Lord in holy attire," the psalmist tells us. Marie-Therese is no longer in hand-smocked dresses on Sunday. But we feel that part of our prayer and witness as a family is reflected by our clothing. No cut-offs and tees even if "everybody else is doing it."

Patrick, our youngest, is preparing for his first reconciliation and first holy communion this year. Unfortunately, for many children there will be no "second reconciliation." They'll receive communion for years without ever confessing their sins. In our family we believe there is such a thing as sin, that we commit it and need to express sorrow for it in regular confession. Al has made it a practice to bring the kids to church for this sacrament.

We pray spontaneously. Our active involvement with Catholic renewal movements has taught us the importance of spontaneous prayer. I'm talking about prayer that's simple, from the heart, in our own words. It's a personal expression of our faith and confidence that Jesus is near us and wants to act on our behalf. From birth (and even while they were *in utero*), we have prayed for our kids in a spontaneous way, often laying on hands as a blessing. You'd be amazed at how readily children learn this kind of prayer. And they put us to shame with their expectant faith.

My friend Ann told me how five-year-old Kevin asked Jesus to "make the rain go away" when it threatened to ruin his baseball game. Ann, seeing the ominous clouds, tried to explain that sometimes our prayers aren't answered the way we want. But Kevin kept on believing and by the first pitch, the sun was shining brilliantly!

Once Al had a headache and our seven-year-old son, Peter, offered to pray with him. "Jesus, please heal Daddy's headache. Thank you, Jesus! Is it gone?" Peter repeated his prayer three times before the headache lifted. That's perseverance! This same Peter, now seventeen, had some car trouble while he was alone on the road. "Did you pray?" I asked him. "You bet I prayed!" came the ready reply. An auto mechanic "just happened" to pass by to offer assistance after that prayer. I've been encouraging him since he first got his driver's license to pray to his guardian angel. In typical teenage fashion, he's shrugged me off. But when he was in need, he remembered to pray and got results!

Marie-Therese and I headed off to buy her confirmation dress last year and I expected a battle. Before getting out of the car, I suggested we pray. "You lead, M.T." Her prayer was to the point. "Jesus, please help us find a dress we can agree on." Do you know what? We did, quickly and painlessly. Without that prayer, we might still be at the shopping center!

We pray on our knees. For the Mansfields, night prayer has always been on our knees... more or less. Sometimes the kids are slumping over a chair with only one knee on the ground, but "knees" are part of our "family tradition." Al has made sure they know the traditional prayers of the church, like the "Soul of Christ." When my four-year-old committed it to memory, I knew I'd better learn it as well. Praying rote prayer may seem boring and uninspired, but we feel it's an important component in training our children in the Catholic faith. At night prayer we've sometimes prayed a novena.

I remember the first year we had a kid in high school and were feeling the pinch. Al made copies of a novena to St. Joseph and we prayed for financial help. On the eighth day of the novena

Peter asked, "Is the money coming tomorrow?" Talk about faith! In fact, a month later, an anonymous donor cancelled our high school debt.

We pray at meals. While the kids eye the food impatiently, we pray the traditional grace before meals, introducing a little variety here and there. At Advent we bring down the wreath and sing, "O Come, O Come, Emmanuel." The kids fight over who lights the candles, but it's still fun. On each person's name day he has the "You Are Special" dinner plate and gets a feast day gift. (Marie-Therese is limited to only one Marian feast!) During the Easter season we sing, "O Queen of Heaven, Be Joyful" (*"Regina Coeli"* in Latin, since we now have two Latin scholars!).

We pray on the road. A car trip of any length for the Mansfields includes the rosary or Divine Mercy chaplet. Many Catholic families incorporate the rosary into their daily prayer. I admire them. My mother recalls how the family rosary was prayed in Italian every night as she was growing up. Sure, the kids are going to squirm or complain. Mine try to sit in the van so I can't see them through the rearview mirror while we're praying. But it's still a way of presenting ourselves and our needs to the Lord through Mary's intercession. And that's powerful.

Pray as you can, not as you can't. How do we pray? As I said at the outset, the Mansfields pray *poorly*. But at least we've decided to "just do it." A good spiritual maxim for every family is this one: "Pray as you can, not as you can't." Forget the ideal. Find what's possible for your family. Ask the Holy Spirit to help you. After all, he is the best teacher of prayer. And he's at work in our children. Every now and again, you can catch a glimpse. Patrick was about four when we were at the airport together. "Look, Mom, there's a man on crutches. He needs our prayer." "Yes, Patrick," I replied, "you lead." Right there this little one prayed aloud, "Dear Jesus, please bless this man and heal his legs. Thank you, Jesus." Where did Patrick learn to pray that way? In a family that prays poorly.

Pray Like These Families

Al and I fell in love while serving in the lay apostolate, so the whole notion of praying together was a given. For most Catholic couples, this isn't the case. One of my friends recently persuaded her husband (a nonpracticing Catholic) to come to church for a brief visit. She desperately wanted to be present as a family unit at a parish Eucharistic adoration service. I shared in her joy on this special occasion. But what pleases me even more is her commitment to family prayer on every other occasion. Every day Ann prays with her two kids. These little ones are growing spiritually because Ann isn't hiding behind her husband's noninvolvement. She's "just doing it."

Or take my friend, Linda, who's divorced and the mother of four. Every day she visits her handicapped twenty-year-old son in a rehabilitation home so that they can pray together. How moved I was on a recent visit to witness the peace and joy in Linda's son. The presence of God in his room seemed palpable. I am in awe of her courage and faith expressed in this daily commitment to family prayer. God's grace shines through in the most broken family situations when even two or three gather in his name. Didn't Jesus promise it? "I will be in the midst of them" (see Matthew 18:19-20).

Patti Gallagher Mansfield

For Discussion

1. Why does the author suggest that parents be satisfied with praying "poorly"?
2. What effect has praying together had on the author's children?

For Reflection

1. In what ways do we pray as a family?
   - at mass?
   - confession?
   - the rosary?
   - in the car?
   - spontaneously?
2. What other ways of praying could we introduce to our family?

Options for Family Prayer

Experiment with different forms of prayer until you find one that suits your family. Then use it regularly.

Bert Ghezzi

Raising kids Catholic requires talking to God about our families and talking to our families about God. Praying together makes us aware of God's presence in our home. Conversations with the Lord involve him in our daily lives. What mom and dad doesn't want to have God's help in caring for their children?

Family prayer times also give families chances to talk about important topics. We can take occasions to speak about God's love, forgiving one another or why we go to mass. Or we can discuss the meaning of a Scripture text or of a prayer. Especially if we have a hard time talking with the family about God, praying together can serve as an icebreaker:

Dad: "Sam, what do you think the Lord's Prayer means by 'Forgive us our trespasses as we forgive those who trespass against us?'"

Sam: "That God wants us to forgive people?"

Mom: "Yes, that's it exactly, Sam. Now let's talk about forgiveness in our family."

Families will not become very Catholic without conversations with God and conversations with each other. That's why family prayer times are essential.

We can take many different approaches to prayer times. Many options are available, and parents should experiment with them. We want to discover what works best for our families. When we find a format that suits us, we should use it regularly for a while. But as families change and children become teens, we will need to look for new ways to pray together. Right now, for example, our family likes a book with psalms, readings and prayers. When our children were little, however, prayer time was very different. It even included dramatizing Bible stories and singing songs with gestures. How many times did I lead choruses such as, "God said to Noah, 'Go build me an arky, arky. Build it out of hickory barky, barky,' children of the Lord"?

Consider some of the following options for family prayer times. Maybe you'll find one that's just right for your family.

Traditional daily prayers. We should teach our kids to pray the great popular prayers of the church. We should start as soon as they are old enough to memorize a few sentences. You'll be on the right track, even if the three-year-old says, "Our Father who art in heaven, how do you know my name?"

There's no better way to build a tradition of Catholic family prayer. So let's be sure our children can pray the Our Father, the Hail Mary, the Apostles' Creed, the Come, Holy Spirit and an act of contrition. You can find these and numerous other prayers suitable for families in many books, such as *The Catholic Prayer Book* (Servant) and *Lord, Hear Our Prayer* (Ave Maria Press).

Scriptural rosary. The rosary is one of the most popular forms of Catholic family devotions. It only takes about ten minutes to pray five decades. If that seems too long, try praying one decade a day. Children seem to like the rhythm and repetition of the prayers. They also like to participate, so have them take turns leading the rosary. The mysteries of the rosary present the life and work of Christ. Thus, they give us many chances to teach our kids. Some prayer books provide an appropriate Bible text for each mystery of the rosary. So we can even use the rosary to introduce our family to Scripture.

Psalms. The psalms are ideal for teaching children how to pray because they are models of conversations with God. The psalms are inspired songs that express every shade of human emotion. They help us talk to God about our desires, fears, sins, anger, loneliness and needs. They also help us praise, thank and worship him. Our family has used the psalms for prayer times with children of all ages. Our kids have always enjoyed alternating verses, Mom leading one group of kids and Dad the other.

Devotionals. Daily devotionals work well for kids of all ages. Devotional books for every day normally provide a Bible text, a story or anecdote, and prayers or reflections. Some are designed to teach faith or morals. Others introduce kids to the Catholic heritage. *The One Year Book of Saints* (Our Sunday Visitor), for example, offers a short biography of a saint, a verse from the Bible and a short, instructive reflection. Check your local Catholic bookstore or Catholic publishers' catalogs. You will find a myriad of devotional books that your family might enjoy.

Conversational prayer. All other prayer formats should lead to just plain talking with God. The core truth of Christianity is that God has come to live in us. He's right there among us in our homes. He waits patiently for us to speak to him. And among other things, he wants to tell us of his love for us. We shouldn't keep him waiting too long. So our family prayer times should include opportunities for each person to talk to God. In his or her own words. Whatever is on his or her heart. Of course, Mom and Dad should set a good example and go first.

We do not always find it easy to pray out loud with others, even our own kids. We may need a little help from the Holy Spirit. Personally, I like to use the opening verses of morning and evening prayer that the church has used for centuries:

Dad: "Lord, open my lips."
Family: "And my mouth shall declare your praise."

Asking for God's help is a great way to start any prayer time.

For Discussion

1. In what ways can prayer times help parents raise their kids Catholic?
2. Why do you think it is important to teach children the traditional Catholic prayers?

3. What is conversational prayer? How do you think it contributes to our relationship with God?

For Reflection
1. What forms of prayer might work well for our family? Have we tried them?
2. What can we do to get in the habit of praying together as a family?
3. What could we do to improve our family prayer time?

25 Ideas for Family Prayer

Let these suggestions awaken you to the many opportunities for family prayer that pop up every day.

Kathy and Mitch Finley

Family prayer is a peculiar experience. Some of the times we tried the hardest for a prayerful experience have bombed, while the spontaneous moments of prayer were some of the best. Most of the ideas mentioned here come from our experience and have ***our*** family seal of approval. We hope these twenty-five ideas will be helpful to ***your*** family in giving you ideas for celebrating the holy in your midst.

A good place to start is with the ***daily*** holy events such as meal prayer and a nightly blessing. At our house, meal prayer is both a frequently chaotic situation and an important one, since we are all gathered together—most of the time—around the table. We take turns (1) by weeks choosing what we will do for the meal prayer, often a bit of silence while holding hands followed by an "Amen." Meanwhile, a lit candle (2) on the table with the overhead light off helps all of us to focus, especially those who choose not to close their eyes. We started that tradition with the Advent wreath (3), and later began using a cross with vigil candles (4) for each week of Lent. Someone in our parish made it.

The nightly blessing (5) has been a powerful way to tuck our now-not-so-little-ones in. We make a sign of the cross on their foreheads while asking God to be with them for the night. Our children give us a similar blessing whenever we go on a trip (6). We know a family that gives a blessing each morning as everyone goes out the door for work and school. Who can guarantee that everyone will make it back safely together by evening?

We can easily overlook the *ordinary* events in our lives, but they contain so many opportunities for family prayer. For example, reading aloud to children (7), beginning a family trip or vacation (8), planting a garden (9), going off to play a game with a team (10), or even a little person finding a new bug or rock (11)—all are ways to see God present in our midst. Our surroundings also sometimes call for a blessing, whether the house or the car (12), especially when new. Or we can even bless the television set (13), before which we spend many hours. We can pray that viewing it stretches our imaginations to help us understand the world better and make it a better place in which to live.

The *seasons* of the year provide many occasions for prayer and celebration from Advent to Thanksgiving (14). What else are we thankful for besides Junior getting rid of his drum set? Time around the Christmas crib or tree (15) is an invaluable time for a sense of family prayer and ritual. Especially on Christmas Eve, we celebrate the Word made flesh in our family with a simple prayer and a Christmas carol. On New Year's Eve, our family has for several years gathered with another family with whom we are friends. After an evening of games and visiting, we bless our clocks and calendars (16) as we remember the year just ending and anticipate the one that is beginning.

Lent is another season that lends itself well to family prayer. Each evening of Lent, if we remember, we give each person a small pretzel (17) on their plate as a reminder that Lent is a time for prayer. The pretzel shape is a reminder of an early posture for prayer, with hands on opposite shoulders and arms crossed over the chest. What about a "tree" out of a bare branch (18) as a centerpiece during Lent to which a leaf of paper is added every day so that by Easter the branch shows new life? Or an evening of charades in which each person acts out one of his or her favorite passages from Scripture (19) while everyone else guesses what it is?

Palm, or Passion, Sunday is a natural for a parade (20) with little ones. We found music with a good march beat, such as "When the Saints Go Marching In," and marched around in our house with rhythm instruments (pans) and the palms we just received at church. We'll never forget our oldest saying, at age five, "This is just like the parade when Jesus entered Jerusalem!"

Family milestones need to be celebrated with prayer, lest they go by too fast. Birthdays (21) are key, a day to celebrate the unrepeatable gift that the birthday person is in our lives. Pulling out some pictures of that person taken over the years can help us celebrate who he or she is becoming. Coming of age (22), although not usually marked in our culture, is worth celebrating with a prayer and a special dinner. From a blessing of the riding toys (23), which we had when our boys were quite young, to the prayer before the first day of school (24), which we still do along with taking a picture in new school clothes, we hope prayer will follow our family through the joys as well as the sorrows and losses, whether the death of a pet, a friend, or a family member (25).

There are *many* more ideas for family prayer than we have shared here. The key is to be watching and listening for the ways in which God is present, sometimes when we least expect it. It's like keeping our spiritual cameras loaded for the spur-of-the-moment "shot" that could never have been planned.

Praying for Our Kids

Next to praying for our children, one of the best things we can do is to tell them we are praying for them.

Mary Ann Kuharski

I remember the first time I told one of my rebellious teens, "I'm praying for you. We raised you to know right from wrong. Now I pray that when the temptations come up, you'll make the right decision."

"Oh, great!" he responded. "What chance does a guy have?"

Telling our young of our prayer may not prevent them from succumbing to sin or bad decisions. After all, there is such a thing as *free will.* But it reminds them that our desire for their well-being is paramount. It says we love them so much that we look to God himself to insure their happiness.

The *Catechism of the Catholic Church* says that "the *Christian family* is the first place of education in prayer...." For young children in particular, daily family prayer is the first witness of the church's living memory as awakened patiently by the Holy Spirit. My husband, John, and I are the parents of thirteen children, ages five to twenty-five. Seven of our children came by "tummy"—as the kids say—and six came by "airport," or adoption. We feel we need all the *awakening* we can muster to help us form them spiritually. You probably feel the same about your family.

The church teaches that God will give us all the grace and tools we need to guide our young. But only if we stay close to the church and ask God's help. And the way we ask is by talking to him in prayer.

Does it guarantee an end to rebellion? No. I remember one particular kid who snapped back with a sharp "Don't bother!" when I told him I was praying for him. This is the same son, a few years later, who asks for prayers before final exams, job interviews or moving decisions. Funny what a few years of maturity can do.

Step Number One is to speak the truth to our children. Take the approach of the spiritual works of mercy, and God will bless our effort even when it appears futile:

- Instruct the Ignorant (if they don't know).
- Counsel the Doubtful (if they are open to your message).
- Admonish the Sinner (when all else fails).

As parents we have a responsibility to remind our young of God's laws, his forgiveness and his love. We must tell a child, ***no matter the age,*** when his or her actions are destructive and sinful.

As one of my friends told her son, who defiantly announced

his decision to live with his girlfriend, "I do not approve of the way you are living your life. I'll have no part in supporting it in any way. But it doesn't change the fact that I'll always love you. *And, I'm going to pray* that you'll stop and do the right thing!"

Step Number Two is to pray. Temptation is a serious thing. It always comes disguised as attractive, alluring and fun. Sin chips away at our will power, attacks our weakest area and is habit forming. But a parent's prayer can be an antidote for a child's temptations.

The kindest, most compassionate thing we can do for one of our wayward children is not to shrug and say, "Well, it's your decision and your life." Strangers do that. Rather, we must love our sinful offspring and hate their sin. An old adage says, "If there's a parent out there praying for you—give it up!" No use trying to live a life of sin and debauchery when someone's praying!

St. Paul repeatedly reminds us to "pray constantly." The new catechism tells us that "prayer comes also from the Holy Spirit" and not from ourselves alone. Now there's consolation and support.

As my Michael recently asked, "Mom, were you praying for me today? I did so well on the test I figured you must have prayed for me!" That's the way I want my kids to remember me. Urging their success and well-being even when I'm not there in person.

One of my favorite prayers is to offer up my daily chores and tasks for one of my children. Thus, every floor I sweep and dish I wash becomes a prayer to God on behalf of one of my sons or daughters. I do not always think to do it, but when I do, my work becomes easier and my worry-load lighter. You should see the smiles when I occasionally say, "Well, Mikey, today was your day. I offered up my laundry and housework just for you. So, I expect to see *great* things from you, kid!"

Catholic parents have a whole arsenal of saints to pray to, to lean on, and to tell our kids about. We have a common union of saints to pray along with us. That's what's meant by the *communion of saints.*

When one of my young adults left home not on the best of terms to "do his own thing," I prayed daily to a small army of saints and his guardian angel to protect him. When he returned months later ready to buckle down, asking for a second chance, I knew who to thank: the Blessed Mother, his patron saint, his guardian angel, a host of others who had interceded for him and our Lord himself, who had heard our pleas.

The one I lean on most, whom I depend on to hear my prayer, plead my case and console my impatient heart is Mary, the Mother of Christ. She is also our mother. Who more than Mary has Christ's ear? And who more than Mary can understand a mother's (or dad's) fears, pains, needs and desires?

All of this is well and good, but what about those children who don't seem to show improvement in spite of our persistent praying? Worse still, the young adults who have chosen a way of life that jeopardizes their very souls? How should one pray for wayward children who use and abuse chemicals, alcohol, gambling or sex? A test of faith, trust and patience in *God's* timing, to be sure. I've been there. We may not see the results of all our prayers. But I know that no prayer goes unheeded.

Have all my prayers been answered? Yes, every one of them. Answered in the way I wanted? No. I have learned through the years that if I relinquish my own will in a given situation, the Holy Spirit is free to bring "all things" to "work together for good for those who love the Lord," as St. Paul so beautifully tells us.

After all, our children are only on loan to us from a heavenly Father who loves them far more than we can even imagine. If we want their happiness and well-being, God wants it even more. Not just on earth but for all eternity.

For Discussion

1. Why should parents tell children that they are praying for them?

2. How can we use the spiritual works of mercy to help our children?

For Reflection

1. Do I pray daily for my children?
2. Do I tell my kids that I am praying for them?

When God's Answer Is Always *Yes*

The Lord wants our kids in his family more than we do, so he cannot refuse our prayers for their salvation.

Bert Ghezzi

At 5:45 A.M. every weekday I head with coffee in hand to my favorite living room couch to pray. Don't feel sorry for me or bad about yourself if you sleep later—I also go to bed early.

After a brief time of worship and maybe a hymn sung at a whisper so as not to disturb anyone, I pray for my family. I say something like, "Father, I come to you united to Christ your Son. In his name I pray for my family." Then I pray for my wife, my seven children and for me. I also include my daughter's husband and my son's intended.

"Lord," I continue, "I expect you to cause us to know, love and serve you and to bring us all to final salvation." Going down the list, I pray specifically about each one's biggest needs, asking for the Lord's direct intervention. It only takes a few minutes. It's worth doing because the Lord's answer to such prayers is always *yes.*

Jesus taught emphatically that when we pray "in his name" he will do what we ask. So we typically conclude prayers with "in Jesus' name. Amen." That's one appropriate application of the Lord's instruction. But at a deeper level, praying in Jesus' name means conforming our prayer to his will. Jesus says that when we pray for what is most on his heart, he will always do it for us.

Of course we must not pretend that we have God in a box and that by pushing a button we can get whatever we want. I might pray to win the Florida lottery, convinced that God should will

"If You Ask Anything in My Name...."

Jesus left no doubt that when we pray in his name he will do what we ask:

- "Whatever you ask in my name, I will do it, that the Father may be glorified in the Son; if you ask anything in my name, I will do it" (John 14:13-14).
- "If you abide in me, and my words abide in you, ask whatever you will, and it shall be done for you" (John 15:7).
- "I chose you and appointed you that you should go and bear fruit, so that whatever you ask the Father in my name, he may give it to you" (John 15:16-17).
- "Truly, truly I say to you, if you ask anything of the Father, he will give it to you in my name... ask and you will receive, that your joy may be full" (John 16:23-24).
- "In that day you will ask in my name; and I do not say to you that I shall pray the Father for you; for the Father himself loves you, because you have loved me and have believed that I came from the Father" (John 16:26-27).

Bert Ghezzi

that for me. But his answer would surely be *no,* since millions of dollars would probably do me spiritual harm. We must conform to God's will, not the other way around.

But nothing is higher on God's list of priorities for human beings than uniting us to himself. Scripture gives us pictures of what he plans for us, since we really cannot think his thoughts. My favorite biblical picture of the divine plan is John's revelation that God is gathering himself a family of men, women and children. "To all who received him [Jesus], who believed in his name, he gave power to become children of God; who were born... not of the will of man, but of God" (John 1:12-13). Jesus brings us to his Father. The Father begets us as daughters and sons, incorporating us into his family through the power of the Holy Spirit.

That's why I'm confident when I pray for my family's salvation. The Lord wants my wife, my sons, my daughters and me in his family. He wants it even more than I do. He loves them more than I do, and saving them is what he is about.

While we can always expect God to say *yes* to prayers for our family's salvation, we must expect answers on his terms. We may be tempted to tell God just how to answer our prayer: "Lord, bring my son back to church. How about this Sunday at the ten o'clock mass?" But we shouldn't. We must pray for our families knowing that God will save them, but that he will do it his way, not ours.

25 Ways to Teach Kids to Pray

First set a good example yourself, then try some of these approaches.

Paul Thigpen

Little Christopher knelt by his bed and prayed softly: "Harold, please bless Mommy and Daddy."

"Harold?" said his father. "Why do you call God 'Harold'?"

"You know," said the boy. "We say it every week in church: '*Harold* be thy name.'"

Most kids are probably like Christopher—they're willing to pray, but they need a little help in learning how to go about it. Here's a smorgasbord of suggestions for teaching your family about talking with God.

1. ***Find a regular time for daily family prayer.*** Pick a time that fits everyone's schedule, then make it a priority. A thousand distractions will try to keep you from establishing this discipline in your home, but persevere. No matter how much you pray alone, your family needs to pray together as well.

   Try setting aside ten minutes a day at first. Once you've formed the habit, you can expand the time easily if you like. The important thing is to get started and stick with it.

2. ***Teach your kids the basic elements of prayer.*** Making requests is only one aspect of talking to God. To remember the other important elements, think of the letters of the word "ACTS":

   A is for Adoration: praising God for who he is.

   C is for Confession: admitting to God our sins and telling him we're sorry.

   T is for Thanksgiving: recalling all that God has done for us.

S is for Supplication: making requests, both intercession for others and petition for ourselves.

Not every prayer needs to have all these elements. But taken as a whole, our prayer times should reflect a balance of them.

3. ***Join family prayers to Scripture.*** Pray a psalm responsively as you do in church. Read together from the Scripture lessons designated for the day and let the words shape your thoughts in prayer.
4. ***Combine spontaneous prayer with fixed forms of prayer*** such as the Our Father, the Hail Mary and the Glory Be. Both kinds of prayer are important. Fixed forms help us find the right words. They remind us of concerns we might otherwise have forgotten and relieve us of the burden of trying to make every prayer new and different. Spontaneous prayer, on the other hand, allows us the flexibility to tailor our prayer to the needs of the moment. It keeps us aware that we're having a conversation with a living Person.
5. ***Make song a part of family prayer.*** Music can lift our hearts to God and allow us to express our feelings in ways the mere spoken word can't even touch. Sing praise songs throughout the day. If no one in your home is musically gifted, don't worry—as one old Bible translation puts it, just "make a joyful *noise* unto the Lord!" (Psalm 66:1; KJV).
6. ***Tell your children that prayer is a two-way conversation.*** We should spend some time listening to God as well as talking to him. Sometimes after a few minutes of silence in his presence we can hear in our minds his words of comfort, discipline or direction. Or we can simply feel his love and concern.
7. ***Teach your kids that prayer is a discipline and a privilege.*** So much in our culture leads them to assume that to be worthwhile an activity must feel good and be entertaining. Let them know that even though prayer is often a pleasure, it is also work. We pray, not for fun, but because it's the right thing to do.
8. ***Divide up intercessory responsibilities*** when you pray together as a family. Make sure each person has at least one concern to focus on, then take turns leading in prayer.

9. ***Have a family prayer list*** on the refrigerator door. Any time family members have a concern they want others to bring to God, have them add it to the list. Pray through the list during family prayer times.
10. ***Take on a prayer project with your kids.*** Discover a need someone has that only God can fill, then commit yourselves to interceding for the situation until you see an answer.
11. ***Encourage your children to start a prayer journal,*** perhaps in the form of letters to God. Writing down their conversation with the Lord can help them clarify their thoughts. Later they'll profit from reading over what they wrote in light of later events.
12. ***Keep a "thanksgiving book"*** of your family's answered prayers. Review it when you need to stir up your faith in God's provision. Swap stories of answered prayer with other families.
13. ***Pray together for people in the news,*** especially government leaders and victims of war or natural disaster.
14. ***Take problems to God as soon as they arise.*** Make it a family habit that prayer is your first response to a challenge, not your last resort.
15. ***Pray about the small things together.*** Whatever concerns your children concerns the Lord. Be specific and concrete in your prayer requests.
16. ***Pray your family table grace in public places*** without embarrassment or apology. Show your kids you're not afraid to let strangers see your faith.
17. ***Be on the lookout for the "prayable moment."*** Maybe you and your teen have just watched the sunrise at the beach, and you feel close to God just now. Perhaps a favorite pet just died and your preschooler needs the Lord's comfort. Some occasions naturally invite us to pause a few minutes and talk with God.
18. ***Put permanent items on your family prayer list,*** such basic perennial concerns as the church, the poor, the sick and the government. Honor the Holy Father's request that children everywhere pray for world peace.

19. ***Praise God on the spot for good news***—the announcement of a new job, the birth of a nephew, top grades on a report card. Give the Lord a round of applause, a rousing cheer, or anything else that says to him, "Thank you!"
20. ***Help your kids make a daily self-examination.*** Bedtime is the traditional time for a brief review of the day, with thanksgiving for God's favors and confession of our failures.
21. ***Discuss the prayers of the mass*** so your kids will understand the meaning of the words they're praying in church.
22. ***Pray the rosary and an occasional novena as a family.*** Talk to your children about how the words of repetitive prayers can press themselves deep into our hearts and free our minds to meditate on the mysteries of faith.
23. ***Teach your children about the saints*** and how God has granted us the great favor of their intercession. Join your family in asking them to pray for you.
24. ***Tell your children about their guardian angel*** and teach them to ask his protection daily. Read to them what the new *Catechism of the Catholic Church* has to say about the role of angels in our lives (see sections 328-336).
25. ***Set a good example of prayer.*** The best way to teach prayer is to model it to your children. Make prayer a way of life. If your family sees that you and God have frequent, intimate conversations, they'll be more likely to want to build their own friendship with him.

Think, Pray & Act

Pray Always

By now I hope you're convinced that talking makes handing on the faith possible. Talking to kids about God. And even more crucial, talking to God about kids. Are you praying regularly for your family? Are you praying regularly with your family? Are you and your family praying enough? Refer to the questions *For Discussion* and *For Reflection*. Should you be doing something differently? Look for the one action that could make the biggest difference in your conversations with God. If you like, use the

Action Idea List (page 41), *Decision Grid* (page 42) and *Action Plan* (page 43).

Resource:

Workshops

- Praying for Our Sons and Daughters, presented by Vernon Robertson. This workshop communicates inspiring and effective strategies and tactics for evangelizing children to Christ and the church. Write Vernon Robertson, 3330 Garibaldi Drive, North Vancouver, British Columbia, Canada V7H 2N9; or call (604) 929-4511.

Publications

- *The Catholic Prayer Book* (Servant Book Express: 313-677-6490).
- *Lord, Hear Our Prayer* (Ave Maria Press: 800-282-1865).
- *Our Family Prayer Book* (Liguori Publications: 800-325-9521, ext. 657).
- Fr. Edward Hayes, *Prayers for the Domestic Church* (Forest of Peace, Inc.: 913-773-8255).
- Mary Ann Kuharski, *Parenting With Prayer* (Our Sunday Visitor: 800-348-2440).

FOUR

Meet Jesus in the Sacraments

Parents must show their children that worship does not end on Sunday morning but extends into daily Christian living.

Remembering the Milestones

Families can remember significant events in the ways that make children feel at home with Christ.

Elizabeth McNamer

Next spring, the youngest of our five children will graduate from college. After thirty-two years of concentrated parenting, Bill and I will be freer than ever to enjoy our married life together. We haven't yet decided how we will celebrate. Perhaps we will take a room for two in a posh hotel and have dinner served in our room, complete with champagne and roses. Then we can delight in the change from the days of crowding all seven of us into one Holiday Inn room and ordering in pizza!

Celebration is such an important part of life, as Jesus himself showed us. He loved to celebrate, and frequently gave his stamp of approval to celebration. He performed his first miracle to gladden a bride and groom at a wedding feast (see John 2:1-11). Once on a hillside in Galilee he treated his friends to a fine picnic of bread and fish. While celebrating the Passover with his disciples, he instituted the Eucharist, leaving us a means of celebrating for all time in the mass.

What we celebrate defines us as a nation: the Fourth of July,

Memorial Day, Thanksgiving. It defines us as a church too: Christmas, Easter, Pentecost, feasts that honor Mary and the saints. Celebration also defines us as a family: wedding anniversaries, baptisms, birthdays, confirmation, graduations, and death days.

Wedding Anniversary. Your wedding day is where your family life began. The saying "the best thing parents can do for their children is to love each other" is indeed true. And a good day to show that love is on your wedding anniversary. On this day make every attempt to attend mass together. Many couples like to renew their wedding vows at this time. Take out the photograph book and show it to your children. When my husband and I were married, a friend recorded the service on audio tape (it was well before the time of videos). We play the tape at breakfast on each anniversary and it brings back all the magical feeling of that day.

Celebrate your wedding often! The graces of the sacrament are freely available, but we need to activate those graces through demonstrated affection, compliments and kindnesses that demonstrate our spouse's importance in our lives. When our children were growing up, I prepared dinner for them early one night a week, and Bill and I ate alone later. It gave us an opportunity to talk. Most often, we talked about problems before they became explosive!

Take inexpensive mini-vacations together whenever you can. Take a walk together on a Sunday afternoon; have lunch together; attend a lecture; enjoy a sports event together. It will change your perspective on your spouse.

Birthdays. We have always made a big fuss over birthdays. When the children were living at home, a big breakfast was served in the dining room, with a special birthday tablecloth and the lighted birthday candle. Presents were piled at the place of the birthday person, who did not come downstairs until the bell was rung. All assembled at the foot of the stairs to give their greetings.

During the meal, each person told what he or she most

appreciated about the birthday person. We recounted stories about the birth and early life of the person. We each thanked God for sending him or her into our lives. Children need all the positive reinforcement they can get, especially from their family. Every so often my husband would say to me, "that child needs a dose of vitamin P" (P for praise), and birthdays are a good time to give it.

Baptisms. Baptism, the time when the child is officially welcomed into the family of faith, is a special family event. Celebrate it by having a meal afterwards and a cake with the child's name. Explain the meaning of baptism to the other children. Remind them that we are all promising to nurture this new soul on his or her faith journey.

We should celebrate the anniversary of baptisms. If possible, invite the godparents to a little party (it does not have to be elaborate). Light the candle that the child received on that great day. On these occasions you could read aloud the story of the child's special saint.

First Holy Communion. Look for ways of enhancing your child's first communion. When my children were about to receive their first communion, I used to go to the school to show the children how to make bread. I left it to rise in the classroom, which always fascinated the children. Then I baked it in the school oven. Later the parish priest blessed it together with some grape juice, and we celebrated a little agape meal. I explained to the children that just as bread becomes part of us, so we become part of Christ's body when we receive Holy Communion.

Make the first communion day special by going out to breakfast or by having a family party. Buy the child a little gift, perhaps a copy of the New Testament. Since first communion is usually in May, why not plant a few pansies to mark the day? The Eucharist is the center of our lives as Catholics. Show this to your child by your own frequent reception.

Confirmation. Confirmation is the other side of the coin of baptism. When the child was baptized, the community accepted responsibility for him or her. Now the child is old enough to accept responsibility for others. You should participate in the instruction of your child. Don't leave this privilege entirely to others. On confirmation day, have each member of the family lay their hands on the person and pray for a gift of the Holy Spirit. At dinner, read and discuss Galatians 5:22-25, which tells of the fruit of the Spirit.

At our house we had a custom on the feast of Pentecost. I cut out paper doves and on the back of each wrote a fruit or gift of the Holy Spirit. For example, "Courage," "Wisdom," "Understanding," "Joy" or "Kindness." Each child received a dove at breakfast and was encouraged to practice during the coming year the gift or fruit written on the back.

Graduation. High-school graduation is an exciting time for everyone involved. It marks the transition to adulthood and usually means a move away from home, whether to a job or to college. We celebrated by having the graduate write out the story of his or her life and put it in a jar along with the tassel from the graduation cap. Then we planted a tree and buried the jar under the roots. Someday a future archaeologist will find it and wonder! Meanwhile the trees are blossoming and spreading and growing strong and serve to remind me (as if a mother can forget) to pray and be thankful.

Death. As Americans we are protected from contact with death. Most people die in hospitals. Funeral homes tend to dull our senses to the realities of death. As Catholics we believe that death is our birth into eternal life. When our children were growing up, I made a point of taking them to visit the sick and dying and to funerals and to houses of the bereaved. At an early age they became comfortable dealing with sad situations. I encouraged them to talk about death with their friends, especially with those who had lost a loved one. They tell me that they are very grateful for this. It never posed a problem and helped relieve anxiety all around.

For a family, death of a loved one will bring too much sorrow to think of celebration. But when that sorrow is abated, why not plant a rosebush in the garden in that person's memory? I started to do this several years ago and now have a magnificent rose garden. When I water the roses on summer mornings, I say a prayer for or to the person for whom it was planted. On the fortieth anniversary of my own first holy communion, I planted a rose for all of those concerned with that day—the teacher who prepared me, the priest who administered the sacrament, the woman who made my dress, as well as my parents. Every summer morning brings me an opportunity to rejoice in the communion of saints, knowing that these people are not gone. They are merely in a different state—and I am spiritually connected to them forever.

Memorial Day provides an excellent opportunity to remember our dead loved ones. Tell the children about a grandmother, uncle or sibling who has died. Children love to hear these stories. Keep our communion of saints alive in their minds. Read the "for everything there is a season" poem in Ecclesiastes 3:1-8, and perhaps have the children learn it by heart.

End Results. Often it seems such a bother to do something. Many a time I have had the tendency to say "skip it." But I really do believe that it is not the things that we have done that will bother us so much as the things we have left undone. The little things add up to a good life. Often now I hear my grown children recall a family custom which I very nearly omitted. As parents, we never know what moment, or memory of us, a child will take and hide away in his or her heart forever. We are creating the past in the present moment. Make your home the happiest place there is. Give your children good memories. You can bestow no greater gift on them. Celebrate often! Particularly the milestones.

For Discussion
What do you think celebrations contribute to family life?

For Reflection
1. How do we celebrate milestones in our family?
2. Are there important personal events our family does not celebrate? Should we celebrate them? How?

Celebrate the Sacraments

The sacraments give parents occasions to exercise spiritual leadership and to transmit the faith to their children.

Fr. Fred R. Gaglia, Ph.D.

"I will celebrate your love forever, Yahweh. Age on age, my words proclaim your love. For I know that love is built to last forever, founded firm your faithfulness."

So the words of Psalm 89 speak to us and tell us to do that with the sacraments: celebrate them, and from age on age, so that we can proclaim the Lord's love for us.

One of the great events for a pastor is the baptism of children. The celebration of a baptism starts a journey of faith for parents and the child. It gives me an opportunity to do more than just baptize the infant. I get a chance to speak to parents about their most important role.

You parents have a most wonderful and awesome responsibility to your children. The church has always understood that you have the primary task of educating your children in the Catholic faith. It asks you to say *yes* to this duty during the baptism ceremony. The *Catechism of the Catholic Church* makes it even clearer: "The role of parents in education is of such importance that it is almost impossible to provide an adequate substitute" (#2221).

All teachers have great power in the lives of those they educate. But Catholic parents have an extraordinary influence on their children by transmitting the treasury of faith to them.

Faith-filled parents are a living inspiration to their children, a living testimony to Christian truth. Inspired parents will raise inspired children. Inspired children will become the inspired parents of the future. They will be the faithful transmitters of Christianity to the next generations. So you parents have a significant service with very long-range benefits. Some of them, in fact, will last forever.

The sacraments are a big help to parents in their role as religious educators. Matrimony gives them the help of the Holy Spirit. His presence in the family makes their job somewhat easier. And the celebrations of the sacraments are important moments in the lives of children. They provide occasions where parents can truly exercise strong leadership. To do this parents must be principle-centered people—centered in the principles of faith.

H Have only a few rules.

Celebrating a sacrament should not stop when the event is over. Families should celebrate the sacraments through the years. For example, families can celebrate the anniversary of a baptism by displaying the child's baptismal candle. Light it at dinner time. Have the child offer a prayer of thanks to God for the gift of faith. As children grow older, help them understand the profession of faith made for them by parents and godparents at the time of their baptism. Ask the godparents to send children cards on their baptism anniversaries, their birthdays into the life of Christ.

Preparing your children for first confession and first communion can be chances for the whole family to grow spiritually. If you are going to talk to your kids about these sacraments, you will have to learn more about them yourself. Getting ready for these sacraments may also show you the need for personal growth in your relationship to God. These are the times when parents should consider making a personal retreat or participating in some Catholic renewal movement, like a parish prayer group or Bible study. Preparing for a child's first confession and first communion should increase parents' appreciation and use of these sacraments. Children won't value the sacraments much if their parents don't receive them.

When your children are ready to receive the sacrament of confirmation, you now have another significant opportunity to influence their lives. Parents should set an example of adult Catholic life by involving themselves in parish programs of service and prayer. Nothing teaches more strongly than example. Young people who see Mom and Dad involved in parish ministry and regular prayer meetings will recognize the authenticity of their parents' faith. They will come to see that such service is important and possible for them too.

Parental spiritual leadership does not end with the sacraments celebrated when children are young. It continues throughout their lives as adults. The witness of your marriage is a model for your children as they prepare for the sacrament of matrimony. You can also influence the young couple to plan a spiritual celebration of the sacrament that will really be a wonderful memory for their family.

> **I** Introduce children to God in a personal way.

Parents should see holy orders as another opportunity for their leadership. They can encourage their sons to be open to a vocation to the priesthood. Parents should be positive about the priesthood and open to sons becoming priests. This will help a young man who is seeking to follow the Lord and may help him choose the priesthood.

The sacrament of the anointing of the sick can be another moment for instructing children in the faith. Have your children present when a family member receives this. It will sensitize them to the reality of sickness and the need to care for the afflicted. It will also help them remember their limits. Nothing will prepare them better for life than an awareness of their own death.

Thus, all sacramental moments are moments of grace. Parents who are filled with a deep sense of these moments will want to share them in the fullest way with their children. The more a family celebrates each of the sacraments, the more that family grows in grace. "I will celebrate your love forever, Yahweh."

For Discussion

How does celebrating the sacraments help parents hand on the faith to their kids?

For Reflection

1. Which sacraments will our family celebrate during the next year?
2. How can we make celebrating these sacraments occasions to help our children grow in faith?

Six Reasons to Cultivate Family Customs

Parents should thoughtfully develop traditions that bring fun and faith to family life.

Paul Thigpen

All eyes are on the tiny basket as it makes its way around the Thanksgiving table. One by one, family members and guests place in it the three small kernels of dried corn we've left beside every dinner plate. With each kernel, they tell one reason why they're thankful that day. It's just a small holiday habit, yet every year it brings us to tears. Lumps rise in our throats as each speaker thanks God for something different—family or friends, health or faith. And when the guests go home in the evening, the comment is always the same: "Next year we'll do that in our home."

The simple practice requires almost no preparation or expense. But its rewards continue long after the meal is over, rippling out from our table into other homes as well. Such is the power and blessing of a family tradition.

Biblical glimpses of family life in ancient Israel reflect God's desire that we strengthen our families with such meaningful customs. When the Israelites left Egypt to become a new nation, the Lord commanded their families to hold special observances in their homes so that they would remember what he had done for them. Perhaps the best-known of these family traditions are the yearly Passover celebration (see Exodus 12:1-20) and the weekly Sabbath observance (see Exodus 20:8-11), both of which Jesus observed (see Matthew 26:17-19; Luke 4:16).

These traditions have endured in the Jewish community for thousands of years. As living reminders of spiritual realities, they have strengthened families throughout the generations.

Why have family traditions? Think back to the first Christmas you and your spouse spent together after you were married. The

Starting Traditions

Some family customs seem to appear spontaneously. You do something once and it just seems so "right" that you do it again and again. Other family traditions are more like habits that grow gradually over a period of time, such as a particular strategy for decorating your tree at Christmas.

These kinds of customs tend to thrive naturally on their own. But others must be intentionally cultivated in order to survive. To establish them and help them grow, you should keep the following things in mind:

- Look for new traditions. Talk to grandparents and other older relatives, especially if they come from the "old country." Discover the traditions other families have. Find books on the subject at the library or bookstore.
- Keep customs simple, since elaborate or expensive rituals may be difficult to maintain. Make sure that the burden of preparation doesn't fall all on one person. Consistency is the key, not complexity.
- Plan and prepare for family traditions well ahead of time—weeks or even months if necessary. Preparation builds anticipation, which is also part of the fun. Avoid canceling or changing plans on the spur of the moment.
- Choose or maintain traditions that focus on values and relationships, rather than on costly gifts or activities.
- Make sure all family members are included in the planning, preparation and observance of every tradition. Also, make sure

most emotionally sensitive conflict in your first year of marriage probably wasn't over money or sex, but rather over how you would celebrate this family holiday.

Would gifts be opened on Christmas morning or Christmas Eve? Would the tree be real or artificial? Would the dinner feature turkey or ham? In every home, each spouse comes into a marriage with an emotional investment in maintaining his or her own traditions. The sparks may fly because our family customs mean more to us than we realize.

But why exactly do they mean so much? What are the benefits of meaningful family traditions? Social research and practical experience both suggest that the families with the strongest ties

that the customs you establish appeal to old and young alike. The benefit of family unity and closeness will be lost if someone is left out.

- Include a few customs that turn your family outward. Many Jewish families, for example, invite a stranger to their table for the Passover meal—an ancient tradition reflecting the biblical command for God's people to remember their exile in Egypt by caring for the alien in their midst (see Exodus 23:9).
- Don't be pressured or rigid about observing traditions. If you have to enforce a tradition, you take the fun out of it. When an idea doesn't work, try a different one. And don't attempt to initiate too many new traditions at once.
- Look for traditions that are tied to recurring events—weekly, monthly, seasonal or annual—which can keep the observances alive naturally.
- Make sure that at least some of your traditions are in some form transferable to later generations.
- Remember that the best customs can be repeated without losing their charm. Their meaning is deepened rather than cheapened by familiarity.
- Finally, be sure to use family traditions to call attention to the significance of an occasion. This is the biblical pattern: Moses told the Israelites that when their children asked why the Passover was kept, the parents were to discuss with the young ones the tradition's special meaning (see Deuteronomy 6:20-21).

Paul Thigpen

tend to have the most traditions because such traditions create and reinforce emotional security in the home in several ways:

1. ***Traditions establish family continuity.*** When something is done again and again over the years and through the generations, it ties together our past and our present. It links year to year, childhood to adulthood, grandparent to child to grandchild, with shared experiences, values and memories.
2. ***Traditions build family stability.*** Consistent family customs provide regular, familiar patterns for a rhythm of life together. Whether it's bedtime stories every night or family games every Sunday afternoon, such customs add an element of predictability to the cycle of family life that is both comfortable and comforting. This is especially important for families who maintain otherwise erratic schedules or who make frequent geographic moves.
3. ***Traditions cultivate family identity.*** Customs that contribute to a family's uniqueness can give its members a sense of who they are and where they belong. This quality is critical as a counterbalance to the intense pressure on today's youths to identify with their peers instead of with their families.
4. ***Traditions enrich family unity.*** Who can forget the warm sense of togetherness that comes when a family gathers for a Christmas morning gift-opening or a Fourth of July reunion? Meaningful customs build a sense of closeness that endures even long after children have grown and may be separated by great distances.
5. ***Traditions reveal the significance of our lives.*** When we set aside the routine for special customs, we focus on what's important to us. All too easily our days can slip by unnoticed until years have passed before we know it. Observing special days and events gives us a chance to pause and reflect on our lives.
6. ***Traditions symbolize how family members feel about one another.*** Family customs are much more than simple words or acts; they give those who take part in them a chance to say

nonverbally: "I love you. I enjoy being with you. You are important to me, and we share with each other what is important in life."

In short, meaningful family traditions make a family strong.

For Discussion

In what ways do you think family customs can help kids grow in faith?

For Reflection

1. What do our family traditions mean to us? Why are they worth maintaining?
2. Have any of our traditions lost their meaning? Why? Should we revitalize them, discontinue them or replace them?
3. Are there any traditions we have lost that we would like to reestablish?
4. Which new traditions would we like to begin?

You Are What You Eat

If we want our kids to stay Catholic, we must see to it that they meet Jesus in the Eucharist.

Fr. Dale J. Fushek

When I was in the seminary, I was assigned to teach a high-school religion class as a field education project. I was a disaster as a teacher. I am sure it was also a disaster for the teens.

There was one bright spot. He was a young man who loved the Lord, read the Bible and gave good answers to my poorly phrased questions. I found out that a few months after class ended, he left the Catholic church and joined another. When I asked him why, he gave me an answer that changed my focus in ministry. He told me he left the church, "Because for 16 years of my life, I never once missed church. And never once while I was there did I feel loved." He said further that, "I'm not sure what this new church believes, but I know they love me." He went on to become a minister in that Christian denomination.

I believe that the key to keeping our kids Catholic is the liturgy and the experience our young people have at mass. Yes, all the traditions and teachings we pass on are important. The prayer and family customs that fill our homes and holidays make a difference in how young people see the dignity of life and religion. And yes, the witness of faith that they see others living is also essential. But our experience of God *at the liturgy* either forms or deforms our understanding of God and of ourselves.

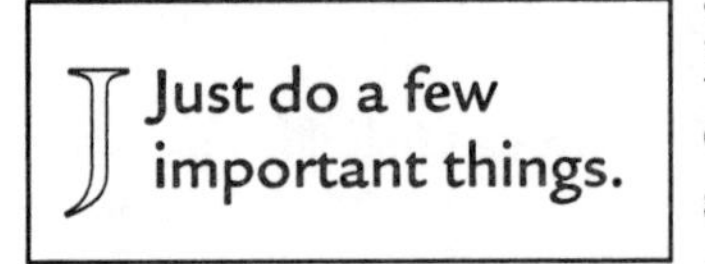

For most of our young people, mass is boring. It's easy to say mass is not supposed to be entertaining. If you want, you can believe that they will grow up and learn to appreciate the mass, but I am sorry, I do not buy that. A few might. But the majority of our youth *leave* the church because *boring* means irrelevant. Something is not boring because it's too long. It's boring because it's meaningless. Most of our youth believe that our *faith* is irrelevant to their lives. Nothing is further from the truth.

The reason most of us stay Catholic is the Eucharist. The Eucharist is the real presence of Jesus Christ. It is the way we accept Christ and experience him. The Eucharist is the center of our faith. It is also a gift that the Catholic church can give us that most other Christian churches cannot. Yet many of us hide the real presence of Christ beneath stacks of missalettes, non-participatory music and irrelevant homilies.

We do not have enough passion for God. We do not have enough passion for the Real Presence. We do not allow the love of God to shine through us enough. Human warmth and healthy human touch are often left out of our celebrations.

Several years back I had the opportunity to do a TV show with Mother Teresa. What an incredible experience! While the cameras were rolling, I asked her what message she had for those who work with American teenagers. She looked at me and said, "Father, bring the young people to adoration." My jaw dropped.

It was not the answer I anticipated. Mother Teresa meant bring young people to the real presence of Jesus in the Eucharist. Help them to feel loved by the Jesus we celebrate in the Eucharist. That should be the goal of every parent, every pastor and every youth worker!

I believe in the old saying, "You are what you eat." It's funny that even teenagers identify themselves with their heritage in terms of food. Teens identify themselves with the food Mom made. They love to eat food from their cultures of origin—pasta, tacos or other national foods. Our Catholic kids need to identify with *our* food. The food of heaven. The Bread of Life. The Eucharist must hold our youth at our table.

To do this our liturgies and masses must come alive. Pastors, priests and liturgists must make our celebrations places of life, not death. Parents must find parishes or work to build parishes that minister liturgically to their children. Parish councils must demand that parishes see the liturgy as the primary place where our families—especially our youth—come to *experience* God's love.

Of course parents must set a good example themselves. They must actively participate in the mass. That means praying out loud, and singing too. Moms and dads must show a real hunger for the Eucharist and devotion to the Real Presence. And they must also *talk* to their teens about their experience at the Lord's table. The best thing parents can give their children is openly sharing their own love for Christ.

We can keep our kids Catholic by giving them a Catholic identity. By all means teach them to love the pope and to regard themselves as Catholics. Teach them gospel values. Teach them to obey the church's moral laws. But above all else, teach them *Who* the Eucharist is. Find a parish where the liturgies are alive and the whole family can participate in the life of the church. Ultimately, sharing these experiences will open the hearts of our youth and form them in the likeness of Christ. Once that happens, they will always hunger for what the church has to offer. And perhaps with grace, they will desire to serve others at the banquet table of the Lord.

How to Encourage Vocations

I was ordained to the priesthood twelve years ago. At my first mass, I thanked my parents for the gift of my vocation. I quoted Pope John Paul II: "And if God does, in fact, call [your children] to the service of his Kingdom, dear fathers and mothers, be generous to him as he has been to you."

On the most recent anniversary of my ordination, the first since my mother died of an extended illness, I recalled the pope's words. As a wife and mother, Mom was "generous to God." It is to her generosity that I owe my priestly vocation.

How did my mom inspire my vocation?

First, the gospel and the teachings of the Catholic church were not impositions in our family life. For my parents, they were the very source of personal and family happiness and freedom. My parents taught me that you could find eternal joy only in the complete abandonment of yourself to the love of God for the sake of others.

Second, my parents nurtured a deep respect and love for priests. They saw priests as guardians of the gospel through their commitment to the church. My parents viewed celibacy as the ultimate expression of that guardianship. They taught me that celibacy was not an obstacle to a fulfilled life. Because it is the total dedication of the self to others, it is the reason for a priest's happiness.

Third, my parents knew that holy priests are raised in the cradle of the family, and from there are offered freely to the Lord and to the church. To make such an offering, they accepted great sacrifice. In so doing, their parental witness to their children was one of constant openness to grace no matter the cost, the sacrifice or the suffering.

Parents today must resist an attitude of selfishness when it comes to their children. Your child is not yours to possess. A child is a great gift to a family. A child is a sacred trust. A child, as Pope John Paul II teaches in his Letter to Families, is a "paschal sign," a sign of the resurrection of Christ and the love of the Father.

Parents today also must be constantly on guard against the temptation to believe that a child's earthly happiness will be found solely in marriage, in a good job or in material success. A child's happiness is found only in holiness. The two are mutually dependent. Faithful acceptance of God's call to a vocation—virginity, celibacy, marriage—is the only path to true happiness. That path begins with parents' generosity to God.

Fr. Edward Buelt

For Discussion

1. Why do you think young people leave the Catholic church?
2. What role does the experience of the Eucharist play in bringing kids up Catholic?

For Reflection

1. Do I participate actively at mass?
2. How do I experience Jesus in the Eucharist? Have I ever told my children about it?
3. What can we do differently to help our children meet Jesus in the Eucharist?

25 Ways to Bring the Sacraments to Life

We meet Jesus in the sacraments and we should do whatever we can to involve him in our daily routines.

Bert Ghezzi

When we approach the sacraments with greater awareness and faith, the Holy Spirit can do more for us. He works through them. Strengthens us for daily living. Nourishes our souls for greater growth. Helps us with family responsibilities.

Here are some ways we and our families can meet the Lord in the sacraments.

1. Make the baptism of babies a family celebration. Talk to everyone about the infant's becoming a child of God. Have a party and involve the whole family in preparing for it.
2. Select an important part of the mass and make it meaningful to your children. For example, explain that at the Great Amen we are offering ourselves with Christ to the Father. Remind them about it during mass.
3. Look for some personal and manageable Christian service you can do with your kids. The sacraments are not supposed to be isolated from life. They're supposed to spill over into our daily relationships.

4. Teach your children to make the sign of the cross. It's a reminder of our baptism. It signifies that we belong to Christ. Use the sign of the cross when you pray as a family. Encourage the children to do it on their own.
5. Study Scripture to expand your understanding of the Christian life. Have an occasional family Bible study. The sacraments are the source of life in Christ. The more we know about them, the better we and our kids can live.
6. Make a family member's confirmation an opportunity for everyone to be renewed in the Holy Spirit. The family can study the sacrament along with the candidate. Encourage all to attend the confirmation service. And to expect the Holy Spirit to work in them too.
7. When driving home from mass, turn off the "Top Forty" and discuss the gospel and homily. Ask family members to share the main thought they took away from the reading. To keep things positive, avoid criticizing the homilist.
8. For a firsthand experience of holy orders, attend an ordination service with your kids. Stay for the reception so you can meet and congratulate the newly ordained priests.
9. Volunteer to be a sponsor for a person in your parish's Rite of Christian Initiation for Adults (RCIA). Regularly tell your family about what you are doing and learning in the program.
10. Pray every day for the Holy Spirit's help in raising your family. This is the way to receive fully the grace that comes to us in the sacrament of matrimony.
11. Teach your children that mass is not just an obligation. It's an opportunity to participate in a special way in the greatest event that has ever happened. At mass we offer ourselves to God with Christ in his perfect sacrifice made present in the sacrament.
12. Attend a communal celebration of the anointing of the sick. Or allow your children to be present when a sick relative or friend receives the sacrament. Discuss with your family the healing power of the Holy Spirit.

13. Talk to the family about the consequences of sins. Explain our need to receive God's forgiveness for them. Review the Ten Commandments as an examination of conscience. Lead the family to the sacrament of reconciliation.
14. Plan to have the family attend the Easter Vigil in your parish this year. This celebration of the resurrection is the high point of the Christian year. New Christians have been preparing for a year for this evening when they will receive the sacraments of initiation—baptism, confirmation and the Eucharist.
15. Use natural signs to explain sacramental signs to your kids. For example, water is a natural sign of cleansing; in baptism water signifies a supernatural cleansing. God uses the water of baptism to produce the purification of our souls.
16. When you don't know how to answer a child's questions about God and the Christian community, expect the Holy Spirit to guide you. Wisdom and knowledge are gifts of the Spirit we received in baptism. He also came to us in matrimony to help us raise our kids
17. Take the whole family to a wake and to a funeral mass for someone they know. It's healthy for children to confront the reality of death. Use the celebration of the mass to teach them about the resurrection.
18. Have everyone gather to pray for family members who are ill. Lay hands on the sick and ask the Lord to heal them. Healing is a gift of the Spirit who dwells in us.
19. Invite inactive Catholics to worship with you at Christmas or Easter. If your parish has a "Remembering Church" program to welcome inactive Catholics, offer to attend it with them. Our Christian life progresses when we widen our hearts to include others.
20. Let your children help you bake bread from scratch. Explain to them that just as bread nourishes our bodies, Jesus is the Bread of Life who nourishes our souls. Tell them, too, that just as many grains of wheat combine to make one loaf of bread, many people are united together in the body of Christ, the church.

21. Save the front page of the newspaper for each child's baptism day. Display it on anniversaries of the baptism. Explain to your kids that their becoming God's children was the most important thing that happened in the world on that day. All other news was less significant because it was passing, but they will live forever.
22. Once a week during Advent or Lent attend mass on a weekday. If possible, take the children too. Let the children know that we don't go to mass because we have to. We do it because we want to.
23. For nine days before Pentecost have the family pray the traditional prayer to the Holy Spirit. Be like the disciples in the upper room who eagerly awaited the outpouring of the Spirit.
24. Create a "ritual" for repairing broken relationships in the family. Help people say "I was wrong, please forgive me" and "You're forgiven." Reconciliation begins in the family.
25. Encourage family members to pray daily for each other. We meet Jesus in the sacraments, and prayer is our way of inviting him to dwell with our families.

Think, Pray & Act
Empowered for Life

The sacraments are for life. They bring us into the Lord's presence. They empower us in the Holy Spirit. Does our family celebrate the sacraments with awareness and faith? Are we getting as much out of them as the Lord wants to give us? Are we meeting Jesus in the sacraments? The questions *For Discussion* and *For Reflection* at the end of the articles in this chapter will help you examine your family's practice. What one thing could you do differently to help family members benefit more from the sacraments? To prioritize your thoughts, use the *Action Idea List* (page 41), *Decision Grid* (page 42), and *Action Plan* (page 43).

Resources

- Peg Bowman, *At Home with the Sacraments: Baptism; Confirmation; Eucharist; Reconciliation* (four booklets; Twenty-third Publications: 800-321-0411).
- Ronda DeSola Chervin and Carla Conley, *The Book of Catholic Customs and Traditions* (Servant Book Express: 313-677-6490).
- Bert Ghezzi, *50 Ways to Tap the Power of the Sacraments* (Our Sunday Visitor: 800-348-2440).
- John Roberto, ed. *Family Rituals and Celebrations* (Don Bosco Multimedia: 914-576-0122).
- Paul and Leisa Thigpen, *52 Simple Ways to Build Family Traditions* (Oliver Nelson: 800-251-4000).

FIVE

Compassion Begins at Home

The more the members of a Christian family reach out to serve others, the more is love multiplied among them.

The Sad Man

To prepare kids to show compassion to the poor and suffering of the world, we must show and teach them love at home.

Eileen C. Marx

"Why is that man so sad?" my three-year-old niece, Patty, asked her mother. She had noticed a small, bearded man while walking to their neighborhood convenience store." He is sad because he doesn't have a home to live in or food to eat," her mother, Alison, answered.

The reply seemed to satisfy Patty. Her mother was relieved that at least this time her inquisitive daughter didn't ask, "*Why* doesn't he have a home or food?"

Later, Alison said to me, "This man looks like he could be any child's grandfather. What would I have told her?" Now each time they walk to the store Patty asks, "Will the sad man be there, or has he found a home yet?"

A few weeks later, my three-year-old son, Bobby, was closely studying a photograph on the front page of our daily newspaper. It was a picture of a child near death being held by his mother in an African relief camp. Pointing to the child, Bobby asked, "What happened?"

Another hungry human being, another person in search of a

home. That evening, and every evening since, we began saying prayers for all the boys and girls who are hungry. Once a month, we also started to pack grocery bags for our parish's pantry for the poor. I wondered what was registering in the hearts and souls of these three-year-old cousins who were learning about the homeless and hungry of the world at such an early age.

These days the questions from our children about the poor and the oppressed are coming at a younger age. In our society the homeless live in our neighborhoods, the plight of refugees from countries ravaged by war is broadcast nightly on the news and racism at its ugliest is captured for all to see on home video cameras.

As Catholic parents, how do we teach our children about the "sad man" in our neighborhood or the dying child in Africa? When our children ask, "Why are people hungry and hurting?" and "Why should we help them?" do we know how we will answer them?

The words of Jesus provide the only answer we need: "Love one another as I have loved you" (John 15:12) and "Whatever you did for one of these least brothers of mine, you did it for me" (Matthew 25:40; NAB). If we are to know how to love one another, first we need to ask ourselves, "How has Jesus loved us?" Mother Teresa of Calcutta reminds us all: "By giving himself to us. This is how we are to love each other: by giving ourselves to each other. Our work calls for us to see Jesus in everyone. He has told us that he is the hungry one. He is the naked one. He is the thirsty one. He is the one without a home. He is the one who is suffering. These are our treasures. They are Jesus. Each one is Jesus in the distressing disguise of the poor."

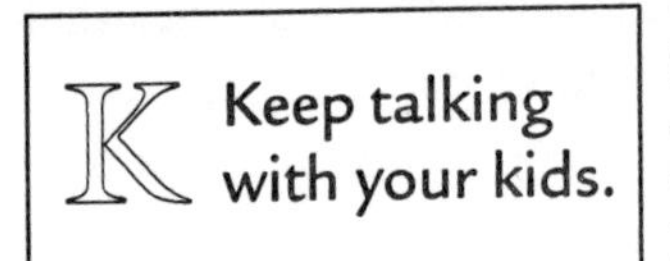

It's important to teach our children that we cannot bring the light and love of Jesus to the "least of these" if he is not first living in our own hearts. Our loving service to others must be grounded in a deep faith in Jesus and in our worship with a community of believers. When we listen to God's word during prayer and worship, we receive our direction—our road map to the kingdom of God. When we receive Jesus in the Eucharist, we are given the nourishment and strength we need for the journey to the kingdom. Mother Teresa tells us, "Our Eucharist is incomplete if it does not lead us to service and love for the poor."

But in the hectic hours of our busy days, it seems we hardly have the time to be there for those in our immediate family. How can we possibly find the time to reach out to a family in need whom we have never met? Yet today's Catholic families are presented with the challenge of discovering Christ in the familiar as well as in the forgotten families of our communities. To bring God's love to a broken world and to truly serve another person requires love, patience and time, all of which are at a premium in our busy lives.

The most important way we educate our children about our faith in God and service to others is by setting examples of love, peacemaking, kindness and justice in our own families. We may talk with our children about the need to send money to a starving child halfway across the world, but if our own children hunger for our love and time, our words and actions are meaningless.

Children can't be forced to care about the poor and the powerless. If we teach love gently through our actions, in time they will discover their own ways to reach out to the hungry, the homeless and the heartbroken. When our children become overwhelmed with the countless needs of our world, we need to tell them that we are not asked to change the world. But with the grace of God, we may change a life or an unjust policy. Mother Teresa says frequently, "What counts is not the number of things we do but the love we put into our actions."

Our responsibility as Catholic parents is to help our children recognize the many faces of the poor and suffering within our families, our communities and our world. There are people who are hungry because there is no food on their table. There are also people who are hungry for faith and love in their hearts. There are children who are thirsty for a drink, and they will wait in line all day for a glass of clean water. But there are far too many children who are thirsty for attention, and they will wait a lifetime for a parent's love.

There are immigrant families who arrive as strangers and need our warm welcome. There are also brothers and sisters in our own families who have become strangers and outcasts through misunderstandings. We need to welcome them home. There are millions of homeless women and children who want nothing more than a place to call home. And for millions of women and children, home is a place that is often more violent and abusive than our roughest neighborhood streets. There are thousands of people living behind bars in our overcrowded jails seeking peace and forgiveness. There are members of our own families and churches who are prisoners of the past—addictions, hatred and prejudice—and need to forgive themselves.

The real hope for restoring peace and compassion to our world is to teach children at an early age that Jesus loves those who are bruised and broken. When we reach out to them, we are touching the heart of Jesus. As we teach our children about the poor, the hungry and the lonely, we discover their responses are often so compassionate and so genuine. Children are willing to open their hearts as well as their homes to other children in need. Perhaps it is because they are so vulnerable themselves that they understand something about those who are most vulnerable in our society. They know what it's like to be dependent on someone else for food and shelter. They know how much they need the love of others.

Recently a homeless man was found dead at the park where my son Bobby and his cousin Patty play pirates and look for buried treasures. It could have been Patty and Bobby rather than an early morning jogger who discovered this "sad man." It was a reminder to me that throughout our children's lives we will be asked to answer some of life's most difficult questions about the poor among us. As parents, we will make our share of mistakes as we strive to teach our children that we must learn to love one another. Often, it will be our children leading us to the kingdom of God.

The final lesson that we can teach our children about God's love for the poor is perhaps the greatest one. When the "sad man" in our neighborhood and the dying child in Africa meet their heavenly Father, at last they will have found a home and they will never be hungry again.

For Discussion

1. What words would you use to explain poverty and suffering to a young child?
2. Why must our compassion be rooted in our relationship to Christ?

For Reflection

What are we doing in our family to teach our children to care for others?

The Hands and Feet of Christ

Involvement in service will help children discover that the church is a living organism, not a deadening organization.

Bert Ghezzi

Feeling that they "don't belong" is one of the main reasons kids leave the church. They say they "don't get anything out of it." The church does not seem to suit their more lively and attractive involvements—people, relationships, doing things with friends—so they are not interested in it.

Many kids feel that way partly because they see the church only as an organization, and organizations are "boring." To them the church is merely a structure, a bureaucratic pyramid. The pope and bishops are on top, everyone else on the bottom, all glued together by rules and regulations. Sunday mass appeals to them as much as would required attendance at a historical society meeting featuring the recently found papers of Edgar Applebee, the county's first superintendent.

Somehow we must help our children discover that the church

is not a lifeless *organization,* but a life-giving *organism.*

Embracing that truth will prepare them to see the church as vital, more interesting, perhaps even appealing enough to find that they belong there. We can accomplish a lot by telling kids about our experience of the church as a community. For example, how Christian friends cared for them when Mom was ill or helped Dad find a new job. Our children might not be ready to live the doctrine of the body of Christ, but they should hear that we are the hands and feet of Christ, extending his love to needy people.

But teaching will not be enough. Since our children learn involuntarily from our behavior, we must set an example by getting involved ourselves. If we want our kids to believe that we are the hands and feet of Christ, we had better get them moving.

No matter how busy we are with work and family, we should find some Christian service that fits into our lives. Not just because our children need us to, but because it's an expression of our faith. As Scripture says, "Be doers of the word and not hearers only" (James 1:22). If *we* parents feel we aren't getting enough out of life in the church, it's probably because we aren't putting enough of ourselves into it.

When looking for service opportunities that are right for you, try to find something that is both manageable and personal. A manageable commitment is one that fits with the rest of our lives. We can perform it routinely and it will not become so burdensome that we will abandon it soon after we start. For example, a busy person might choose to be a lector because he or she can make an important contribution—proclaiming God's word—and it only takes two hours a month to prepare for it, outside of mass.

Our service should also be personal, if possible, so that we and our children can learn to be other Christs to real people. If someone told you that there were five hundred AIDS babies in your city, asking what you were going to do about it, you would probably be overwhelmed. You would be unable to respond because you would not know where to begin. But if someone asked you to spend a half hour a week visiting Luke, an eleven-year-old AIDS victim, you would probably welcome the chance to be merciful.

When possible, we should include our children in our service. Involving a child in some work of mercy, for example, may not produce an immediate change of behavior, but the message will get through. Author and columnist Dolores Curran tells of involving her family one blustery Christmas Eve at a Catholic Worker soup kitchen in Denver. "My nineteen-year-old took off his $40 Reeboks and gave them to a street person who had flapping soles on his wet canvas shoes."

That's the way we want all our kids to get involved.

For Discussion

1. Why should parents involve their kids in Christian service?
2. Why should service be manageable? Why should it be personal?

For Reflection

1. Am I involved in some kind of Christian service or social action? What could I do to become more involved?
2. How can I involve my children in service or social action?

Violence: Can We Lower the Level?

The place to begin is right in our own homes.

Paul R. Leingang

She was standing at the door with something shiny in her hand. I hadn't noticed what it was when I first arrived.

I was standing on the top row of a wobbly set of concrete blocks. My confidence was shaky too.

The sun was bright. Whoever was inside the house could see me clearly as I shifted from foot to foot, not quite balanced and far from comfortable.

If I turned from side to side, I could see the neighborhood. The houses, narrow and small. A car with a broken window. A piece of a fence that kept nothing in, nothing out. A dusty path through a littered front yard. There would be a sidewalk along the street in a more prosperous neighborhood. There would be grass in the front yard, and a fence that would do more than mark a boundary line that no one honored.

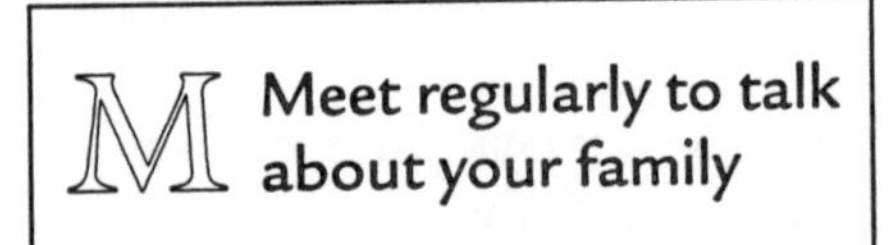

I could see the peeling paint and poverty. But my eyes could not see past the glare of the storm door glass, or into the uncertain darkness on the other side of it.

I said "Hello," as loud as I could, while trying to remain polite. There was no answer, only movement. I said "Hello" again, wishing whoever it was would open the storm door so we could talk to each other.

I spoke to the figure who leaned forward, peering closer to the glass which separated us. "I'm from the church down the street," I said. "I am helping with the census," I said. There was movement, but no answer. No door opened—not the one to the house, nor the one to the person inside in the darkness.

She did not want to invite me in, nor to come to talk outside on the steps. She did not answer my questions, or tell me her name.

Looking down at my feet in failure, I began a cautious turn to go away. That's when I saw with great embarrassment why there had never been a reason for me to shout through the storm door. There was no glass at the bottom. No screen. No barrier at all to the loudness of my presence.

The barrier between us had been much more substantial than any door of glass or metal. At the bottom of the steps, I looked back. No glass glare hid my view of the woman at the door. She was old, with fear in her eyes, and a butcher knife in her hand.

Violence has shut the door of the American home. The fear of violence has built a barrier more powerful than steel bars and dead-bolt locks.

* * *

Is there something we can do about the level of violence in our world?

The members of the Christian Family Movement use a three-step process: observe the world around you, judge what you see in the light of gospel values, and then act.

I invite you to use this Christian Family Movement approach as you reflect on violence in the world today.

What is your reaction to the story about the census worker and the woman with the knife? If there are children in your home, ask them for their reactions.

What is your experience? How has violence—or the threat of violence—affected you? How has it affected your children, your neighborhood? The world?

* * *

How did Jesus respond to violence in culture and society? We are often tempted to think of Jesus as meek and mild, the one who went to his death without protest. Such was his strength, not his weakness: we cannot forget that Jesus is the one who told Peter to put away his sword. Jesus is the one who chose not to call legions of angels to assist him.

This is the same Jesus who faced a crowd of angry men intent on killing a woman caught in adultery—and he sent the men away, no longer violent, but deeply ashamed of their own sins.

This is the same Jesus who praised the Samaritan outsider who had responded to the needs of a victim of a violent beating and robbery.

This is the same Jesus who encouraged his followers to tend to the needs of all victims of violence—the hungry, the thirsty, the sick and the lonely.

* * *

What can you do about it? A lot, even if it is a little at a time.

Start at home. Lessen the level of violence in your voice. Refuse to join in the killing of another person's character. Encourage others in your home to reject violence—and teach by your example.

Select an area where you and your family can take a stand against the violence you have observed.

- Select worthwhile television programs and movies; support programs of value and those who provide them.
- Encourage your church or your community to begin or improve a program to assist victims of spouse abuse. Do what you can to help.
- Get to know your neighbors. Get together with them and decide what you can do to reduce the level of violence you have observed.

And get to know the children in your neighborhood. Some neighborhoods establish a place where children can go for safety, if there are no adults available at their own homes. Look around; judge what you see in the light of Christ's teaching. Do something about it.

Take the time to make a difference.

For Discussion

How can individuals and families reduce the level of violence in the world?

For Reflection

What can I and my family do concretely to replace violence with peace in our city? neighborhood? home?

Involving Kids in Service

Parents have many opportunities to teach children compassion, especially by serving right alongside them.

Lisa and Steve Walker

Our job as parents is to challenge, guide and equip young people into the mission proclaimed by Jesus. The story of sheep and goats told by Jesus in Matthew 25 says that the way we treat people and serve others will be the measure by which we are judged. So involving our children in the mission of Christ and making them aware of the needs of others is one of our primary responsibilities as parents.

Fifteen years' experience as youth ministers has taught us the importance of involving kids in service. Service projects give our teens opportunities to help others *and* allow them to sense God's love acting through them at the same time. And getting them to do something is more effective than talking to them about the importance of service.

For example, we often have teens work at a shelter for the homeless. Seeing crowds of people lined up for food or cots to sleep on teaches kids about the responsibility that comes with the gifts they have been given. The teens involved in preparing and serving food come face to face with the stark reality of how fortunate they are. Sometimes they are frustrated by the poverty, pain and injustice they encounter and are motivated to figure out how to do something about it.

Every summer we bring hundreds of teenagers to Catholic HEART Workcamps in Orlando, Florida, and other cities. The kids who participate say that working together to serve someone helps them grow in faith. What has surprised us most is that the kids say that service is fun. Doing something for others actually feels good. The youth receive much more from the experience than the people they are serving. In some mysterious way, their *yes* to Jesus' call to help others imprints the spirit of God's love on their hearts. It changes their lives.

Parents can point their children in the right direction by forming generous attitudes in the family. We constantly model ideals that are more *caught* than *taught*. We teach our children to care for others by demonstrating it within our homes. Children will see the importance of compassion when their parents live it. When we get a chance, we should also talk to them about it.

Our six-year-old son, Zachary, attended one of our monthly youth-ministry-sponsored trips to the soup kitchen. He served hot chocolate to homeless people. We talked about our shared experience on the way home in the car. Zach said he thought that people were homeless because they were lazy and spent all their money on alcohol and drugs. I was glad for the chance to correct his mistaken idea. I told him that some people may have squandered their money, but most homeless were good people who were overtaken by things they couldn't handle. I think I made my point clearest when I said we were one paycheck away from being homeless too. Zach got the message. The following week he gave his allowance to a homeless man who was begging on the corner.

Parents can reap great benefits by serving alongside their children. Here are some suggestions:

1. Spring clean for a shut-in.
2. Write Christmas cards to senior citizens without family.
3. Make Easter baskets for people living alone.
4. Visit or sing Christmas carols at a nursing home.
5. Volunteer to work on a parish service project.
6. Become a big brother or sister to a needy child or parish newcomer.
7. Babysit during church services.
8. Put up Christmas decorations for shut-ins or senior citizens.
9. Participate in a day or week of service (cleaning, repairing or building) in an impoverished area.
10. Drop off clothes or blankets to the local homeless center.
11. Organize a canned goods drive for a local service center.
12. Work with organizations such as Habitat for Humanity.
13. Join a local walk for hunger.
14. Help with Special Olympics for handicapped youth.
15. Teach disadvantaged children how to read and write.

Our families have the potential to be love, to be joy, to be hope, to be light to those who need to be lifted up. Our families are called to follow Christ. Following in Jesus' footsteps always means putting others first. Not an easy task for us or for our children. It will mean missing some favorite TV programs or a few hours of Nintendo. We may have to skip that extra hour of sleep. But in return we are involved in something much greater—bringing the reality of God's love to others.

For Discussion
Why should parents participate in service with their children?

For Refection
What opportunities for service do we have as a family?

25 Ways to Teach Children Compassion

If you are wondering how to teach your children to care for others and how to prepare them to serve the poor and needy, start with some of these suggestions.

Eileen C. Marx

There are many ways to begin teaching Christian service to our children that don't require a lot of our time, only a commitment to faith and love. Married couples and single parents alike need to find ways to remind themselves and their children to follow Jesus' invitation to "love one another." If you would like to do this with your family, but aren't sure where to begin, here are twenty-five ideas that family, friends, parishioners, priests, sisters and teachers have helped me to discover:

Adopt a poor child in a mission program, with every family member making a small contribution each month.

Bake a cake with your kids and share it with a lonely neighbor.

Compliment your son or daughter when you notice they are sharing.

Donate food and unwanted clothing or furniture to Catholic Charities.

Encourage your children to use patience and fairness in resolving conflicts with their friends.

Fight against hatred and prejudice. Refuse to tolerate hateful attitudes, racial and ethnic jokes and slurs in your own family or anywhere else.

Give an hour each week to a family member or friend who is struggling with an addiction or raising a child alone. Visit with them, send a kind note and pray for them.

Host a baby shower with your neighbors and donate the items to a local program for unwed mothers.

Invite a friend for dinner who has recently lost his or her job. Listen to the person's fears and explore ways that you may be able to assist him or her in finding employment.

Jot a note, write a letter or pick up the telephone to protest federal, state or local legislation that undermines human life and dignity.

Kiss and hug your children often. Love begins at home.

Look for examples of racism, sexism and violence when watching TV with your child, and discuss them.

Make a meal for someone in need—a person suffering from AIDS, a single mother or father, a friend who has lost a loved one.

Nurture your children's gifts of kindness, forgiveness and love, celebrate the many ways they express them.

Offer to go food shopping for a neighbor or a parishioner who is recovering from an illness.

Pray regularly as a family, especially for the needs of the poor, the lonely and the oppressed.

Quit saying how you wish you had the time to volunteer, and do something small.

Read and discuss books with your children that emphasize compassion for others, such as a story of a saint or a champion of social justice.

Smile at your children when you see they are showing love and compassion to a grandparent, a neighbor or sibling.

Take your older children to a nursing home or soup kitchen. Hold hands with an elderly woman or a homeless man while you're there.

Use your talents to offer assistance in your parish, your child's school, the Special Olympics or a non-profit organization.

Volunteer as a family once a week, once a month or once a year.

Welcome new neighbors of all cultures into your community and new parishioners into your church with joy and warmth. Welcome them in your home too.

Catholic Organizations Where Families Can Help

1. *Catholic Charities USA* (703-549-1390, ext. 21) provides information and action alerts on issues of poverty and human services: 1731 King Street, Suite 200, Alexandria, Virginia 22314

2. *Catholic Relief Services (CRS)* (410-625-2220) is the U.S. Bishops' overseas development agency. It organizes Operation Rice Bowl, which involves family prayer, education and almsgiving during Lent for families in the Third World: 209 W. Fayette Street, Baltimore, Maryland 21201-3443

3. *Holy Childhood Association* (202-775-8637) provides children's offering boxes during Advent, Halloween and Lent, encouraging them to give to needy children in more than one hundred countries: 1720 Massachusetts Avenue, N.W., Washington, D.C. 20036

4. *The Campaign for Human Development* (202-541-3210) is the U.S. Bishops' anti-poverty program: 3211 Fourth Street, N.E., Washington, D.C. 20017

5. *The National Council of Catholic Women (NCCW)* (202-682-0334) cosponsors Help-a-Child with Catholic Relief Services. It offers the opportunity to reach out to poor children with a one-time contribution or through monthly sponsorship: 1275 K Street, N.W. Suite 975, Washington, D.C. 20005

6. *Food for the Poor* (305-427-2222) provides food and other essentials to the poor in Haiti and throughout the Caribbean: 550 SW 12th Avenue, Building 4, Deerfield Beach, FL 33442.

7. *Call your diocesan Office of Social Concerns* or Catholic Charities to find out how you can reach out to those in your local community.

Xerox an article which focuses on love, peace or justice, send it to a family member, a friend or a priest.
Yield not to society's pressures to buy excessive material things, especially at Christmas and on birthdays.
Z Of course in this book there is no "Z," but you can **Z**oom in on many other possibilities to teach your kids about service!

It is in simple acts of kindness such as these that we can create for our children a profound awareness of and sensitivity to all those in need.

Think, Pray & Act

The Heart of the Matter

Love is the test of our family's Christianity. How we care for others matters more than anything else. Which way is your family turned—inward or outward? In what ways do you serve your neighbors? the elderly? people in need? Use the questions *For Discussion* and *For Reflection* at the end of articles in this chapter to review your Christian behavior. How could your family be more involved in caring for people? Is there one thing you could do differently? Consider using the *Action Idea List, Decision Grid* and *Action Plan.*

Resources

- Heart Catholic Work Camps. Every summer Catholic teens have an opportunity to serve the poor in Orlando, Florida; Pittsburgh, Pennsylvania; and other cities. Heart Catholic Work Camps combine service, worship, fellowship, instruction and fun. Your teens can work through the year to save money to pay for the chance to help others. For information call 407-740-0791, or write Heart Catholic Work Camps, P.O. Box 3291, Winter Park, FL 32790.

Publications

- *A Century of Social Teaching: A Common Heritage, A Continuing Challenge,* Statement by the U.S. Catholic

Bishops. A video, "Bring Down the Walls," which summarizes one hundred years of Catholic social teaching, is also available. (U.S.C.C. Office for Publishing and Promotion: 800-235-USCC).

- Bert Ghezzi, *Keeping Your Kids Catholic* (Servant Book Express: 313-677-6490).
- Bert Ghezzi, *Sharing Your Faith: A User's Guide to Evangelization* (Our Sunday Visitor: 800-348-2440).
- Virgil Gulker, *Helping You Is Helping Me* (Servant Book Express: 313-677-6490).
- Pope John Paul II, *The Mission of the Redeemer*, and Pope Paul VI, *Evangelization in the Modern World* (Paulist National Catholic Evangelization Association: 800-237-5515).
- Mother Teresa, *Heart of Joy: The Transforming Power of Self-Giving* (Servant Book Express: 313-677-6490).

SIX

Catholic Minds and Hearts

Catholic parents are the primary religious educators of their children, but they get plenty of help from the church and the Holy Spirit.

Teaching Your Kids

Using the natural stuff of daily life to convey supernatural truth—that is what parental instruction is all about.

Keith Fournier

One Sunday in early spring, several years ago, our family decided to go on a picnic after mass. It was one of those rare days when the sky was brilliant blue, the sun was shining as brightly as I ever remember and everyone was in a great mood. We just had to be outside on such a perfect day. So we headed to a nearby favorite spot in the beautiful hills of West Virginia. We stopped at a picnic area and ate our lunch. While my wife, Laurine, played with our infant son, Joel, I threw the frisbee with our three eldest.

After some time, I noticed that our fourth child, Mary Ellen, had wandered over the hill and was picking dandelions, which she maintains are the most beautiful flowers that grow. Of course, until that morning I thought they were a weed, but the simple insights of a child are heartwarming, aren't they? We all eventually joined her, roaming through the meadow, drinking deeply of the beauty of the hillside and drawing strength from this obvious display of God's presence in the world. The children were frantically picking the wild flowers that adorned the hillside.

Eventually they bound together all of their pickings in one bunch and presented the bouquet to their mom.

My son Keith then remembered a story about four-leaf clovers and good luck and leprechauns. He became increasingly excited as he talked and finally bounded back into the meadow in search of his very own four-leaf clover. Of course the rest of the kids followed. One by one, they returned to the huge picnic blanket, claiming that they had found a four-leaf clover. I knew that probably none of them had, so I told them a story that gave the ordinary clover a special charm.

I held up a clover for them to see and asked two questions: *How many clovers do I have?* and *How many leaves does it have?* The responses were one and three, respectively. I then explained to them how a bishop named Patrick had once explained the Trinity to the Irish people with just such a clover. Did my children understand the intellectual underpinnings of the theology of the Trinity? I doubt it. Great theologians have tried through the ages to clarify this mystery, to no avail. But it was a healthy start. Using the natural stuff of daily life to convey supernatural truth—that is what parental instruction is all about.

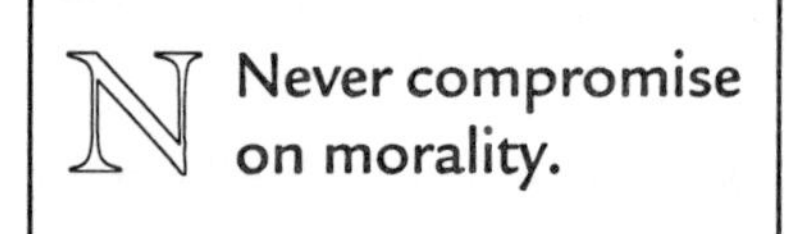

Parents are meant to be vessels for their children's salvation, imparting to them the truths of the faith. One way we do that is by teaching. We are called to instruct our children in the faith. The role of teacher is a very critical role and one that isn't understood or talked about as much as it should be; but being the first teachers of our children is actually our primary vocation as parents.

John Paul II states that "for Christian parents the mission to educate, a mission rooted... in their participation in God's creating activity, has a new specific source in the Sacrament of Marriage, which consecrates them for the strictly Christian education of their children."

That means we cannot leave the education of our children to

the schools or to the Sunday school teachers. It means we as parents have been given the means to be the main educators of our children. In marriage we are set apart. As mothers and fathers we are set apart to educate our children.

The Book of Judges contains a story that I believe speaks to all parents and their responsibility to their children. The story is of Manoah and his wife and an angel's prediction of their offspring. Upon hearing the news, Manoah prayed that God would send the angel to instruct him as to how to care for the child. God did send the angel, and Manoah petitioned him saying, "How shall we order the child? And how shall we do unto him?" (Judges 13:12).

Andrew Murray reflects on this Scripture in his book *How to Raise Your Children for Christ.* Murray is touched by Manoah's abiding sense of holy responsibility in the training of his child. Murray points to Manoah's humility; he is a man not necessarily trusting his own ability, but desiring God's full wisdom. He suggests that Manoah's approach to parenthood is quite a contrast to the thoughtless self-confidence with which many Christian parents undertake the training of their children. How much effort do we make to realize the importance and solemnity of this work? How much do we pray for the preparation of the Spirit to fit us for it? How much do we surrender to a life for God? Not enough, says Murray.

Isn't this what we need for our families—reverence for the task of parenthood, prayer and surrender? Writers on the family agree that the ideas and behaviors formed in the first seven years are often permanent values. Parents need to utilize that time in the best way. Teach your children truth. Guide them toward everlasting life.

How are we to go about the Christian education of our children? We must present to our children the truths of life, the truths of God. These are mysteries that cannot be grasped through verbal teaching alone. They must become a way of life. If they are a way of life for parents, the home will become the sacred school it is meant to be. Words can never be the only method of expression of our faith. We must also teach through the example of our lives.

To teach our children with authority, we parents must first know the teaching in our own hearts. We must know what it means to live as baptized Christians: we have submerged the old nature and have emerged from the living waters as new creations. We need to know that we are full members of God's family and will be eternally. We need to cultivate our relationship with the

Tell It Like It Is

Some years ago I presented a workshop on the Ten Commandments at a youth conference. I chose that topic because of my experience in Catholic youth ministry. Hundreds of conversations with college-age men and women showed me that they did not have the full picture. Many of our young people have heard about God's love and forgiveness. But they do not seem to have a clear concept of what's right and wrong in the Lord's eyes. They give themselves permission to do things God has forbidden. They don't seem to realize that their actions have serious spiritual and personal consequences. They have lost, or have never been taught, a sense of sin. I was pleasantly surprised when four hundred young people showed up for what I thought would be an unpopular workshop.

My presentation was a straightforward review of the Ten Commandments. I stated each commandment and explained what it meant. I told them, for example, that the worship of strange gods outlawed in the first commandment included the gods of our age. I asked them if any of them were tempted to worship sex, money or power. If they were, I warned them, they needed to take another look at the first commandment. "You may think you are worshiping the Lord," I said. "But he may be telling you that you are really worshiping one of the strange gods of our day."

As I went through the commandments, I demonstrated with statistics how disobedience produces miserable consequences. For example, I showed that disregard for the fourth commandment—honor your father and mother—has left our elderly disrespected and destitute. "One in twenty Americans over sixty-five," I said, "are subject to physical and psychological abuse and financial exploitation by their own children. One-

Lord, to know his intimacy. If we live these truths from the heart, our children will be affected. So we must live our faith fervently, lovingly and consistently before it will mean anything to our children. The holiness of our own lives and the openness of our love for God will spill over to them.

My early childhood memories are filled with people who truly loved God. My first-grade teacher, Sister William Patricia, talked about Jesus as though he were her best friend. She told me I

and-a-half-million cases of elderly abuse are reported annually." In the fifth and sixth commandments, I said, the Lord forbade murder and sexual relations outside of marriage. "But we don't seem to be paying attention. Look at the numbers. In this country we have one murder every twenty-two minutes; violent crimes have increased by 560 percent since 1960; and 1.7 million babies are aborted every year."

"And what are the consequences of our disobedience of God's laws on sex?" I asked. "Since 1960 the divorce rate has quadrupled. The number of children raised in single-parent homes has risen from 8 percent to 22 percent. One half of all children will experience their parents' divorce, and one in ten will experience three divorces."

As I was proceeding through the commandments, an extraordinary sense of the Lord's presence began to fill the room and touch the students. Their response took me by surprise. Young men and women started to get down on their knees. Many of them wept audibly. As I was nearing the end of the talk, three-quarters of the audience were kneeling. I heard some of them praying and calling on the name of Jesus. We concluded by spending a considerable time in prayer, which was not part of my plan for the workshop. The whole thing startled me. I thought I was filling in some of the gaps in these kids' Catholic formation. But the Lord had a bigger idea and took hold of their hearts.

This experience framed my conviction that we must tell our youth about God's laws as well as his love. Tell them that the Lord loves them so much that he wants them to avoid any behavior that could keep them from him. And that, if they should have the misfortune to sin, out of his love he has arranged a way for them to repent and to repair the damage. We must tell it like it is.

Ann Shields

could do the same, and I did. Although I wandered from the faith as a teenager, I later came home to the church. Her open witness to God had a great deal to do with it.

My grandmother Ida was also a woman of great faith. At age seventeen, when I returned to the Lord, I went to tell my grandmother about my new faith. She hugged me tightly and wept. "If you only knew," she said, "how many years I've prayed for you!"

Their lives, and many others, have shaped my faith, and I am grateful for their examples. This is what parenting is all about.

For Discussion

What do you think parents need most to prepare them to instruct their kids in the faith?

For Reflection

1. Do I live the kind of Catholic life I want my children to embrace?
2. Is there one thing I could do to give my life more fully to God?

Power Tools for Shaping Kids Catholic

Helping our children acquire the cardinal virtues is a means of forming them in the faith.

Bert Ghezzi

Sometimes I look at my kids and wonder about the Lord's saying that unless you become like little children you cannot enter the kingdom of heaven. *Not like my children,* I have thought. They could turn the heavenly banquet into a food fight.

Little children have attractive qualities. They're trusting, docile and affectionate. But they are also selfish, willful and mean. As they grow up their lives continue to reflect this conflict of good and bad. "Your teens are so helpful," a friend once told me. "Oh, really?" I said. "Are we talking about the same individuals who seem to evaporate when there's work to be done at my house?"

When our children are baptized, they receive a share of divine life. I don't need to prove to you that God's life in them does not automatically transform their behavior. Getting children to grow up as faithful Catholics takes both grace and effort. The Lord gives us plenty of help, but we must actively train them in Christian ways of speaking and acting.

Trouble is, we don't always know what to do. Forming kids as Catholic Christians requires attention to many areas. If we try to deal with everything in detail we can easily become overwhelmed and give up. What we need for the job are a few principles that sum up Christian behavior and give us guidelines for helping our kids take a Catholic approach to life.

These concerns are not new. The church wrestled with them centuries ago and gave us tools we can use every day to shape our kids Catholic. The church identified a set of virtues that, when acquired, help a person approach daily life in a Catholic way. These are the cardinal virtues, which the older ones among us learned in the *Baltimore Catechism, Number Two:* temperance, justice, prudence and fortitude.

"Cardinal" comes from a Latin word that means "hinge." These virtues are cardinal because all life hinges on them. Since they affect everything, parents can use them to cut through the complexities of forming children as Catholics. We can evaluate our kids' lives against these virtues as standards. For example, we can measure their conduct against the requirements of justice to see if they are giving others their due. Then we can help them learn whatever behaviors they are missing.

Let's look at the cardinal virtues as helps in raising kids Catholic.

Temperance. Little humans, as well as big ones, have a font of evil desires that bubbles up inside. That's why the same adorable four-year-old can turn from hugging his mom and wallop his sister on the back of the head. That's what prompts a lovely teenage girl to look for thrills in drugs or shoplifting.

Jesus taught that "out of the heart come evil thoughts, murder, adultery, fornication, theft, false witness, slander"

(Matthew 15:19). Paul calls this stream of evil inclinations "the flesh" (Galatians 5:19-22). James says these desires lure us into temptation and cause us to sin (James 1:14-15).

Temperance disciplines these internal impulses. We acquire it as we build in ourselves and our children a set of behaviors that controls our more rambunctious desires. We and our kids become temperate as we learn how to defuse destructive feelings and turn them to good.

Here are some ways to help kids get control of troublesome desires:

- *Self-denial.* Train family members in self-denial by doing without something during Lent or for another period of time. For example, pull the plug on the TV or eliminate snacking.
- *Boundaries.* Set limits that require children to say "no" to something they want. You could require them to have homework done before entertainment is allowed. Or restrict phone calls to a certain hour each day.
- *Help with feelings.* Teach children how to express feelings appropriately. For example, we should make it OK for a child to say that something is making him feel angry. But we should train our kids not to express anger by bashing a toy against a wall or by hitting someone.

You will think of many additional ways to teach temperance. But doing things will not be enough. To form children in any of the cardinal virtues, you must explain *why* you are doing it. Understanding the reasons will help the children acquire the behavior. "On Wednesdays in Lent," you can say, "we are only going to eat a cup of rice and broth. No snacks allowed afterward. We are doing this to remember Christ's passion and to help us grow in self-control." After the grumbling dies down, encourage questions and discussion.

Justice. To get through every day, all humans—children included—have to relate to others. We communicate. We listen. We respond. We help and ask for help. We serve. We work. We go to school, and so on. Relationships are the fabric of human life.

Because our families are a part of the Christian community, relationships are even more important. As sons and daughters of God we are committed to relate rightly to everyone. The laws and teaching that govern our Christian lives are substantially concerned with relationships. Of the Ten Commandments, for example, the first three deal with relating rightly to God, the last seven with relating rightly to other people. Jesus summed it up when he taught that we must love God with all our heart, soul, mind and strength and that we must love our neighbors as ourselves (see Mark 13:30-31).

Justice is the virtue that requires us to give each person his due. It helps us apply the law of love to all of our relationships. We become just by ensuring that we do the right and loving thing in every situation.

Parents are responsible to show their children how to relate properly to everyone. Here are some ways we can enlist justice as a helper in the task:

- *Worship.* Teach children that we worship God because honor is due him. That's why we celebrate the liturgy, have family prayer and pray personally.
- *Obedience.* Have it as a family rule that children must obey a parent's direct orders. Let them know what the penalties will be for disobeying. Be careful to give direct orders sparingly.
- *Repairing relationships.* Teach kids to say "I'm sorry" and "I forgive you." When they have conflicts with friends, help them fix the relationships.
- *Social justice.* Involve your kids with you in a local outreach that serves the needy. They must learn that justice extends from personal to social relationships.

Prudence. Every day our children make many choices. Some are inconsequential. But as they grow older some will be life-shaping, like choice of friends, school and job. Their moral choices are of even more consequence. For a time parents can guide children to make the right choices. Sometimes we can even decide for them. But ultimately our kids will have to make their own decisions.

They will have to choose to follow the Lord and live their lives as his faithful disciples. That's all according to the Lord's plan. He wants sons and daughters who freely choose to love him and serve him.

Prudence is the virtue that helps us make the right choices. We and our kids need a lot of it. It is the practical wisdom that James says produces a good life marked by humility (see James 3:13). We acquire prudence by repeatedly making careful decisions in light of what is reasonable and what is expected by God. We are not left to ourselves in the process because the Lord sent us the Holy Spirit as a helper in choosing rightly (see John 14:25).

Parents must educate kids in making sound decisions. We can teach younger children prudence by explaining choices we make for them. But we should look for opportunities to let them practice decision-making for themselves.

Here are some suggestions for helping the family grow in prudence.

- *Prayer for guidance.* Make prayer to the Holy Spirit for wisdom a regular part of family life. When a family member is making an important decision, involve everyone in praying for the Spirit's direction.
- *Study.* Do a family Bible study on the Book of Proverbs, which is a training guide in practical wisdom. Have everyone look for a favorite proverb and tell why they like it. Invite everyone to apply their proverb through a week. At a family meal, ask each person to share what happened.
- *Decision-making.* Watch for chances to guide a child through decisions he or she must make. Teach children to analyze the situations and to judge their options reasonably. Help them figure out the possible consequences of their choices. Let them choose. Let them make a mistake if it is not life-threatening. Then review and follow up.

Fortitude. Living as a Christian is not easy. In our social environments it's getting harder. We and our children need backbone to be faithful disciples of Christ. The cardinal virtue that puts spiritual starch in our spines is fortitude. It is an antidote to fear that gives us courage to do the right thing. Social pressure makes our children afraid to be different. But if they are to grow up Catholic, they must do many things differently. A youngster, for example, needs fortitude to decide not to fight in response to a bully's taunts. When a teen has decided to remain a virgin, he or she will need courage to stick by that choice. Or a teen who has returned to sanity from a wild fling with drugs will need fortitude to stay clean.

Parents should teach kids that they can still be courageous if they feel afraid. Courage sidles up to fear and defuses its power. It enables us to do the right thing even when fear tells us we cannot.

Here are some ways to encourage kids to grow in courage:

- *Being different.* Watch for opportunities to help a child overcome social fears. Something as simple as helping them wear a bike helmet when other kids are not. Be sure to explain your reasons.
- *Study.* Do a family Bible study on Luke 22, John 21 and Acts 1-3, focusing on how Peter acquired fortitude.

Virtues are habits. We get them by repeating appropriate actions until we do them almost without thinking. The process of helping our children to become temperate, just, prudent and courageous will take years. We should get ready for the long haul. When our children become young adults we will still be helping them make wise decisions or working to get them to curb a wild desire. And let's not forget to grow ourselves. These virtues are cardinal for parents too.

For Discussion

1. What are the advantages of using the cardinal virtues to form our kids as Catholics?
2. Which of the cardinal virtues do you think is most helpful for the task of raising kids Catholic?

For Reflection

1. Right now, focusing on which of the cardinal virtues would help me most in caring for my children? Why?
2. What one thing could we do differently to contribute to our kids' Catholic formation?

Should We Send Our Kids to Catholic Schools?

Parents should give serious consideration to sending their children to Catholic schools.

Janet Alampi

By the time a toddler starts uttering two-syllable words, middle-class American parents have started thinking about school choice.

As I was growing up, the decision wasn't very difficult. We had a pastor in Louisiana who announced regularly from the pulpit that if parents weren't on welfare, they should be sending their kids to the parochial school. If they failed to do so, he continued, they were destined for a place hotter than Cajun country. Shaky theology, scary thought. All the classes were filled.

Some, not all, of my memories of Catholic school are pleasant. Nuns and a few lay people taught us in elementary school, and the assistant pastor was both high-school girls' basketball coach and religion teacher. It was the heyday of Catholic schools. Tuition was low because the religious sisters worked for next to nothing, and the handful of lay teachers labored for a few dollars more than next to nothing. Discipline was still an acceptable word, religion class was still a must, and weekly mass on a school morning was still a given.

In the midst of my elementary years came Vatican II, and along with the many good changes in the church, there emerged some negative ones in Catholic schools. Gradually, there were fewer and fewer sisters and brothers teaching. Consequently, more and more classes were being taught by lay persons who, because of family obligations, could not put in as many hours or work for as little pay as had the religious. Tuition rapidly rose, and middle-class parents could not always handle the increases. The results were often heartwrenching: many Catholic schools had to be closed.

But recent years have seen a gradual reversal. There's no turning the clock back, of course. Catholic school tuition is still out of reach for many families; there are fewer religious teaching than ever, but still there is good news. According to a report issued by the National Catholic Educational Association (NCEA), Catholic preschool enrollment has increased by nearly 400 percent in the last decade. At this writing, there were more than two and a half million students in Catholic schools. Minorities made up 24 percent of the Catholic school enrollees. The pupil-teacher ratio in Catholic schools for prekindergarten through grade 12 was 17 to 1. Catholic school enrollment in elementary or secondary schools was up in forty-six states.

Obviously, many parents are opting for Catholic schools, despite the double whammy policy currently in effect in our country. Besides the burden of supporting the public school system through taxes, these parents also choose to support their Catholic school. In doing so, the NCEA points out, these parents save other taxpayers $14.5 billion a year.

While it is reassuring that many parents have confidence in the Catholic school system, it is important to remember two important realities:

- No two schools—Catholic or otherwise—are created equal.
- Parents are, as Vatican II and the Holy Father remind us, the number one educators of their children. This duty and privilege should be considered nontransferable.

School Evaluation

There are often waiting lists for Catholic schools, so it is wise to start your evaluation well in advance. Just how far in advance can be determined by a call to the school to see how long its list happens to be.

If you are fortunate enough to have more than one Catholic school a convenient distance from your home, you will want to gather information about both and do some "comparison shopping." If you simply stop at the bottom line and find that one is objectively "cheaper" than the other, you may spend less—

but you may also get a lot less. Use as much diligence comparing features of a school (or a homeschooling curriculum) as you would when shopping for a new car.

Of course, there are some nondenominational private schools that provide quality education. Often, however, their tuition is much higher than that of Catholic schools.

As you consider various options, make a list of those qualities of education you consider indispensable and those you consider "extras."

Suppose you find that the public school is serious about educating kids, upholds traditional values and has managed to keep guns and drugs out. You conclude the major difference between it and the Catholic school is that the latter also offers religion classes. You then need to ask yourself whether you are willing to pay the tuition principally for that class. (You also need to send the rest of us the location of such a public school.)

Your evaluation of the Catholic school should likewise include a tour of the facility itself, to form a judgment about its attentiveness to safety and security as well as its provision for recreation and sports.

Find out what the school offers to familiarize parents with its programs. But don't settle for brochures or a one-hour media presentation. Ask questions of other parents who are sending their kids to the school.

In short, be a smart buyer. If the Catholic school or schools in your area are not distinctively Catholic, serious about providing students with quality programs, then judge whether they are worth the money. If you find that you are somewhat satisfied with what the school offers but would like to see improvement, don't discard the idea of sending your child there. Catholic schools are an invaluable part of the heritage of the church in America. They have educated great men and women, principally because parents as well as staff have recognized that kids cannot learn in a vacuum. They either inhale the oxygen of a moral atmosphere or they breathe in the gases of a toxic culture. Catholic schools were founded to show youngsters that religion cannot be relegated to Sundays but must permeate life as a whole.

Some schools that claim to be Catholic teach anything but Catholicism. For that reason, examining the textbooks its teachers use for religion class is a most important aspect of evaluating a Catholic school. If you like what you see, this is a strong pull to enroll your child. If you find the texts lacking on some points, you may choose to supplement with some home instruction. One thing to keep in mind is that sometimes "unteaching" what a person in authority has impressed upon a child is a lot harder than teaching it in the first place. If the religion class causes confusion in your child, consider taking him or her out completely.

The Nontransferable Job

While it is important to choose the best schools we can for our children, it is even more important to keep our own role in perspective. When we enroll our kids, we are not shifting all responsibility to teachers. We are merely delegating some duties to others, while remaining the primary educators. This distinction is crucial.

Parents are far more likely to find recognition of their unique role when dealing with Catholic school faculty than with public school staff. After all, the doctrine permeates church documents on parenthood.

Awareness of this responsibility prompts parents to show genuine interest in the education of their children and to express this concern in action. Often a school is enhanced as much by the parents as by the staff themselves. Parents who reinforce learning at home and who are active in school activities can make a huge difference, not only in the education of their own children but in the overall quality of the school itself.

When parents choose to send their children to an authentically Catholic school for some or all of their formative years, they are laying a foundation that is deep and strong. Such a choice often means years of sacrifice and of fund-raisers. But the rewards can be enormous. There is much to be said for a school that is in touch with realities beyond this life—a school where prayer doesn't have to be approved by a legislature; where Christmas, Easter and other holy days can be freely celebrated; where children can look at a crucifix or other holy image while learning about the Creator and his wonderful works. This is education with a soul, and no price tag can be put on that.

For Discussion

1. Why should parents consider sending their children to Catholic schools?
2. What should parents look for in selecting a school for their children?

For Reflection

1. Is there a Catholic school available to our family?
2. Have we considered sending our children there?

The Homeschool Option

Some parents choose to educate their children at home to ensure that they learn to practice the faith and to view things from a Catholic perspective.

Leslie Payne

Today parents who desire to raise their children to be devout Catholics, prepared to stand up to a self-destructive secular culture, will have to work hard to add a Catholic vision to the education (academic and cultural) their children receive in a typical mainstream setting.

Some Catholic parents have decided that, rather than going to all the trouble of following along with each child's instruction—adding to or subtracting from it as necessary—they might as well keep the children home and teach them themselves. Other reasons parents might decide to homeschool include:

- financial constraints
- avoidance of peer pressure

- facilitating a child's special interests (competitive athletics, music, art, and so on
- providing advanced academic studies

Catholics who choose home education can take advantage of the advances made by the burgeoning national homeschooling movement. It consists mainly of evangelicals who pulled their children out of school over issues such as evolution and sex education. But it also has a sizable contingent of "alternative education" proponents who view institutional school structure and methods as ineffective and harmful. Thanks to the efforts of these pioneers, homeschooling is legal in all fifty states and has earned a reputation for providing a high-quality education.

Within the homeschooling movement, there are different educational philosophies and teaching styles. They range from the "school-at-home" people whose children sit at desks four or five hours per day, to the "unschoolers" who believe children should learn by unhindered exploration of their environment, rather than formal teaching. There is also a teaching method known as "unit study," with the children concentrating on one "unit" (for example, electricity and magnetism, the Crusades, nineteenth-century English literature) for a period of time until they learn everything they can about that one subject. Many homeschoolers mix and match among these various techniques.

A number of companies sell complete home study packages, with textbooks, lesson plans, grading of tests, report cards and professional teachers available for consultation. The three major Catholic curriculum providers are Seton School in Front Royal, Virginia; Our Lady of the Rosary School in Bardstown, Kentucky; and Kolbe Academy in Napa, California. The former two companies rely largely on out-of-print Catholic school materials from the 1950s. The latter school focuses on a "great books"-based classical liberal education, with no lesson plans, but with a more flexible program. For example, the parents are not necessarily required to use the recommended textbooks, or even to cover each subject offered. In addition, there are numerous resource companies—Catholic, Protestant and secular—with literally hundreds of resource choices for each school subject available to parents who wish to design their own curricula.

Homeschooling parents learn to work with each individual child's learning style, strengths and weaknesses. They integrate academics, discipline, catechesis and love. For example, a day's study of some historical event can be interrupted to relate the subject to Catholic principles, to the child's personal concerns or to current events. "What do you think the Christians in Pompeii did when Vesuvius erupted?" you might ask. Or, "This story reminds me of the fight you had with your best friend yesterday." Or, "How did the Roman practices of abortion and infanticide affect the empire's moral situation? How is that similar to the effects of abortion in America today?"

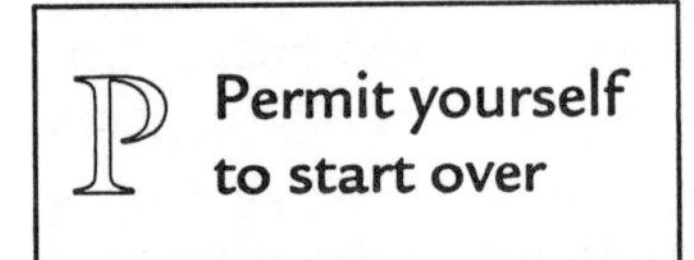

Two common concerns about homeschooling are whether home-taught children learn as much as children in organized schools and how homeschooled children can learn socialization.

Fortunately, the twenty-plus years' history of the homeschooling movement in America has demonstrated that homeschoolers come out ahead on both these counts. The time spent in one-on-one instruction in a classroom setting is minimal. A couple of hours of intensive home study imparts more information—and in such a way that it is more readily retained—than one typical school day. The children can also take a few days off from their studies to rest, or concentrate on one favorite subject for a while, without getting behind. Furthermore, home-educated children enjoy greater intellectual freedom and can develop their gifts more thoroughly than their counterparts in school, who must bend their minds to fit multiple-choice standardized tests. This is to say nothing of the lessons taught by the important activities of daily life—gardening, singing, playing with the baby, baking bread—which children in school have less time to enjoy.

Concerning the issue of socialization, homeschooled children generally have high self-esteem, excellent leadership skills and an ability to relate well to people of all ages, because they are not being placed in the very artificial situation of segregation by age. Even when interacting with friends of the same age, they are less susceptible to the peer pressures that would be overwhelming at school.

Most importantly, the homeschool and local homeschooling support group form a sort of Catholic counterculture, in which families can enjoy all the richness of the Catholic religion. Support groups organize celebrations of saints' feast days, first Friday masses, May crownings, rosary processions and other all-but-forgotten jewels of Catholic life. Homeschooling families can work ancient Catholic traditions—such as the Liturgy of the Hours, the rosary and the Angelus—into their daily lives. All the children of a family can work together on projects for special feast days or seasons—making tortillas for the feast of Our Lady of Guadalupe, designing symbols for the Jesse tree during Advent, or creating costumes for an All Saints' Day party.

One word of caution: any time you go outside the mainstream, you may run into people on the fringe whose ideas differ greatly from yours. While people with extreme ideas sometimes make themselves more visible, the overwhelming majority of Catholic homeschoolers are good Catholics, good parents and good citizens who believe they are called to teach their children at home. They want to raise up children who will be lights of the world. They hope their kids might help bring about a renewal of a faithful, unified Catholic culture in this country.

For Discussion

1. Why do some people choose the homeschooling option?
2. How can homeschooling help form a Catholic culture for a family?

For Reflection

1. Have we considered the homeschooling option?
2. What is the best education option for our family circumstances?

For More information about Homeschooling

Catholic homeschooling information, resources and contacts can be obtained from the National Association of Catholic Home Educators (NACHE). Membership in NACHE is $12 per year and includes a quarterly magazine, The Catholic Home Educator. Write: NACHE, Post Office Box 420225, San Diego, California 92142.

25 Teachable Moments

Use these suggestions to start conversations about Christ and the church with your kids

Bill Dodds

It's easy to feel intimidated when it comes to teaching our children about the Catholic faith, to feel inadequate. Most of us don't have a degree in theology. (And those who do aren't necessarily sure how to translate a college-level concept into kid-level language.)

But throughout the year there are family events—natural opportunities—that can be springboards for moms and dads to talk to their children about the church. (Sometimes we may need to do a little brushing up on the material ahead of time, but that's all right.)

Here are some to consider:

- When a new baby brother or sister, a cousin or a friend is getting baptized, tell your children why you chose baptism for them. Explain that the water represents new life in the Holy Spirit.
- Most family calendars have birthdays penciled in. Include baptism days, as well. There's no need to give a gift; just offer congratulations. A happy anniversary marks the day your child became a Catholic.
- First Reconciliation isn't as frightening for most kids now as it was when you were little. But at the same time, it's still a big event for your son or daughter. A good way for the family to get ready—and for you to make a point about the importance

of this sacrament—is for the older members to go to confession the weekend before the celebration.

- To bring home the notion of celebration (as in the parable of the prodigal son (see Luke 15:11-32), some families go out for ice cream or another treat after they have visited the church together on a Saturday afternoon and gone to confession.
- When a son or daughter is receiving first holy communion it's a natural time to talk about the Eucharist and what this sacrament has meant to you.
- When a grandparent, an elderly neighbor or an older parishioner dies, kids want to know what comes next for that person. The idea of heaven sounds wonderful because it is.
- For birthdays (and Christmas), give your child a little religious gift in addition to the usual present. It might be a small crucifix for the bedroom, a medal with his or her patron saint on it, a rosary or a children's book about saints' lives.
- Speaking of saints, have a little celebration to mark the feast of your child's patron saint. If he or she wasn't named for a saint, let him or her choose a favorite one and mark that saint's feast day.
- Rent a religious video. For example, *The Song of Bernadette* for the younger kids or *A Man for All Seasons* for older ones.
- When everyone is in the car at the beginning of a vacation, say a Hail Mary or Our Father together asking for a safe trip and a good time.
- While on vacation, be sure to go to Sunday mass at the local parish. (Kids need to learn that we don't take vacations from our faith.)
- As Halloween approaches, talk to your kids about "All Hallows Eve," (that is, All Saints' Day) and how Catholics believe we can pray for and love—and be prayed for and loved by—those who have died. The creed refers to this as the "communion of saints."
- Say a "homemade" grace before dinner and let each child offer a prayer of petition or thanksgiving.
- Encourage your children to pray for their friends.
- During Advent, read a little bit each night from the beginning

of Luke's Gospel after lighting the Advent wreath candles.

- Take your children with you as you go door-to-door collecting canned goods for a Thanksgiving or Christmas food drive. Or when you're out collecting for the cancer or heart society or some other charity. Tell them why you are doing this.
- Ask your children to say a short prayer for whoever needs help when a fire truck or aid car passes by with its siren going.
- When your son or daughter receives an award, talk about the parable of the talents (see Matthew 25:14-30) and how God has given each of us special gifts he wants us to use to help others.
- That's also a good parable to use when noting the differences in skills that members of your child's ball team may have. It helps children understand the idea of "using what God has given you."
- When a son or daughter is studying to receive the sacrament of confirmation, use the time for the whole family to talk about the Holy Spirit and how the Spirit can fill each person's life. Read about the first Pentecost in chapter two of the Acts of the Apostles.
- Show your children what it means to "honor your father and your mother" by treating your own parents with respect.
- When the family is attending a wedding, explain how, from the Catholic point of view, getting married is more than simply "signing a piece of paper." It's a sacrament.
- During Lent, help your children become more aware of the needy by using the Rice Bowl program that is sponsored by Catholic Relief Services.
- When your son or daughter has an important test at school, tell your child you will say a prayer for him or her. Ask your kids to pray for you.
- Do not hesitate to talk to your child about the spiritual side of life. About faith. About mystery. The more you do it, the easier it will become. (And the more you will learn!)

Remember that like a patient gardener, you are planting seeds of faith and it may be years before they take root, grow and blossom.

Think, Pray & Act

Planting Faith Seeds

Catholic parents have the primary responsibility to introduce their children to the faith. We plant the seeds and the Holy Spirit brings the water of life to their souls. How are we doing as religious educators? Do we speak to our children about Christian truths? About our own experience of God and the church? Use the *For Discussion* and *For Reflection* questions at the end of this chapter's articles to help you gauge the effectiveness of your efforts. Is there one thing you could do differently to improve your faith planting? You may find the tools, located at the end of chapter one, helpful in sorting out your ideas.

Resources

- *The Catechism of the Catholic Church* (Servant Book Express: 313-677-6490).
- Mary Kay Clark, Ph.D., *Catholic Home Schooling* (Tan Books: 800-437-5876).
- Bert Ghezzi, *50 Ways to Tap the Power of the Sacraments* (Our Sunday Visitor: 800-348-2440).
- John A. Hardon, S.J., *The Faith: A Popular Guide Based on the Catechism of the Catholic Church* (Servant Book Express: 313-677-6490).
- Karl Keating, *What Catholics Really Believe* (Servant Book Express: 313-677-6490).
- Edward D. O'Connor, C.S.C., *The Catholic Vision* (Our Sunday Visitor: 800-348-2440).
- Alan Schreck, *Catholic and Christian* (Servant Book Express: 313-677-6490).

SEVEN

Care to Discipline

Catholic parents should use discipline wisely, in order to prepare their children to become disciples of Christ.

Six Compromises Parents Must Never Make

Train your children in Catholic morality by helping them conform to a few carefully chosen ideals.

Bert Ghezzi

Sometimes I wish that slick powers of negotiation were among the graces of matrimony. Regularly, for example, I find myself squaring off with Mary, my thirteen-year-old daughter, for whom the word "no" is not a decision, but a matter of opinion. "What part of that word *no* don't you understand, Mary?" asked an older brother recently from the sidelines. One of Mary's favorite words is *options.* If I say no to one option, she wants to reach a compromise on another.

A parent may compromise with a child when all the choices are good or neutral. For example, I may deny Mary permission to visit a friend but agree to allow her to invite a friend to our home. However, there are compromises parents must never make. In some areas, there are no acceptable options except doing the right thing, so compromise is not possible. You can probably think of numerous situations where this is the case. I want to talk about three moral compromises parents must not make with kids and three spiritual compromises that parents must not make with themselves.

Three Moral Compromises Parents Must Avoid

Like you, Mary Lou and I struggle daily with the challenges of raising moral kids in a blatantly immoral world. Recently, for example, I had to tell my daughter Mary she could not dance to a ditty called "Shake Your Body" in a school talent show. We try to limit such interventions to situations in which immoral opportunities are about to become occasions of sin for one of our kids. However, we have decided that because evil attractions are so plentiful, we cannot protect our children by policing every situation.

Instead, we decided to hold up a few ideals that would set a high moral standard for our family. We looked for qualities that summed up the moral law in simple words. Our choices were love, obedience and truth. We established these ideals as behavioral guidelines for our children.

Love, obedience and truth are absolutes. They represent the incontrovertible fundamentals of Christian living, expressing the Ten Commandments in an abbreviated form. Your own short list of absolutes may include other terms such as justice or mercy. But whatever words we choose, parents must not compromise with their children on Christian basics.

Love. Jesus commanded his followers to love God above all, and to love others unconditionally. Since he made love the test of all Christian behavior, parents can form their children in Christian morality by training them to do the loving thing in every situation. Together in our families we learn how to express affection, how to serve others selflessly and how to make choices based on love.

The Lord set a high standard of love and we must hold each other to it. So parents must not compromise with kids by tolerating any unloving behavior. Not so easy a task when you remember that, unlike the one-sided, nice characters in some TV families, we and our kids have a not-so-nice underside that causes conflict. Mary Lou and I have only a few family rules, but the main one has always outlawed hurting other human beings. If

Ghezzi family members—Mom and Dad included—do or say anything that injures another, they must ask forgiveness and set it right.

Obedience. By requiring our children to obey us, we are preparing them to obey God, which ultimately is a matter of life or death. Jesus says his Father rewards us with eternal life not for great accomplishments, outstanding Christian service or even miracles, but for obedience to his will (see Matthew 7:21-23).

Training children to obey requires consistency and can admit no compromise. Parents need wisdom here, because if we try to control our kids by demanding obedience on too many issues, we'll crush them and make them rebels. We do better to have only a few rules on matters of importance to us. Mary Lou and I also try to give direct orders to kids only when we must. Once we give a command, we must follow through by expecting obedience. Teaching kids to obey is worth doing right because obedience, like love, is a life-shaping Christian ideal.

Truth. Parents must not allow their kids to compromise the truth. Deception damages our relationship with God. Lying to ourselves and others prevents our dealing with sinful behavior patterns. It also ruins our personal relationships. But Jesus said that the truth sets us free (see John 8:32). For example, take the Samaritan woman. When the Lord made her face the truth, she was able to break with sin and turn to God (see John 4:28-9; 41-2). To build respect for the truth in our children, we must set an example. We need to rid our own lives of every dishonesty.

Dealing with deception in a child is one of the toughest tasks parents face. The best advice anyone ever gave Mary Lou and me about handling it was "proceed with caution." Lies fog our perception. We must not act until we figure out what's really going on. We don't want to make children lie in self-defense by coming down too hard on them or by falsely accusing them.

Training our children in truth, obedience and love puts their lives on a Christian course. These ideals work together as an internal guidance system, a moral gyroscope, that keeps them on the right path. Each time our children choose to be loving, obedient or truthful, their lives take on a little more distinctly Catholic Christian shape. We don't want to compromise that in any way.

Three Spiritual Compromises Parents Must Avoid

To keep our children on firm spiritual ground, we must refuse to compromise our own relationship with the Lord. Let's talk about maintaining the strength of three significant elements in our divine relationship—faith, hope and love. We know these qualities as the theological virtues. They represent graces that are essential for parents in the job of bringing kids to God.

Love. Parents' love for God must be obvious to their kids. Little brothers and sisters are watching. They must see us honoring the Lord in the way we live every day. If we put something else first in our lives instead of God, believe me, they'll know. Kids seem to have sensors that tell them when their parents' spiritual lives are off. "I don't see you reading the Bible as much as you used to," a kid said to me once, triggering an immediate change of behavior.

Parents' love for their kids must also be obvious. Our children must feel it in their bones that we love them no matter what. For a lifetime we must love all our kids generously. We must not hold back even from those who may withdraw from us. The father in the film *A River Runs Through It* dearly loved a troubled son, who could never take the spiritual gifts the dad had to offer. Like that father, we need to love our children, renegades included, without conditions or compromises.

Faith. The stability of our relationship with God plays a big role in our handing on the faith to our children. Remaining faithful for years to a God who sometimes seems unconcerned about us is an invaluable witness for our kids. Our children must make their own faith choices. But our example of refusing to compromise our fidelity to God will appeal to their innate desire to give their lives to something worth dying for. Like Monica's faith of thirty years that attracted Augustine to the Lord, our faith, too, will work like a magnet, drawing our children to God.

Hope. More than anything else, parents need a daily dose of hope. We must not compromise it by losing heart. Mary Lou and I, for example, scan the lives of our seven children, noting their needs and our wants for them. Then we do what we can and hope that everything turns out all right. If the outcome of our childrearing depended entirely on us, we wouldn't be able to stop trembling in fear. However, God is intimately involved in our families. He is very interested in bringing our kids to himself, so there is every reason for hope.

During World War II, when all seemed lost and it seemed certain that Nazi forces would defeat the Allies, British Prime Minister Winston Churchill gave a moving speech to the Western world. His message of hope was a simple three-word chorus: Never give up! Never give up! Never give up! When things get especially bad and some dark disaster seems to hang over a family member, I remember Churchill's exhortation. I put my hope in the invisible God who is my Father and the real Father of my children.

Paul says that faith, hope and love are the "three things that last" (1 Corinthians 13:13). Let's live them as fully as we can, with no compromise, so that they may channel a flood of grace to us and our children.

For Discussion

1. How can holding kids to a few Christian ideals help form them in Catholic morality?
2. What effect do you think a parent's commitment to Christ and spiritual life have on a child?

For Reflection

1. What are we doing in our family to help the kids conform to Christian moral standards?

2. What one thing could we do differently to improve the moral training of our children?
3. What is the status of my relationship to the Lord?
4. What one action could I take to strengthen it?

When Compromise Is OK

Parents can open their kids to grace by holding them to high moral standards and taking a more flexible approach to their own arbitrarily defined expectations.

Bert Ghezzi

We don't like making compromises. When we do, we feel like we are settling for something less than what's right. That is the case when we compromise an absolute like one of the Ten Commandments. But many compromises parents face are neutral or even good.

We make a compromise when we concede to behavior lower than that set by some standard. Thinking about standards will help us learn to make wise compromises. A standard is something set up as a model for behavior. It establishes a requirement that we can measure ourselves and others against. Standards may be laws, conventions or rules that we get from an authority or by our consent. Here are some examples:

- At table it is polite to place your napkin on your lap and wait until everyone is served before you start to eat.
- The Ghezzi family worships together at Sunday mass.
- On most highways, the state of Florida requires that you maintain a speed above forty miles an hour that does not exceed sixty-five miles an hour.
- Members of the honor society must maintain a 3.5 grade point average.
- "I give you a new commandment," Jesus said, "love one another. As I have loved you, so you also should love one another" (John 13:34-35).

We feel that concessions to such standards are always bad,

because they appear to be failures. We don't like it when we don't measure up.

As we saw in the previous article, some compromises are always bad. Any concession to the law of Christian love is unacceptable because it offends the Lord. Parents must never compromise with children or themselves on moral and spiritual absolutes like love, faith, obedience and justice that are pillars of Christian living.

Every day, however, parents use standards that don't carry God's supreme authority. Some, like manners, are conventions we get from society. Others, like standards of achievement or orderliness, are rules we define for ourselves that stand only on our authority. For example, we set expectations for our kids' academic, artistic or athletic accomplishments and we establish the boundaries for their neatness. Compromising standards such as these is not only possible; sometimes it is good, wise and necessary.

Learning to compromise on my own standards has not come easy for me. When I was a novice dad, I was always strict with the children. My family attributes that trait to my authoritarian Italian genes. Whatever the source, I was uncompromising and it almost wrecked my relationship with some of my children.

When one of my older sons reached adolescence and began to test his limits, I measured him against high standards in every area—eating habits, manners, dress, the condition of his room, school work, you name it. "You are all over him for everything," a friend told me. "If you don't back off, you are going to push him into real rebellion."

My friend taught me an important distinction that has helped me apply standards wisely. He said I had to learn to distinguish being *strict* from being *firm*. When you are strict, he said, you hold someone to the highest possible standard. But you can accept a lower standard and hold someone to it. That's being firm.

He recommended that I be strict with this son only on moral matters. In other less important areas, he said I should lower my standards. I should compromise. He assured me that being firm did not mean "giving up," but having moderate expectations. Worry less about his manners, his dress and his room. Be concerned to help him do good and avoid sin.

Over the next few years in my relationship with this son, I learned how to use compromise as a parenting tool. I was able to moderate my requirements in most areas and hold fast in the few that really counted. I changed my behavior in time to preserve my relationship with my son, but I have had to learn the lessons over repeatedly. My tendency to strictness keeps popping up and other kids have different needs or circumstances, requiring me to review and adjust my standards.

I suggest that parents freely modify standards that they have set when concession seems necessary or beneficial. Give some ground in a nonessential area to help gain or maintain ground in another, more important, area. Think about setting standards at the right level in these areas:

Orderliness. Most children are naturally messy. Parents fight a constant battle to have them keep their rooms in order. It gets even worse when they become teenagers. But this is an area where compromise may be necessary. Standards here are arbitrary and concessions are neutral, unless their rooms become health hazards.

When I told a friend that my wife, Mary Lou, and I no longer expected kids' rooms to be picked up at all times, he laughed and said he had done that long ago. "I just take photographs of their rooms," he said. "When they ask what I'm doing, I say that I'm saving the photos for their children."

Dress. Parents can also compromise on their standards of dress. We can allow kids to wear styles of clothes that are popular with their friends. But there are limits, and our family's boundaries may be different than yours. For example, we have permitted teens to experiment with weird haircuts because we know hair grows back. When one son came home with his hair sticking out on top in a uniform rim over completely shaved sides, I whispered to Mary Lou, "I think he looks like a zinnia, don't you?" All of our daughters and one son have pierced ears, but we don't allow them to mark their bodies in any other way that may be permanent or damaging.

Manners. Manners are important. Teaching a child courtesy prepares her or him to learn virtues like kindness that require disciplined behavior. But we can gradually form a child in proper social behavior. First, respect for adults, then table etiquette, then telephone courtesy, and so on. When the battle rages thick in another area, we can compromise by relaxing our efforts to police this one.

Achievement. Parents must learn how to set expectations that draw the best out of their kids, stretching them to the limits of their ability without pressuring them unfairly. But the standard must be flexible. For example, we should reward the "Bs" and "Cs" of an average student as generously as we do the "As" of a more gifted one. Other concessions may be necessary. Recently, for example, I encouraged a teenage daughter to drop an academic subject to make room for driver's education because I thought it was important for her self-confidence.

The arts and sports are other areas where parents may have to compromise their standards of achievement. At long last Mary Lou, for example, has had to abandon the subtle pressure she put on our sons to become professional athletes. Alas, never will she see a son on television, giving the high sign and mouthing, "Hi, Mom!" (But she is still heard to shout, "Be a hitter!" to our youngest daughter, who excels at softball. So she still has a spark of hope.)

Making acceptable compromises in areas such as these helps parents hold the line on standards of behavior that do not admit compromise. However, our lowering some expectations and asserting *no compromise* on moral standards does not guarantee that our kids will make the right moral choices. Parents must forbid behavior that breaks the laws of God or the church. Parents can teach, exhort and point the way. When children do something wrong—when they compromise a moral absolute—we can correct them, instruct them about the dangers of sin, punish them and help them repent and repair the damage. But we cannot control our children's actions, even when they are young. Parents can be uncompromising on moral and spiritual standards, but that won't keep the kids from compromising them. Parents need the wisdom of Solomon to make the right compromises. But since the Lord gives us wisdom freely, we can expect to be able to make sound choices.

For Discussion

1. When is it OK to compromise on standards?
2. What is the difference between being strict and being firm?

For Reflection

1. What expectations do we have for our children?
2. Are we strict or firm in upholding our standards?
3. Should we take any steps to adjust our expectations? Should we raise them or lower them?

Discipline Without Feeling Guilty

If parent fail to discipline their children, others will do it later with no trace of love or gentleness.

Ray Guarendi, Ph.D.

Some parents who write me say that while discipline is important, it makes them feel guilty. They mistakenly think that all discipline is mean.

The prime motive for discipline is this: You are the most kind, gentle teacher that your children will ever have. Never again will they be taught how to get along in life by someone with even a fraction of your love. If you don't discipline now, for whatever reason—because you feel guilty, too strict, afraid of doing something "wrong," or because it's just easier to let things go—then who will ultimately discipline your children? The world. And the world is neither a kind nor gentle place to learn lessons.

If a parent doesn't teach qualities like self-control, respect for others, consideration, and the ability to follow rules, then the teaching is thrust upon others: a teacher, employer, landlord, army sergeant, police officer, judge. Who of these has the emotional attachment to your child that you do? Who loves your child as much as you do? Who will forgive and forget as many times as you will?

When a child is five, eight, or twelve years old and talks mean, what do you do? Put him in a chair, swat his bottom, send him to his room, fine him fifty cents or make him write a two-hundred-word apology? When he's twenty-five and talks mean, what happens? He could get beat up, fired or arrested. He may have to sleep on the couch! And the stakes get higher as we get older. No matter how mean you might think you are for enforcing limits and expectations, you are a whole lot less mean than life.

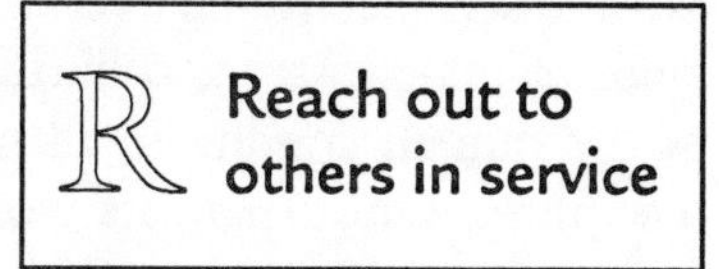

Life delivers consequences solely on the basis of how we act. It seldom takes into consideration mitigating factors like, "Oh, she's cranky because she's tired." Or, "What do you expect, he's a middle child." Try telling your boss after you've verbally unloaded on him or her, "I'm sorry. I went to bed late last night and woke up crabby—with a headache, no less. On top of that, I don't think I'm fully over my birth trauma yet." I'm not sure he or she will just have a good laugh and make allowances.

Parents make allowances. We love without limits because we see mitigating circumstances, sometimes even when there are none. That's the beauty of parenthood. It's what makes our discipline have heart, our lessons come with soft landings. All the more crucial then that we not surrender our privilege—no, our duty—to discipline. We alone are uniquely suited to teach little humans, when it's easiest on them and when they are most durable.

A mother once told me, "I think the worst thing I could do to my son would be to allow him to be unlikable." In the short term, an undisciplined child aims most of the unlikable behavior at the parents. They suffer the immediate brunt of demands and unruliness, but in the long term, if left uncorrected the child suffers. Others quickly tire of difficult behavior and avoid people because of it. Long after Mom or Dad have left the scene, such a person is left to learn on his or her own how to relate maturely to others.

A critical distinction must be made between discipline in and of itself as mean, and mean discipline. Certainly we can be mean as we discipline. We can verbally pummel, demand and fling all kinds of unnecessary and hurtful words and emotions. By virtue of the human condition, all parents are prone to some mean discipline. Good parents work hard for years to reduce its presence. But setting firm limits and holding children accountable for their actions is not mean at all. It is love in action. Perhaps it is a love difficult for children to comprehend. Nonetheless, it is a love that will endure long beyond our passing, in the character of the mature person we leave on this earth.

For Discussion

Why must parents discipline their children?

For Reflection

1. How well do we discipline our children?
2. Does disciplining my children make me feel mean or guilty? How can I deal with those feelings?

Three Rules for Restoring Love

With patient effort parents can teach kids to honestly admit their wrongdoing, to replace bad behavior with good and to repair broken relationships with forgiveness.

Mark Berchem

Our goal is to provide our children a loving home. A place where they know they are loved. A place where all can live together in harmony. We strive to live out the Christian ideal—loving one another as Christ loved us.

Unfortunately, we screw up! Our children mess up! Try as we might, we are unable to maintain loving relationships all the time. We fall short of the ideal. Dad gets impatient with Mom. Hannah says an unkind word to John. John takes Claire's book. Claire complains about what's for dinner.

My wife and I have three rules that we use to deal with failures to love that constantly occur in our home. Some evenings after the children are in bed, exasperated by the most recent failure, we sit down to remind ourselves of these principles. The first rule is so obvious that it is almost comical:

Rule #1— Don't be surprised when you or your children fail to love. It happens!

Yet how often are we amazed by our children's lack of love! This is especially true with the younger ones. It can be shocking when that sweet little angel gets mad and wallops his sister.

We get lulled into thinking the kids have mastered the art of loving when they have a few good days or weeks of getting along. Then *bam*! All of a sudden they are totally different, seemingly void of all rules of civility. Don't be surprised. At times like this, the temptation is to think: *I have failed somehow as a parent. What did I do wrong? What should I have done? What happened?*

What happened is called *sin*. Despite our best efforts to teach them to love, our children still suffer the effects of original sin. Of course, so do Mom and Dad. As we strive for the ideal of loving as Christ loved, we will stumble and fall. The key is to not get all bent out of shape. Get back up and start anew. Christian life is a race. It's not the person who stumbles and falls that loses, but rather the one who doesn't get back up and continue on.

Rule #2—Don't lower the standards of love.

Scripture gives plentiful advice for parents on training children in the school of love. St. Paul's exhortation to Timothy to remain faithful to his ministry is particularly helpful. "Stay with the task whether convenient or inconvenient—correcting, reproving, appealing—constantly teaching and never losing patience" (see 2 Timothy 4:2). Stay with the task! Never lose patience! Why is this so important? Because when our children are failing to love one another we face the temptation to lower the standard.

We get tired of constantly correcting, reproving, appealing and teaching. We forget it takes a lifetime to learn to love. We want results now. When we don't get them, we get discouraged. At times like this, we feel like giving up and settling for less love in our family. When we're about to wave the white flag of defeat, we need to battle the temptation.

My wife and I have found two things that help us stay with the task. First, we pray hard. We turn to the Lord often for strength and wisdom. Second, we get support from other Catholic parents. Visiting regularly with couples who share our commitment renews our patience and gives us the encouragement to continue on.

Rule #3—Provide a way to reconcile relationships and restore love.

Training our children to conform to the love ideal requires us to have a way to reconcile relationships and restore love. My wife and I have found a simple four-part process that we use to help our children get back on track. Our whole family uses it when anyone has been unkind, disrespectful or mean to one another or to Mom and Dad. Our process involves:

1. being honest
2. deciding to change
3. asking forgiveness
4. showing love

Being honest is a critical first step in restoring damaged family relationships. Three of the hardest words for our children to say are "I did it."

"John, did you hit your sister?"

"Well, she took my book."

"Claire, did you call Hannah stupid?"

"Sort of. She was bothering me when I was reading."

Just like their first parents in the Bible, children learn to blame others. If you ask my kids, it's always someone else's fault. But cultivating the virtue of honesty is vital. You can't reconcile a broken relationship until you take personal responsibility for what you have done.

You cultivate honesty in your children by your example and by your word. Parents must acknowledge their own mistakes and failures. We must also talk with kids about the virtue of honesty and truthfulness. We must help our children understand that their doing something wrong doesn't change our love for them. When children are confident of their parents' love, they will find it easier to be honest about their failings.

Deciding to change is the second step in restoring relationships. The church has traditionally called this *repentance.*

Repentance is not mainly feeling sorry for what you have done that has hurt someone. Rather, it's choosing to no longer speak or act in that hurtful way. Helping our children decide to change is a teaching moment in our family. It's an opportunity to talk about Christ's desires for our lives. It's also an opportunity to help our children rethink their actions and come up with positive alternatives.

"John, instead of hitting your sister when she takes your book, what could you do?"

"Claire, what's a more loving way to speak to Hannah when she interrupts your reading time?"

This is the spot where parents really have to be staying with the task. If your children are like mine, they keep doing the same wrong thing over and over again. We have to patiently remind, explain, teach and encourage the new behavior we hope will replace the unloving one.

Asking forgiveness comes next. After being honest about what they have done and recognizing how to change, the children are ready for this step.

My wife and I have taught our children a simple formula to use in asking forgiveness.

"I am sorry for (state the offense). Will you forgive me?"

"Claire, I am sorry for hitting you. Will you forgive me?"

"Hannah, I'm sorry for calling you a bad name. Will you forgive me?"

This does not have to be a painful process. In fact, asking forgiveness should be a regular occurrence in a family's life. Our children should see me asking my wife for forgiveness when I am impatient or irritable. They should experience me asking for their forgiveness if I'm too harsh with them or ignore them. And they should experience my patiently prodding them to ask forgiveness when they have been unloving.

Reconciliation is a gift from God. It provides us, as a family, a way to undo wrongs, heal hurts and repair brokenness. We should be eager to restore love to our relationships. We should constantly extend mercy to one another, as our Father is rich in mercy towards us. When we hear the words, "Will you forgive me?" we have a great opportunity to demonstrate Christ's love.

"Yes, John, I forgive you."

"Yes, Hannah, I forgive you."

"Yes, Dad, I forgive you."

Showing affection always ends our little reconciling moment. We usually hug and say "I love you." We want a small sign that the relationship has been restored and we are all back on track. My wife and I are gratified to watch our children begin to instinctively use the steps to repair a rupture in their relationships. Of course, it has taken years of perseverance. Yet by staying with the task, we're starting to hear "Will you forgive me?" as much as we hear "I love you."

For Discussion

1. Why is it important to honestly admit that we have done something wrong?
2. Why do you think family members should ask forgiveness when they have hurt each other?

For Reflection

1. How do we help our children deal with their wrongdoing?
2. Does our family have a way of repairing broken relationships?

The Apple Does Not Fall Far from the Tree

Since our kids imitate us, parents must rely on the Holy Spirit to help us replace our bad behaviors with good ones.

Bert Ghezzi

Our kids resemble us in more than just physical ways. Ghezzi kids, for example, tend to be short in stature and short on patience—like their dad who stands tall at five feet five inches and struggles daily with his anger. They also tend to be both sports fanatics and good sports—like their mom who caught the bug early, watching the Pittsburgh Pirates at Forbes Field when she was twelve.

Genetics, of course, plays a big role in determining our kids' traits. When my teenage boys complained that their ears stuck out, my wife obligingly explained the cause by showing them my high-school picture. But the family environment plays an even bigger role in making our kids like us. That's where they acquire their behavioral traits. Family is the school for character. Kids become a lot like their parents just by living with them.

Our children learn how to live by imitating us either consciously or unconsciously. Along the way they pick up both our good qualities and our bad tendencies. From my dad, for example, I learned dedication to caring for my family. He worked twelve-hour days to provide for us, rarely relaxing. He never took a vacation. But along with his paternal concern I also got a big dose of his intensity. After my dad died, my mom prayed her way through raising four children as a single parent. Her example taught me faithfulness to God. But I also caught her irritability. Like her, I get furious over petty things.

Because our kids are modeling their behavior on ours, we have to become the kind of people we want them to be. We must aspire to be like St. Joseph, the exemplar for all parents, who, according to Scripture, always did what was right (Matthew 1:19). But we do not need to be candidates for canonization, just moms and dads who are doing their best to obey God's will. That way we will give our children more good qualities than bad tendencies to imitate.

For this job we need integrity. This means that parents must do what they say the kids must do. Kids model on our actions, not our words. Recently my youngest daughter refused to kiss me good night because I had said no to something she wanted to do.

"Mary," I said, "you can't withhold affection just because you're angry with me."

"Why not?" she shot back. "You do."

Then she reminded me of another recent situation when I had refused to kiss her because I was frustrated by her vigorous campaign to change my mind on something. Startled, I apologized on the spot. I told her my behavior had been wrong and asked her forgiveness. When we don't measure up to our standards, repenting to our children repairs the damage of our bad example. It brings our actions back into line with our words.

Becoming appropriate role models for our children is not as difficult as it might seem. That's because we get our good qualities the same way they do—from our relationship with a us by living in our presence, we become like our Father by living in his presence. Scripture says that Christians are being renewed in the image of the Creator (see Colossians 3:10). That's the work of the Holy Spirit, who changes us into God's likeness, Paul says, "from one degree of glory to another" (2 Corinthians 3:17-18).

When the Father begot us as his daughters and sons, he put his own life in us. Thus he arranged for mere humans to enjoy a family resemblance to him. Living the divine life disposes us to do the right thing in every situation. We can act kindly to someone who asks a favor when we really feel like being mean. Or we can patiently endure little inconveniences, like overcoming angry urges to curse drivers who pull ahead of us in traffic. Or, again, we can temper our justice with mercy when a teenager apologizes for coming home late. We call behaviors like kindness, patience and mercy the fruit of the Spirit (see Galatians 5:22) because they are the products of God's life in us. Jesus himself taught that we bear such fruit by living in him (see John 15:5).

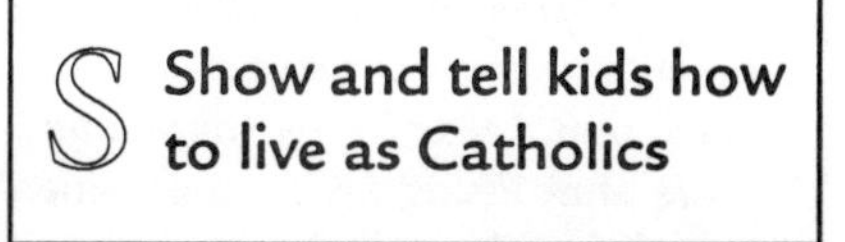

An old proverb says, "The apple does not fall far from the tree." It applies equally to the kids in our families and to all of us, the children in God's family.

For Discussion

1. What is integrity? Why do we need it for our role as parents?
2. What makes it possible for us to do the right thing even when we don't feel like it?

For Reflection

1. In what ways are my children becoming like me?
2. Am I the kind of Catholic Christian I want my children to become?
3. Which of my bad tendencies ought I to work at eliminating before my kids pick it up?

Parents in White Hats

"Mom," my grown daughter complained during one of our weekly telephone conversations, "I caught myself sounding just like you the other day. It was really weird."

Of course, I found it quite amusing that my first-born child, who had struggled fiercely to be her own person, was now being visited with a realization that eventually hits most adults: Like it or not, we absorb much more from our parents than we realize.

This same conclusion had hit me later in life, too late for my parents to enjoy the sweet satisfaction I felt after my daughter's revelation. I was in my thirties and burying my father just five years after losing my mother, when one of Dad's good friends stopped at the wake to say simply, "Your dad wore the bulgiest white hat ever."

Now, I was a kid who grew up with 1950s black-and-white westerns at the neighborhood theater. So I knew instantly what she meant. The villains usually wore black, but the good guys always wore white hats. And it finally hit me that most of the values I cling to so tenaciously today—or at least try to—were learned by observing how my father and mother lived, not just from what they said.

I never thought too much about it when Dad quit more than one accounting job because the bosses wanted him to juggle the books. It seemed like the thing to do when my parents

25 Ways to Form Kids in Catholic Morality

Which of these possibilities is best suited to help you train your children in Christian behvior?

Therese Boucher

1. Each of us has a list of *shoulds* that we use to evaluate our actions. For example, we should "keep the peace" or "forgive each other." The cornerstone of Catholic morality is a vital relationship with Father, Son and Holy Spirit, lived out within the church community. This is the greatest *should* for Catholic families. Find out how faith can be more of a criteria for your actions and parenting.

loaned money to down-and-out friends, even though Mom and Dad were struggling to support their own family. And I thought it was just typical for a family to drive three miles out of the way to take a widow friend to mass every Sunday. Be honest, share what you have, help other people and keep the faith: This simply was the message my parents lived, day in and day out.

But now that I'm a parent, I find that it is intimidating to know that your children are watching your every move and are learning their values from what you do as well as from what you say. During casual dinner-table conversations, a parent can see the little wheels in the children's heads turning, and even a toddler will notice the slightest event. What parent hasn't been amazed to have a child imitate some action the parent wasn't even aware the child had observed? What mother isn't mortified to hear her child scold her doll with the same angry words Mother had used on the child the day before? What father hasn't heard his child casually use a swear word that Dad had let slip out once?

Being parents means making mistakes, and I remember quite a few mistakes that my parents made too. But the consistency of their day-to-day behavior is what I remember most. That's what seems to affect children in the long run.

So, when children surprise themselves by imitating Dad or Mom, may they imitate something that only the good guys in the white hats would have done.

Ann Carey

Kids can learn to think!

2. Encourage children to think about their actions and experiences. Help kids evaluate life for themselves. For example, look at an ad together (print, TV, or billboard). Ask, "What does this ad say about people? What does it tell us to do?" It might say, "It's important to be beautiful, or to drive a new car." It might tell us to consume or to overindulge.
3. Teach respect—which means to look twice. Have your children list ways that a person or an object is valuable to them, the family and the world. Involve kids in outreach to the poor, the homeless or neighboring elderly.

4. Teaching new behavior involves transforming a child's thinking. It's internal, not external, and harder than changing clothes. Tell yourself, "This will take at least two hundred attempts." Pray for patience. Aren't there things you are still learning too?
5. Apologize for your own failings. Provide a model of humility and conversion. Kids need to watch how you tap into the unbounded mercy of God.
6. Help children examine their conscience. Help form the criteria they use for reviewing their actions. Ask, "What were you thinking and feeling at the time? How did your actions affect others? How could you be more loving if you were in this situation again?"
7. Use television to discuss moral choices. Watch a show up to its climax. Turn off the TV and tape the rest. Discuss the choices that characters face. What would each family member do? Ask kids first. Then watch the ending. Discuss the difference between your projected choices and what happens.

Kids can learn to choose what's good!

8. What specific behaviors (what list of *shoulds*) do you have for your children? Are they realistic and achievable? Do these behaviors foster your long-range parenting goals? You may want a child to make his bed and dispose of dirty clothes, not just "clean your room!" The long-range goal is personal organization and discipline.
9. Admit that your child is capable of sin, wrongdoing and inappropriate behavior. Try to respond to each accordingly, without going berserk. Correct actions without blame and name calling. Try "I'm sorry this happened. What do you think should happen next?" Help kids accept the consequences of their actions.
10. Provide regular opportunities for making choices and accepting responsibility. We once gave our teenagers expense money for a three-day family vacation. Each one paid for meals in restaurants, as well as entertainment. Their decisions were comical, but very revealing.

11. Give specific directions that describe ways to love others. Avoid saying vague things like, "I want you to share." Try saying, "I want you to take turns using that wagon."
12. Teach kids to obey directions. My husband gives "sitting lessons" at the supper table. He tells preschoolers to use "behind glue" and listen for the stillness their bodies need to digest food. He reminds older kids of our common need for conversation.

    Once our two-year-old Mary bolted down a pier at a fishing port, ready to jump in the deep water. John boomed out her name, and she froze in her tracks just a few inches from the edge. What a lesson in the value of obedience!
13. Realize that kids will not be consistent in their actions. They are on the move from parent control to kid control. You can provide suggestions for an inner script that's in tune with God's voice. One of my favorite lines is, "People are more important than things." In time, kids must choose their own *shoulds* and develop a personal inner divinely shaped script.
14. Let kids make mistakes. They need to have a private world of their own. Let them learn by doing.
15. Catholic morality is a covenant and communal affair, not just a private experience. It's even global and ecological in scope. Expose young people to regular contact with the local faith community so they can meet people with values shaped by the gospel. Encourage them to experience the sacraments of the Eucharist and reconciliation often.

Kids can learn to love!

16. All Catholic morality is about love, and abiding in God as the source of love. Highlight moral successes. Affirm the good that children do and the love that they attempt. These are the beginnings of virtue.
17. Encourage children to take responsibility for the emotions that lead to actions—anger, fear, joy, desire. Teach them to name their feelings, and state what they want. They will learn to think and communicate before acting. They may be able

to decide against bad actions. Hopefully, they will ask others the same questions.

18. Criticize the behavior, not the person. "Slamming the door in your sister's face makes me angry. Her nose could have been broken." Help young people discuss what happens when they express understanding and forgiveness accompanied by some sign of affection.
19. Encourage privacy, silence, reflection and personal prayer. Noise pollution leads to mind pollution. As a part of our stance about solitude, we regulate TV viewing and don't allow televisions in bedrooms. Teach kids to keep a diary or journal that includes letters to Jesus.
20. Encourage kids to look at Jesus and the way he acted in Scripture. Imagine your whole family was present during a Sunday gospel's events. Discuss the feelings and the *why* behind each character's actions. Act out a Scripture together, like foot washing on Holy Thursday.
21. Teach kids a balance between the good of the individual and the person or community at hand. Instill thoughtful compassion for each person, as well as concern for the needs of the family.

Because God said so!

22. Be careful not to use God as a club to bully children into submission. They don't need a "super-parent." Instead, invite them to experience God's life, God's strength and God's plan for human beings.
23. The Father has created each of our children as fundamentally good. God made us what we are and continues to mold us. Help kids discover the abilities they have been given. A stubborn child has a raw gift of perseverance. Ask our Father to nurture and direct that gift.
24. Jesus has broken into human history and into each child's personal history with baptismal life. He is my child's most important teacher. Jesus is the way, the truth and the life for

each member of our family. Talk to him out loud with your child. Pray to him as a family.

25. The Holy Spirit is the source of all moral strength. The Spirit gives us an inner energy to love and be our best self. Cultivate a love for the Spirit in the family. Fruits of the Spirit like peace, patience, joy, wisdom, and fortitude will rub off on us and our children. We can rely on God for the desire to begin a new moral life as often as we need.

Think, Pray & Act

As Twigs Are Bent...

Parents who care are parents who discipline. We form our children's characters with deeds and words. Holding up ideals. Setting boundaries. Rewarding good. Punishing evil. Forgiving and being forgiven. What kind of character are you molding in your kids? What kind of character are you modeling for your kids? Take a moment to review the questions *For Discussion* and *For Reflection* at the end of the articles in this unit. They will help you get a picture of your approach to discipline. Have you come up with an action idea that could improve your practice? The tools presented in chapter one may help you select the right action.

Resources

- Foster Cline and Jim Fay, *Parenting With Love and Logic* (Piñon Press: 719-548-9222).
- Bert Ghezzi, *The Angry Christian* (St. Paul Books & Media: 800-876-4463)
- Ray Guarendi, Ph.D. *Back to the Family* (Villard Books: 800-733-3000).
- Ray Guarendi, Ph.D. *You're a Better Parent Than You Think* (Fireside/Simon & Schuster: 212-698-7000).

EIGHT

In the World, but Not *of* It

Our families are immersed in a society that swirls with good and bad, and we must teach our kids to love the good and avoid the evil.

Must We Rock around the Clock?

Wise parents will manage media influences without driving their teens away.

Angela Elwell Hunt

Few people would dispute music's persuasive power. Music has the ability to teach, to change moods and to subtly influence society. It can be used to uplift and inspire. But perhaps never before has music had the potential for harm that it has today. Rock music—born in the era of Elvis Presley, poodle skirts and greasy hair—has progressively and aggressively pushed the limits of good taste and morality.

Rock's outrageousness should not surprise anyone who has ever switched on MTV and witnessed a rock band performing with a six-foot male sex organ. Parents shake their heads and mutter. Kids clutch their radios and plead, "But it's not all bad! I don't pay attention to the really bad stuff."

They are right—it's not all bad. Songs can, for example, raise society's consciousness concerning ills that need to be addressed. Some songs express our deepest feelings and offer—even if only on a natural level—a certain peace and intimacy. But other songs are deadly.

On August 1, 1981, the Warner-Annex Satellite Entertainment Company launched the first full-time rock video network on American television—MTV, as it has come to be known. MTV broadcasts a powerful message into our homes. It entices teens to stake their identities on the acquisition of products like clothes, beer, perfume or music.

How can parents manage the potential menace?

There is no substitute for becoming and staying informed. Jennifer Norwood, director of the Virginia-based Parents Music Resource Center, says that parents are "dropping their twelve-year-olds off at concerts to have the Beastie Boys spit beer on them and sing about 'trusting crack.' Why don't parents have the knowledge about what's going on?"

Many of us may believe our families are safely out of rock music's reach. After all, we do not make a habit of listening to raunchy rock. Perhaps we prohibit rock albums from entering our homes. The songs we casually overhear in shopping malls are garbled, and we rarely take the time to analyze lyrics. "Sure, the kids hear that stuff on the radio," we reason, "but it isn't really going to affect them, is it? Is it really worse than the music *we* listen to?"

Twenty years ago parents and their kids argued over long hair, mini-skirts and the blue jeans worn by rock idols. Today's rock stars encourage everything from sex and drug use to suicide. Mike Diamond of the Beastie Boys told *People* magazine, "We're probably a parent's worst nightmare." Can a junior high school student listen to lyrics like "I met a girl at a party and she started to flirt/I told her some rhymes and she pulled up her skirt" as simple fun and nonsense?

Today's music scene promotes drugs, alcohol, violence and sex. People in the industry, however, deny the possible harmful effects of their music. "That lyrics affect children is a fantasy," said musician Frank Zappa. But parents know that children are affected by virtually everything they see and hear.

The power of much of today's music rests in its ability to appeal to the emotions. One MTV executive says, "If you can get their emotions going, [make them] forget their logic, you've got 'em."

Drop into any teen hang-out and you'll discover the power of teen music: You can't just *listen* to it—you have to *become* the music. Dancing until they are exhausted, sometimes high on drugs or alcohol, kids let the music vibrate and pulse through their whole being. They are often mesmerized by psychedelic lights and laser shows. Many kids find in this kind of music a source of "peace" and escape. One pop musician even said, "Rock music can have a greater influence over people's souls than primitive Christianity." Among American youth today, those words seem to ring true. Think about it. Who do young people consider to be a more popular figure—Jesus Christ or Madonna?

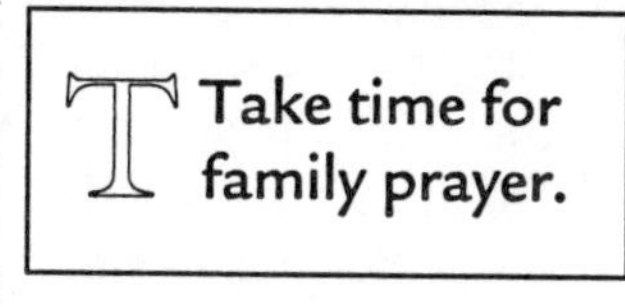

What's a parent to do? Teenagers aren't about to settle for a radical change of diet from rock music to religious hymns. Nor do they need to. Here are a few practical tips:

1. ***Decide to manage your family's music,*** but don't go on a purification binge. If you have allowed your children to listen to music indiscriminately, they will not understand why you've suddenly thrown out all their records and disconnected every radio in the house. Be rational. Explain that you feel some music is beneficial, some is not.

2. ***Help your children analyze the lyrics*** of some popular songs. Take an hour or two with your children to write out the lyrics. Help your child understand the meaning of the songs. Explain why they must reject ideas that contradict good taste and morality.

3. ***With your children, establish principles and guidelines*** for what is acceptable in your home. Some songs may be perfectly acceptable but need to be discussed. Some songs and certain

programs on MTV are objectionable because of the sensations and desires they arouse in the listener. They sometimes seduce the teen to partake vicariously in an experience that may not be morally acceptable.

4. ***Investigate popular musicians*** in a variety of musical fields. Are the artists' lifestyles worthy of emulation? Are they themselves happy with their marriages, families and success? Do the artists, including Christian performers, earn respect off the platform as well as on it?

5. ***Expand your family's music options.*** Play all kinds of music in the house: classical, jazz, blues, opera, contemporary Christian music, instrumentals and, yes, some well-chosen popular music. Attend the symphony, recitals, musicals and other performances. Consider providing your children music lessons. Or enroll them in the school band.

6. ***Beware of MTV and its imitators.*** Music wears a deeper groove into your child's subconscious when visual images accompany it. Watch an hour of MTV programming one afternoon. Take note of the network's cynicism and its promotion of consumption-based novelty and change. Its values are inadequate and inappropriate for building true community, personal identity, intimacy, relationships and high moral motivation. Do MTV programs celebrate life and give hope? Do they enrich youth culture or corrupt it?

   Watch MTV with your teen and talk about these issues. You may even arrange to keep MTV from coming into your home. But since your kids will see it somewhere, you should speak to them about it.

7. ***Encourage your teens to take some regular quiet time.*** Consider having a time or a place where the electronic media are not used. Maybe you could agree not to listen to the radio when you are together in the car. Someday, they may learn to appreciate the silence.

8. ***Help your kids find a Catholic peer group.*** Community with other teens can be an antidote to MTV culture. In a peer group of committed Catholics, they can confront together what they have heard and seen. Community promotes the intimacy, selflessness and relationships lost by an individualistic, isolated generation of young people mesmerized by the sounds and visual images of rock music.

For Discussion

1. Why do you think rock music has such an impact on our teens?
2. Why are rock music videos such a threat to Christian values?
3. What can parents do to manage music in their families?

For Reflection

1. What kind of music do we listen to in our home?
2. Have we discussed the youth culture, especially rock music, with our children?
3. What steps should we take to help our kids sort the good from the bad in pop music?

"C" Is for Chastity (Not Condoms)

Parents have the power to take back their teens and teach them the beauty of sex and self-control.

Molly Kelly

Like Peter Pan, our teens live in Never-Never Land. Think about it. Teens are no longer children, and they are not yet adults. They are in between. Yet, how do we as parents often treat them? Sometimes we treat them like children, and sometimes like adults. Let's keep in mind that they are teens, and those years can be exciting and terrifying years for them and for us.

Teens tend to magnify everything. They magnify success, failure, rejection (a really big one) and even pimples. Teens also want to be more in control of their lives. They don't share much with parents, while wanting us to *trust* them more. Yet, they are living in a society that doesn't trust them to be able to control their sexual desires. That works against their natural desire to want more control. So let's give them the right messages and challenge them to take control.

Don't give teens "mixed messages." How does this sound to you? "Don't use drugs, you can control yourself! Don't drink alcohol, you can control yourself! But when it comes to sex, you can't control yourself, so here's a drug!" And the girl is handed a prescription for birth control pills. Confusing? Then that's exactly how it sounds to our teens. In fact, here's how it translates to them: "Don't take drugs/here's a drug! Control yourself/you can't control yourself!" And we wonder why they are confused! Unmix the messages and give them the right one, the *chastity* message!

Why is it so hard for some adults to give the chastity message? First, some people don't know what chastity means. Second, you don't challenge teens to do something you don't believe they can do.

Chastity has to do with *self-empowerment* and building *self-esteem*. We all need to be loved, and teens need it in large doses. If they don't get it at home, they will seek it in all the wrong places: sex, drugs, alcohol and unhealthy relationships. Teens need to know that sex and love are not interchangeable.

Love is built on giving, which is the basis for friendship and commitment. Sex outside of marriage can ruin a friendship, because it takes rather than gives. Chastity is not a product; it can't be sold! Chastity is a virtue with no industry behind it. "Safe sex" is a lie with an industry promoting it!

What exactly does chastity mean? Isn't abstinence a better word? Abstinence is a well-meaning word. But it has a negative connotation. It means not doing something. People can abstain from candy, cookies, smoking, drinking, sex. And abstinence sets no boundaries. People can abstain today and indulge themselves tomorrow.

Chastity, however, is a positive word, a *yes* word! It means *yes* to the idea that sex is so good it's worth waiting for, and marriage is the place it belongs. Chastity does not mean never having sex; it means keeping sex where it belongs—in a marriage relationship. So chastity applies to married people, too, who must protect their relationships with their spouses.

Let's remind our kids that there is a difference between "desire" and "need." We have a need for food and water, but we don't have a need for sex, as strong as our sexual desires may be. Needs must be met; desires can be controlled. Chastity means *sexual self-control.* It means understanding our sexuality and the healthiest way to enjoy it. It means refraining from sex before marriage and placing sexual intercourse in marriage, where God intended it to be. Our teens have heard the *safe sex* message from society. Now they need to hear chastity—the *saved sex* message. They need to know that if they have already given it away they can start saving again!

Why is the *safe sex* message a lie? There is absolutely no contraceptive pill, drug or device that is 100 percent effective. None of them claim to be. The *safe sex* message tells teens they need to take something, wear something on or insert something in their bodies to be protected against pregnancy and disease, including AIDS, the deadliest disease of all. Yet just about every study maintains that the median failure rate for condoms is 10 to 17 percent. Would you fly on an airplane with those odds? Our children are our most precious gifts. Shouldn't we challenge them to the 100 percent protection that chastity provides?

Plus, what about the emotional and spiritual consequences of sex? Teens engaging in premarital sex often experience fear, frustration, guilt, anger, rejection, heartbreak and despair. What can condoms and birth control pills do for their emotions or their spiritual lives except hurt them more?

Why does "safe sex" get more play in the media than chastity? Hey, which one brings in more money? Keep in mind that chastity is not a product. It can't be put in pill form, or packaged as some kind of repellent. "Safe sex," which is a contradiction in terms, brings in big bucks.

> The ABCs of Chastity
>
> Our children are our most precious gifts. Tell them that sexual intercourse is a gift, a gift with a designer's label that says, "Do not open until marriage." And if teens have unwrapped it prematurely, tell them that they can wrap it up again. That's the beauty of chastity. It's for everyone! Here are the ABCs of it:
>
> A. Affirm teens in their innate goodness.
> B. Believe in them.
> C. Communicate with them.
>
> Molly Kelly

Who impacts most on teens' lives? The four groups of people who impact most on teens' lives are: parents, teachers, peers and the media. Who loves teens the most, and talks the least about sexuality? *Parents.* Who loves teens the least, but talks the most about sexuality? *The media.*

What we need to do as parents is to take back our children. Parents need to communicate with their teens. Keep in mind that communication involves both talking and listening. Parents need to work with teachers and to know exactly what their children are being taught in school about sexuality. Parents need to explain to their teens that peer pressure can be a positive force instead of the negative force it always seems to be.

And parents need to expose the media for the sex-selling, money-minded business that it is. The role models children see in the media are often "sexy," but also sex-crazed. The most important role models our children have are their parents. If we give them the safe sex message, then we have caved in on them.

Can parents rely on the schools to teach their teens about sexuality? Yes and no. *Yes,* teens will learn about sexuality in school. *No,* parents cannot totally leave it up to the schools. In fact, parents should carefully go over exactly what the school's curriculum is teaching about sexuality. Is the "safe sex" message being taught? Are your values being undermined by a "value-free" curriculum? Is abstinence presented as the best lifestyle for teens? Is chastity even mentioned? If you don't like the answers to these questions, go to the school and do something about it. There are very good abstinence-chastity curriculums available for private and public schools. If your children are in a religious-based school, then make sure that God's plan for sexuality is the only plan taught.

How can parents bring up the subject of sex? My suggestion is to use teachable moments. If you are watching TV with your teen and an uncomfortable sexual scene comes on, talk about it. I ask mine, "Would you want someone watching you and your husband (or wife) having sex?" Tell them that sex is not a spectator sport—it's a sacred act between two people who have made a lifetime marriage commitment to each other. And if your child says, "What if they're not married?" you should reply, "Then they shouldn't be doing it!"

If an ad comes on using sex to sell a product, point that out to your teen. They need to realize that sex is a multibillion dollar industry. It sells cars, clothes, shampoo. It also keeps family planning and abortion clinics in business. These places would go bankrupt if chastity became the "in thing."

Expose the sexual lyrics in songs, explaining that they degrade the beautiful gift of sexuality and desensitize the listener. But don't make your teen think that you want to go back to "the good old days." Today's teens are wonderful, bright and precious people. You want to tell them the truth so they can be spared the spiritual, emotional and physical harm caused by premarital sex. Your message: "Sex is so good, it's worth waiting for. And you're so good, *you* are worth the waiting!"

Should a parent discuss "how far do you go?" with his or her teen? You bet! What a fair question, and one that needs to be answered in a way that teens will understand. I tell teens that if they rev up the car motor, they intend to go; and if they rev each other up, it will be real tough to turn the motor off. Teens need to know that foreplay leads to sexual intercourse. If they don't want to arrive at a destination, they should not keep going down the road. You need to tell them the difference between *affection* and *arousal*. If they cross over into the arousal stage—necking, petting, prolonged kissing—then it's harder for them to turn back. If they mix it with alcohol, it's deadly. Alcohol numbs the conscience and heightens the passions.

How can we get teens to say *no* to sex outside of marriage? Our young people today have been given the *tools* to have sex (pills, condoms, spermicide, Norplant, and so on). What they really need are the tools to say *no*. Why, when *no* was one of the very first words they ever said, and a word they have practiced so often in their growing up years, do we now think they can't say it?

Teens need to be taught that there are three kinds of language: verbal, body and clothes language. They can say *no*, but does it come off as a *maybe*? They can also say *no* while their body language is saying *yes*. A sexual c'mon can be given by our eyes, our hands, our whole body. Also, whether we are male or female, we send a sexual message by what we wear or don't wear. Clothes can be sexually inviting. Modesty is a word that parents should be using. It doesn't mean that we want our teens to cover themselves from head to toe. Rather, it means that the more they show, the more difficult it is to say *no*. If they mean *no* they should say it, act it and wear it.

For Discussion

1. Why is it better for parents to hold up the ideal of chastity instead of abstinence?
2. How should a parent relate to a child who is sexually active?

For Reflection

1. Do I have a positive and open relationship with my teens?
2. Do I have conversations with my teens about sexuality and sexual control?

3. What do I need to do to replace with myself the other sources influencing my teen on sex?

The Parent-to-Parent Covenant

To establish some reasonable boundaries for teen social events, parents should generate a little peer pressure of their own.

Sr. Ann Regan

Parents and educators cite peer pressure to describe, defend, explain or expose youngsters' behavior. It is often given as the reason for a young person's choice of language, taste in clothes and music, and form of entertainment. Surely no one doubts the effects of peer pressure on adolescent behavior.

A much less talked about phenomenon is "parent peer pressure." Busy professional parents, who can handle office pressure quite well, often buckle under home accusations such as "You are the meanest parent in the world" or "Everyone else can do it."

Differences in opinion between parents and children may range from minor matters such as clothes and hairstyle to major decisions such as the use of alcohol or drugs. Allowing children to make some choices can be the right thing to do. However, too often a pattern is set that leads to ignoring more serious concerns.

At the Academy of the Holy Names in Tampa, Florida, an open-door policy between the administrators and parents made the reality of this potential problem all too clear. Parents were concerned about certain weekend parties that their middle-school-aged children were attending. Some were well-chaperoned and appropriate. Others were questionable. Parents needed a way of knowing the details of home parties, as well as the support of other parents willing to say "no" when their children's choice of entertainment was at odds with family values.

The school administrators took the first step by inviting all parents of sixth- through eighth-grade students to a meeting. After outlining the physical, spiritual, intellectual and social characteristics of eleven- to fourteen-year-olds, the administrators spoke about the dangers of teenage drinking at unchaperoned parties.

Since school-sponsored activities were not the problem, the administrators then turned the meeting over to the parents, suggesting they consider questions such as: What can you do about this problem? How can the school help?

In the discussion that followed, parents shared their concerns and hopes. A core group volunteered to work further, and the result was the Parent-to-Parent Covenant. This document seems to answer parental concerns.

Now that the program is set up, the school's part is merely secretarial. Each September, parents of students in grades six to eight receive two copies of the covenant. If they wish, they sign them and return one to school. A list of all covenant signers, as well as their home phone numbers, is then returned to the signees.

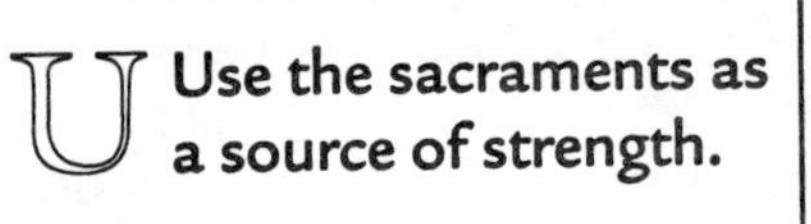

This Parent-to-Parent Covenant has given those who choose to follow it an opportunity to use parent peer pressure as a positive force for discernment and support during the challenging years of raising young adolescents.

For Discussion

What is the Parent-to-Parent Covenant? How does it work?

For Reflection

1. What would it take to install a Parent-to-Parent Covenant in our school or church?
2. Can I do something to make it happen?

The Parent-to-Parent Covenant

In keeping with the tradition and educational goals of the Academy of the Holy Names, I join this Parent-to-Parent Covenant, sharing in both love and concern for the well-being and safety of all students, and will share in building a relationship of adult to student and student to adult, by accepting the following Covenant:

1. Parents have the right to phone the sponsors of parties, to come into the party when they drop their student off and meet the chaperones, to make inquiry about the number of chaperones, students and party facilities. In general, those who sponsor parties will welcome other parents as concerned parents.

2. Parents agree that any alcohol will be out of sight, either locked away or properly under control of a chaperone. No alcohol will be available to students or allowed to be brought to the party by students. No drugs will be available to students or allowed to be brought to the party by students.

3. Adult chaperones will be visible at all times during the party. They will actively supervise inside and outside activities.

4. Parents will leave phone numbers with the host where they (or a relative-adult neighbor) can be reached in case of emergency.

5. Entertainment will be monitored so that "R-," and "X-" rated, or otherwise inappropriate, videos and music will not be available.

I offer my support and participation in the planning and chaperoning of those social activities important to the students of the Academy of the Holy Names. I hope to share with the students the excitement and joy of celebrating their youthfulness and future.

____________________	____________________
Mother	Father
____________________	____________________
Address	Phone
____________________	____________________
Name and Grade of Student	Date

Ending the Tyranny of Too Much TV

Limiting family TV consumption can add productive years to your lives.

Michael Medved

How would you respond to a reliable promise of eight, ten, or even sixteen extra years of life? Wouldn't you jump at the chance to extend your precious time for loving and laughing and learning and savoring this glorious world God has given us?

The life extension offered here has nothing to do with vitamin supplements, exercise programs, special diets, magical serums or scientific breakthroughs. Instead, it will flow unfailingly from a simple decision, which you can reach in the few minutes it takes to read this column.

That decision involves reducing the amount of time you invest each day in watching television.

If you are a typical American, you now spend twenty-eight hours every week in front of the tube. Statistics show that half of us spend *more* than twenty-eight weekly hours—more than four hours every day—staring at this all-powerful machine.

It's easy to calculate the commitment of time this represents over the course of a life. Assuming a typical life span of seventy-two years, an average American therefore spends twelve uninterrupted years watching flickering images on a cathode ray tube. If you allow for minimal breaks of just six hours a night for sleeping, this means a normal citizen devotes sixteen years of eighteen-hour days—seven days a week, fifty-two weeks a year—to viewing television.

Imagine a gravestone with the inscription: "Here lies our loving husband and father, who selflessly gave sixteen years of his life to his TV set."

This investment of our time is seldom conscious; it creeps up on us as we turn on the tube while we're eating breakfast or falling asleep, or we reach for the remote control to cope with moments of boredom, restlessness or sheer exhaustion.

According to every available survey, this electronic accompaniment to our daily rounds brings us very little satisfaction. Despite a proliferation of new alternatives on cable and pay-TV, a 1990 *Parents* magazine poll showed a staggering 71 percent who rated today's television as "fair, poor or terrible." A 1991 Gallup Poll located only 3 percent who believed that TV portrays "very positive" values. A major study for *Channels* magazine in 1988 revealed that 48.5 percent of all viewers engage in the practice known as "grazing"—regularly changing programs during a show. As James Webster, professor of communications at Northwestern University explained, "Grazing is by definition a sign of dissatisfaction."

The obvious cure for this dissatisfaction is to take conscious control of our television viewing and to begin rationing the hours we spend in front of the tube.

A simple technique could save you countless hours of wasted time, while increasing your pleasure in the televised entertainment you do choose to watch. On Sundays, the great majority of American newspapers offer listings of the television programs to be broadcast in the week ahead—or else *TV Guide* is universally available. At some point on Sunday, try sitting down as a family to discuss those programs that you care about and want to be sure to see.

In planning your week's TV consumption, it's a good idea to agree on a maximum time commitment for your family—say, for the sake of argument, twelve hours a week. This figure allows for at least ninety minutes of viewing on all four week nights, plus another six hours over the weekend. No one could suggest that this viewing schedule will deprive your family of outstanding televised entertainment. In fact, on many weeks you may be hard-pressed to find twelve hours of truly worthwhile TV to place on your personal program. In any event, once you've decided which shows deserve your attention, write out a weekly schedule and post it on the door of your refrigerator.

The most important aspect of this plan is to follow your calendar faithfully, and to resist the impulse to turn on the TV set at all times other than those you have planned.

At first, you may feel yourself instinctively reaching for that remote control—like a nicotine addict unconsciously fumbling in his pocket for the cigarettes he's trying to give up. After a few days, however, you'll grow accustomed to the idea of using TV as a form of preplanned entertainment, not as a distraction for idle moments or as background noise for the rest of your life.

Following this simple resolution will bring all sorts of side

Ten TV Alternatives for Teens

When parents limit a teen's television or other media consumption, they should provide attractive alternatives. Suppose you restrict media use to one or two hours a day. Or even dare to pull the plug on the TV permanently. What can teens do constructively with the time they used to spend glued to the electronic box? Here are some ideas families have found useful.

1. Chores. Parents should expect teens to do regular work around the house and yard. It helps to have a schedule that lists daily duties. Some parents also have a jar full of slips with special tasks. They prescribe taking them as an antidotes to complaints of boredom.
2. Part-time Jobs. Consider helping your teen find part-time employment. Many kids can handle ten to fifteen hours a week at jobs like clerking or providing child care. Parents sometimes have teenagers save half of their earnings for special events, travel or education.
3. Youth Enterprises. Junior Achievement and 4-H Clubs are examples of organizations that involve youth in enterprises that prepare them for future work. Such activities can spark any kid's interest. It may even get him or her to start a small business, like a lawn mowing service or floral arranging.
4. Service. Teenagers can make a significant contribution by volunteering to serve others. Sometimes elderly neighbors need household assistance or transportation. Or teens can volunteer at local hospitals or social agencies. They will get more out of serving than they put in.
5. Time-out with a Parent. Parents should consider spending regular time one-on-one with their teens. Go for a walk. Drive to an ice-cream shop for a visit. Here's a chance to replace solitary staring at the TV with valuable conversations.

benefits. At breakfast, husbands and wives may even be forced to talk to one another, rather than listening to the chatter of Bryant Gumbel. All members of the family will suddenly discover more free time to catch up with newspapers and periodicals, rather than switching channels between *A Current Affair* and *Who's the Boss?* reruns.

6. Family Reading Hour. Good reading is a great alternative to TV. Parents should always have some good books around the house for kids to pick up. Consider setting aside a regular family reading time, say 7 P.M. to 8 P.M. every week night. Maybe even read and talk about the same books.
7. Games. Replace relating to the television with relating to each other while playing games. Stock up on a few board games like Taboo, Scattergories, Pictionary and Scrabble. Learn Charades, Twenty Questions and other games that require no monetary investment at all. Most libraries have a selection of family game books that will increase your options.
8. Hobbies. Encourage all family members to develop a hobby. Collections, puzzles, crafts, writing and sports are prominent possibilities. Sometimes local high schools or colleges offer special evening courses that launch or enhance such activities.
9. Teen-Friendly Home. Parents ought to encourage teens to have their friends over frequently. That means that our homes must be teen-friendly. Parents will need to provide a place to meet, things to do, clearly defined rules, some snacks, and so on. And the parents should welcome their teen's friends warmly and show genuine interest in them. (See Neta Jackson, "Is Your Home Teenager-Friendly?" page 56.)
10. Family Night. Many families set aside a weekly or biweekly evening to do something together. All family members are expected to participate, teens included. Possible elements include brief prayer and Scripture study, games, family sports events, excursions to museums, parks or performances, and so on. Occasionally allowing children to invite a guest makes the time more fun for them. Most families top off the night with special snacks or desserts.

To help teens fill up the time freed by shutting off the TV, you will only need to select a few of these wholesome alternatives. Go to it.

Bert Ghezzi

And on those occasions when you do sit down together to watch something of entertainment or educational value, viewing will be more satisfying because it has been consciously planned and eagerly anticipated.

Meanwhile, think of the long-term benefits: A child who is born into a home that limits its TV watching to twelve hours a week, and who then follows that practice into adulthood, will have more than eight *extra* years of life—to enjoy loved ones, to do homework, to play ball, to cook, build, talk or make music—that an average American won't have.

There is no greater gift that you could give your child—or yourself—than to set careful and conscious and strictly observed limits to your family's TV watching. You will establish once and for all that you own that amazing entertainment machine in the living room—but you will never allow it to own *you*.

For Discussion

1. What are some benefits of limiting TV viewing?
2. How many hours of TV per week do you think is "enough" for any family member?

For Reflection

1. How many hours of TV per week does each family member watch?
2. Should we reduce TV consumption at our house? If so, what limits should we establish?

25 TV-Free Ways to Entertain Your Kids

Break the TV habit with one of these family fun activities.

Catherine M. Odell

"There's nothing to do...." Even though TVs are switched on across America for an average seven or more hours a day, children still often become bored. Instinctively, they realize that TV really doesn't give them anything to do. Instead, like a bossy playmate, TV does all the talking and makes all the rules. Adults understand better than kids that there are other things to do. But parents must be completely convinced about that. And they must be prepared to prove it to their children. There really is life—and fun—beyond TV.

Here are twenty-five ideas to help you make your case and enjoy TV-free fun with your children.

Out of the House Entertainment

1. ***Take your child to the museum.*** Most communities have a museum, park, aquarium, nature center or zoo. It is good for children of all ages to see and learn about things outside of their daily experience. And it's fun! Research your community and neighboring communities to find out what's available.
2. ***Attend an area festival.*** Most communities have summer or Fourth of July festivals. Many also have harvest festivals, Octoberfests and even winter events, such as a maple sugar festival. Mark those events on a calendar for ready reference.
3. ***Tour a local business, factory or farm.*** Check with a Chamber of Commerce office to find out if any businesses, the post office, bakeries or factories give public tours. Or locate farmers who welcome visits to their fields, barns, vineyards, orchards, and so on.
4. ***Visit a local artist, photographer or musician.*** Choose one who will be happy to show your children how his or her artwork is done. Seeing how a potter makes a pot or how a musician practices may inspire your children to try out an art that attracts them.
5. ***Attend a sports event.*** Try school baseball games, wrestling matches or swim meets. Or your family might enjoy watching cross-town high-school rivals battle it out on the basketball court or football field.
6. ***Go swimming.*** Spending a summer morning or afternoon with kids near sun and water is a God-given gift for the

season. In the "off-seasons," go to the local YMCA pool. Most pools allow guest visits for a small fee. High schools or colleges often offer pool times for public use.

7. ***Go to a concert.*** Many orchestras offer annual children's concerts. Free summer concerts are often offered in city parks. High schools and junior highs often offer Christmas or spring concerts. If younger children might be disruptive, sit in the back or stay only until intermission.
8. ***Go for hikes or bike rides.*** Locate a scenic park path or trail that suits your young hikers or bikers. Pack a picnic lunch and put it in back packs. Don't push too hard, and try to arrange a ride home for weary walkers or bikers.
9. ***Go fishing or boating.*** Spending time near the water gives kids a whole new way to look at the world. Contact your parks to locate places where you can rent or use a canoe, rowboat, paddleboat or motorboat. Combine boating with fishing, if you wish. Make sure, of course, that your kids are well protected with life vests and jackets.
10. ***Browse through a new- or used-book store.*** Locate a bookstore that does not object if your reading-aged child flips through some books. Spend an hour or so looking at books. Splurge on a book or two that caught your youngster's eye, perhaps one you could read together.
11. ***Visit an antique shop.*** With school-aged children, spend an afternoon visiting an antique shop. Ask shop personnel to answer your children's questions about the history or use of various items. Before you tour, check about ground rules that may apply in a store with irreplaceable and fragile merchandise.
12. ***Go roller skating or ice skating.*** Skating is too much fun to leave it to the kids. Almost any adult can sustain the wear and tear on the knees and ankles. Children love to skate at rinks, and most rinks provide skates small enough for preschool kids. Take some of your children's friends and they can help support one another.

At Home Entertainment

13. ***Make a home video about a favorite book or Bible story.*** Help your kids choose a story that they would like to present on video. Rehearse some lines and make some suggestions for costumes and staging. But be ready for ad-libbing and highly individualized performances. Then, let the camera roll.... (Many rental businesses stock videocameras.)
14. ***Make candles.*** Candle-making is an especially good project to do with kids at Easter or Christmas. Kids like to give them as gifts. Sand candles, candles made in molds or even in glass jars are easy variations. Take the children to the library to find books on niftier techniques and candle-dipping.
15. ***Make bread.*** Most children get involved in cookie-baking. However, assisting in a bread-baking project might be more exciting. Try yeasted breads when you have more time. Allow children to knead the bread and create new bread shapes—alphabet bread sticks, animal-shaped dinner rolls and so on. Take the occasion to talk about the Eucharist.
16. ***Make a papier-mâché family bank.*** Have the children make a family piggy bank to save for treats or outings. Many crafts books have recipes for papier-mâché. Or challenge kids to create birds over aluminum foil bases for a mobile. When the creations are dry, have the kids paint them.
17. ***Create a new family photo album.*** Almost every family has a drawer or box of photos. Brainstorm with the kids about a new theme for an album. It might focus on summer activities. Or it could be a display of family faces.
18. ***Learn some new card games.*** Or play the old favorites. Find a book that suggests games you can play for various age groups. Very young children like the face cards and can play games like Slap Jack if they're given plenty of help. A dish of popcorn adds to the fun.
19. ***Tape recorder fun.*** A sturdy children's tape recorder can provide kids with hours of fun. Taped books can be purchased or borrowed from libraries. Kids can also record

their own "mystery" stories with different voices and sound effects. Another enjoyable project might be to tape messages for an out-of-town grandparent, aunt or uncle.

20. ***Family silhouettes.*** Have an older child trace silhouettes of each family member on white paper taped to the wall. Since the subject must remain still, the project may not work for very little kids.
21. ***Modeling with clay.*** Purchase professional modeling clay through an art supply store. (It's fairly cheap.) Working on a flat, protected surface, encourage the young sculptors and potters to play with the clay for a while. Then suggest that they make something they might like to keep. As the clay dries, it hardens. A local potter might agree to fire the finished works of art.
22. ***Create a family collage.*** Use photos of everyone, including pets, and special paper items (certificates of merit, "A" school papers, drawings or paintings, and so on). Mount them securely on poster board. Later, frame the finished product and display it where the family and visitors can see and enjoy it.
23. ***Make a terrarium.*** Build a terrarium with a fish tank or another big glass container. Take time to plant your garden in a jar. Take the kids to talk to a local florist about appropriate plants and soil. Have the children help plant the terrarium and decorate it with shells and ceramics.
24. ***Make sock puppets.*** Retrieve socks headed for the rag box and recycle them for some fun. With colored bits of felt, buttons and other items, help your children sew on simple faces. Stuff the ends of socks with cotton balls to give them fuller shapes. When the cast of characters is done, drape a sheet or blanket across some chairs and have a puppet performance.
25. ***Ping-Pong ball Olympics.*** With a half dozen ping-pong balls, challenge kids to increasingly difficult feats on a predetermined course in or outside the house. Have them carry a ball on a spoon while hopping or jogging. Then, have competitors carry the ball on a baby spoon as they do

household tasks such as setting the table, hanging up clothes, shelving books. Reward the contestants with special snacks and with home-made gold, silver and bronze medals.

Think, Pray & Act

Worldly Wise

Our kids are tossed about in a world full of attractive choices, some good and some bad. Parents must be worldly wise and teach their kids to be discerning, too. Are you on top of the "world"? What must you do differently to do better with it? The questions at the end of the articles in this chapter will increase your wisdom about the world. They will help you take stock of your family situation. What action idea strikes you as a possibility to improve your family's approach to contemporary culture? Consider making use of the *Action Idea List, Decision Grid* and *Action Plan* that were presented in chapter one.

Resources

Teen Ministry

- Cultivation Ministries (800-513-8244) helps parishes and dioceses establish youth ministry programs: P.O. Box 662, St. Charles, IL 60174.
- LIFE TEEN (602-838-8844) is a nationally supported, Eucharist-based parish evangelistic program: 1730 W. Guadaloupe Rd., Mesa, AZ 85202.
- National Evangelization Teams (612-450-6833) sends teams of college-age men and women to evangelize teens in dioceses and parishes: 110 Crusader Avenue West, West St. Paul, MN 55118-4427.

Publications

- *Catholic Parent* magazine has a regular media review section, including Michael Medved's regular column (800-348-2440).
- *YOU* magazine (800-359-0177) is an upbeat Catholic magazine for teens.
- Bert Ghezzi, *Keeping Your Kids Catholic* (Servant Book Express: 313-677-6490).

- Michael Medved, *Hollywood vs. America* (Harper Collins: 800-342-7737).
- John Roberto, ed. *Media, Faith and Families: A Parent's Guide to Viewing* (Don Bosco Multimedia: 914-576-0122).

NINE

When the Going Gets Rough

Grace and special assistance are available to help families work through problems of all sizes.

Raising Rebellious Teens

Journeys through chaos to faith

Richard F. Easton

I sometimes wonder what experience would have better prepared my wife and me to raise a teenaged daughter and two sons. I had studied at universities for years to teach thinking skills and persuasion. I had also studied all the great literature, a lot of which was about families. And my wife, Pat, seemed to be more prepared than I. She had elected a psychology major in college. Now she actually wrote children's books. She even had written one novel—about a troubled teen—that had been considered for an award.

But our confidence in ourselves as teachers ebbed away as our laughing, pink-faced infants one by one transmuted into teens. The first became a tightly jeaned bombshell who professed a love for horses and cowboys but not school work; the second, a hairy, six-feet-four-inch, electric-guitar-playing Buddhist; and the third, a six-foot, hygiene-and-fashion-obsessed soccer player-scholar. The latter's movie star looks (even beneath the pimples) have unknown girls phoning our unlisted number day and night.

I wondered for months whether combat training would have prepared me to lead my wife to confront "the enemy teens" in the upside-down rec room. Could we force them back, maybe at bayonet point, past the emptied and devastated kitchen, to corner them finally in their ruined bedrooms? Because I dreamed that we parents were stronger, we would shout the terms of surrender. The teens would capitulate and rejoin the commonwealth of civilized peoples.

During the first phase of the teen wars, which did begin with a lot of shouting, my wife and I discovered we were pacifists at heart. We couldn't *civilize* the teens by becoming *uncivilized*. If we acted crazy, the teens simply got crazier. In fact, if we did manage through endless punishments and constant bedroom patrols to control one, the others in the unholy alliance unleashed new attacks—threats of hair dying, body piercing, tattooing, running away and quitting school came daily. And all of this was happening in what my wife and I thought was a nice Christian home where we all dined together every night, attended church weekly, and went on annual family vacations.

My wife and I became teen-shocked refugees of the war, hiding in corners of our house, hugging each other but quibbling over which of us had caused this mess. Fortunately, we finally withdrew from the battlefield to discuss how we were going to deal with our teenagers, help to form them into recognizable human beings, and so regain peace in our family. Instead of karate lessons, we got some counseling. We read medical and psychological texts on raising teens. Our labors last to this very hour. Any knowledge we have gained is imperfect, but we are willing to offer it, in hopes of stimulating other parents to be better prepared.

The most basic lesson Pat and I learned came from our faith. Our family had to learn to love in mature ways. After all, the Lord had said loving God and one another were the greatest commandments and all the rest would follow. Pat and I agreed that our home shouldn't become a dictatorship in which we enforced the commandments with sour faces and stern punishments. Our home provided the children, even as teens, with their basic experience of love and the celebration of life.

Somehow in the face of their worst rebelliousness, the teenagers had to feel loved and secure. We are convinced that if they do not experience love and security at home, they may never find it life long, no matter where they search. But comforting a squalling baby with a bottle and hugs brought us both emotional and even physical fulfillment. We find comforting a squalling teen much more complicated, often a matter of thought and will rather than heart.

The challenge of how to love teenagers puts stress every day on the love relationship of their parents. When the kids were infants, Pat and I idealized each other as lover and parent. Even our friends, including the college's psychology department chairman, judged us the perfect parents. Our teens-in-turmoil left Pat and me feeling very imperfect. Our teens' rebelliousness has made us become more searchingly honest about our own selves and with each other. We have had to learn to communicate and compromise more completely than ever before.

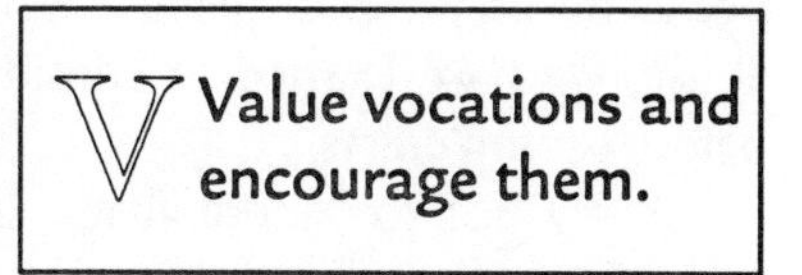

For example, we have discovered that I tend to offer intellectual and physical order, while Pat provides creative and emotional spontaneity. Our infants thrived with these approaches. As teenagers, though, they began to manipulate us because of our differences. "Dad's too tough, Mom." "But, Dad, Mom already said I could." Teens are dealing with the bewildering transition from infancy to adulthood, and their parents often are not only dealing with the teens but also their own transitions from youth to middle age. Sometimes we have found that all we can do is love blindly, with faith that we'll get through another day when there is so much change going on in one household of 2,500 square feet.

Pat and I have discovered some guidelines to ease the roughest moments, though. Parents must never disagree about the treatment of the teenagers in front of them. Such disagreements invite the "enemy" to enter into manipulation and nine times out of ten to get their own way. Pat has had to learn not to be so quick in handing out permissions to our teenagers. I have had to learn that what I see as softness won't destroy. Pat and I can balance each other, as we used to, if we discuss our differences privately, compromise, and present a united front to the teens—always.

We have also learned that there is an art to offering consequences to bad behavior. Parents must say what they mean and do what they say. Therefore, we must be very careful in any consequence we threaten. Another parent in a support group we attended offered, "If you threaten to break their arms, you'd better be prepared to do it." Since we never condone physical abuse, we have learned to consider consequences very carefully before issuing edicts.

We try not to "shoot from the lip" while a misbehavior is occurring. We inform the offender that we will consider the consequences and inform him or her later. The coolness of consideration can lead to more appropriate consequences than "You're grounded for the rest of your life," or the more realistic, "No television this evening." After hearing one of our kids announce, "I've never been hit, but I've spent half my life in my room," we started to explore positive consequences. A rude, hateful complaint now requires that the offender compose a list of people, events and objects for which he or she is grateful.

Parents whose teens rebel more seriously have to face the fact that the consequences they serve up will have to be tough. Teenagers have to understand that there are behaviors that will not be tolerated. The use of drugs or alcohol, physical or verbal violence, running away, truancy or stealing—any criminal act—cannot be tolerated.

For instance, when one of ours skipped school, we immediately notified the school of the truancy, picked up the truant, and delivered her into the waiting jaws of the assistant principal. We never had another skipped day of school by one of our teens. One of our habitual curfew offenders was firmly told, "The next time you'll find the house locked." He entered the door one night just as Pat was locking it. Realizing how close he'd come to spending that rainy night on the lawn, he has ever since arrived well before his curfew. Our kids describe these new tough line policies as "Your way or the highway." And they know we mean them.

Such firm resolve is crucial when dealing with drug and alcohol abusers. Pat and I think they should be offered the choice of rehabilitation or the outside of the front door. Addiction is a progressive disease that kills if not treated. Even though throwing your addict out of the house seems harsh, coddling this disease is tantamount to cosigning his or her death warrant. In some states, addicted teens can be committed to a treatment facility. If you are having trouble, learn your state's laws and your rights over your child. Despite media portrayals, law enforcement agencies are usually filled with caring, supportive people and helpful information.

Do not worry about ruining your children's future college or job opportunities. Treatment is often confidential; without treatment teen addicts cannot prosper in their futures and probably will not live to have it. Whether their teens get help or not, parents in such a situation need the help of the many international support groups available, such as Al-Anon, Nar-Anon, POTADA (Parents of Teenage Alcohol and Drug Abusers) and Toughlove International.

Parents who face any degree of teen rebelliousness need to understand over which issues in child rearing they have power and over which they are powerless. The acceptance that we finally are *powerless* over our own flesh and blood comes as a hard lesson. But, after all, the parents' job is to make independent the wholly dependent. We become unnecessary guides to a young adult especially if we have been effective parents. Parents of rebels need to put the destiny of their young—and themselves—in the hands of God. As Pat often reminds me, "Relax, God isn't finished with them yet."

If we obsess over a child's difficult behavior or the failure of our dreams, we will cause more rebelliousness. How can a teen learn to worry about himself if his parents are doing all the worrying? We know of many parents who are learning this painful lesson late in life—their thirty-year-old children still living on the dole at home, perhaps addicted to drugs or alcohol, unable to complete an education or hold a purposeful job.

Besides learning to say *no* and to depend on God, a parent who obsesses over a teen's behavior and future most frequently

Love—No Matter What

Parents experience no greater pain than they do over children whose lives get derailed. Years of long-suffering prayer and support can produce positive results. But what can a dad and mom do when they are right in the thick of the turmoil?

1. *Love the child no matter what.* We rarely feel good about the mess a renegade makes. But we must stand by him or her and do whatever is the loving thing in each situation. Sometimes love means saying no. As in "No, son, I can't help you pay off your speeding tickets. You earned them. You need to handle them yourself." But love always means expressing affection, which we should do even when we find it difficult or when the child feigns disinterest.

2. *Deal with anger constructively.* To guard against blowups and screaming fits, we should learn to express anger under control. For example, when children cross us, instead of either suppressing anger or dumping on them, we should tell them how their behavior makes us feel. "You know that I love you, but you lied to me. And being deceived makes me angry."

3. *Maintain self-esteem.* This goes both for parents and for kids. Most rebellious kids have such low self-esteem that it drags the bottom of the ocean. We need to look for ways to lift up the spirits of our renegades. Hugs, words of encouragement and praise for accomplishments, regularly applied, will help a lot.

Many things conspire in the derailing of a child's life. Parents must avoid blaming themselves entirely. Remember, original sin is alive and well. It collaborates with our kids' freedom of choice to produce much havoc.

needs to focus on the quality of his or her own life. To deal with the changes of middle age, parents must deal with their own well-being. Parents are entitled to the joys of their own healthy, adjusted lives! We can think of no better way to guide teenagers than to offer the model of faith-filled, cheerful, responsible adulthood.

4. *Find out if there is a physical cause.* Ask about allergies, celiac disease, chronic ear infection, hearing impairment, minimal brain damage, epilepsy or any of your own observations. If your doctor brushes your concerns aside, ask a trusted friend or someone at your child's school to recommend a different doctor. Or write for referrals to the American Academy of Pediatrics: 141 Northwest Point Blvd., P. O. Box 927, Elk Grove, IL 60009-0927.

5. *Get help.* Parents should not try to handle alone all the fallout caused by a difficult child. Contact Toughlove International, a support group for parents of difficult-to-deal-with teens, at 900-333-1069. Ask at your parish or archdiocesan office or your child's school for support groups for parents. If your spouse refuses to go, then go alone. And get professional help if you need it, for your child and for yourself. Counselors can diagnose problems (for example, identify a learning disability that's the real root of a kid's misbehavior), and they can help parents with strategy and tactics for relating to the child.

6. *Communicate with your child or teen.* Share what is important to you. Mass attendance, school, or refraining from substance abuse or immorality (pick one at a time). Don't lecture. Five minutes' worth of sharing is enough. Allow plenty of time to really listen to your child's perspective. If you can't agree or find a compromise that's OK, you're still ahead by the decision to communicate.

7. *Never give up hope.* The Lord wants our little renegades as his children, too. So we should pray confidently for their salvation and for their present circumstances to change. When we pray for something God himself wants, his answer must be yes. So never give up. Just resist the temptation to tell God exactly how to work things out. He can handle it.

Bert Ghezzi and Meg Raul

Obviously parents must do a great deal more than say *no* and offer consequences to deal with difficult teens. All teens want as much independence as they can get. Some have difficulty perceiving that independence is earned by becoming more responsible. Most of us want to make our children feel loved. Some of us mistake doing and buying everything for our children as a way to make them feel love. This is not simply a problem for the rich; in our culture it is a problem for the middle class and the poor, too.

Teachers and writers are not the most generously paid in our society, but Pat and I overdid our bit in trying to make our kids feel *privileged*. The results were "Mom and Dad will do it—buy it—fix it," and we did. Today Pat and I are struggling to make the kids perceive that it is a privilege and a joy for them to work for themselves and for the family. Certain chores are now a must and we pay no allowance for them. House, lawn, and automobile care are being shared. We sense that everyone, parents included, has more gratitude for possessions.

Family behaviors change slowly but during the teen years responsibilities mount—financial, educational, sexual, emotional and religious. The teen who bears his or her share will become a responsible adult, not just an independent individual. And again, careful consequences for responsibilities not met will prod the overly individualistic teen into becoming a team player.

Parents who know what behaviors and values they want and ask for them simply and directly, often get what they want. If they don't, they can at least find joy in themselves and life if they stick to their values and trust in the support of God. Confident, relaxed, optimistic parents make better headway with teens than stressed, nagging, pessimistic ones. Of course, achieving serenity with teenagers in the household often comes like faith—a journey of small, imperfect steps.

Pat and I have made headway in our own faith journey. We communicate better with each other and with God. Signposts of our improvement also include much better communication with our teenagers. Of course, they are becoming more responsible.

Our jeaned girl, who loved horses and hated school, enrolled in a reputable four-year college with an equestrian program. She is getting a liberal arts education while learning to train children on performance horses and manage a stable operation of her own.

Our rock-and-roll mountain of a teen waited a year before enrolling in school. He said, "I need to learn how to work or I'll mess up college." His hair shortened and beard shaven, he works in a fast food restaurant. After the third day, he came home and picked up a book—he's read a book a day for the past two weeks. When I casually asked him what was up he said, "I have to do something for my mind; I am definitely going to school next year." He had just come in from mowing the lawn, after being asked only once!

And our youngest teen is going to high school, studying every night, playing soccer, and swearing he doesn't even want a steady girl friend. This poor fellow, who gets the benefit of all our new-found wisdom, still hugs us a lot and actually told us the other day, "I'm really very happy." A happy teenager—miracles do occur!

Pat and I have found that we have to learn and share many more responsibilities. We try to worry less and live day to day in the faith that God has a plan for us and our children. We are all imperfect children on a challenging but hopeful journey to meet a Father who, after time, will reveal to us his own perfection and love.

For Discussion

1. What do you think is the most important thing parents can do for a rebellious teen?
2. How do you think parents should deal with a teen who abuses drugs? Commits a crime?

For Reflection

1. Are any of my children rebelling or headed for rebellion?
2. Am I prepared to use a *tough love* approach to help a rebellious teen?

Family Nonconformists

Is there room for wildflowers in your garden?

Dolores Curran

A gardener went out to sow his seeds. As the weeks went by, he tenderly watered each tiny shoot because he loved them all. Soon they grew into a bed of glorious red blossoms. But, to the gardener's dismay, there bloomed among them a single golden flower, unlike the others in every way.

As people passed by, he was gratified to hear them comment on the beauty of his garden. But all seemed to have some opinion on his golden beauty. "Look at that beautiful flower, so different from the others," a few said. Most, however, were critical. "Why is that golden flower there?" they asked.

Disheartened, the gardener uprooted his beloved golden beauty and tossed it away, but its roots left a hole in the symmetry that he could not fill. People stopped pausing to look on his garden, only saying as they rushed by, "Pretty flowers." Some said, "I wonder what was in that hole?"

And he would tell them about the golden flower because he could not forget it. Long after the red blossoms withered and died, he wondered about the golden beauty. "Where had it come from? What would have become of it if I had nurtured it? Why did I kill it?" In his heart lay a hole as deep as the one in his bed of flowers.

The nonconformists in our families know what it's like to be a golden flower in a bed of red blossoms, and parents know what it's like to be the gardener. Where did this weed come from? It's not like the rest of us. Should we be proud of its uniqueness or embarrassed by its differentness? Should we change it, nurture it or uproot it so that people will view us as normal, respectable, symmetrical? Will it leave a hole in our hearts if we refuse to allow it to flourish in its own fashion?

Few families want to have a nonconformist. It's simply easier to rear and relate to offspring who are like us in every way. At times, I hear parents say, "Tommy is our different one," in tones ranging from apology to pride. And they will go on to explain that unlike his siblings he prefers art to Little League or being a loner to being part of the gang. Tommy knows he is different from the others in his family, perhaps different from others in his school, church and community, and he wonders why. In his young mind different implies defective, so he begins a lifetime of self-blame. He may try to conform to the expectations of others, to win their approval and love, but his nature resists.

His unenviable choices are to succumb to others by developing a false self or to risk losing others by remaining true to himself. If he chooses the former, he faces a life of unhappiness and inner disharmony. If he chooses the latter, he faces the very real possibility of losing his family, church, and other relationships, usually in that order.

How the family responds to differentness is basic to the unique individual's lifelong self-esteem. If nonconformist children feel accepted and even prized for their uniqueness within the family circle, they will tend to see the church and the world as positive and accepting environments. Even if they face intolerance, they tend to dismiss it as an aberration on the part of a few. If, however, their family has stamped a negative label on their character, they will see the church and world as unfriendly and intolerant environments in which they are—weeds.

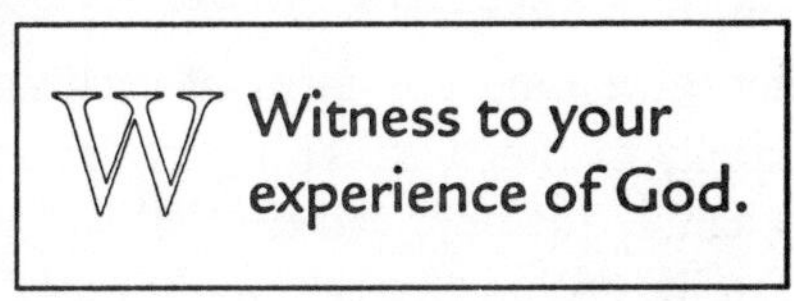

Nonconformists come in many family configurations. There's the pacifist in the military family, the bigot in the egalitarian family, the cultist or nonbeliever in the mainline religious family, the gay or lesbian in the straight family, the cohabitor in the marriage-vowed family, the honor-roll student in a C-plus family, the alcoholic in the temperance family, the nonconsumer in the stress-for-success family, the introvert in an extroverted family, the nonacademic in the Ph.D. family, the missionary in the mercenary family, the artist in the business-minded family, the conservative in the liberal family, the feminist in the traditional-role family—the list seems endless.

It takes an inordinately strong inner self to counter parental, religious and societal condemnation to remain true to oneself. Author e.e. cummings wrote, "To be nobody but yourself in a world which is doing its best, night and day, to make you everybody else means to fight the hardest battle any human being can fight; and never stop fighting."

Some children possess wills strong enough to resist the temptation of giving up their true selves to please their parents. Others learn quickly that their parents' love is conditional, and they embark on a lifelong quest to alter their nature to win their parents' and society's approval. The result is often unhappiness, depression, addiction or even suicide.

Keep it together. In his book, *Power of the Family,* Dr. Paul Pearsall lists twelve articles of faith to which healthy families commit. The first reads, "Everyone in my family belongs in my family. Nothing will ever change this, and this article of faith is our first and most basic rule. This shows reverence for the family by preventing any form of exclusion or threat of exclusion of a family member, either in fact or in gesture. There is nothing that a family member can do that would isolate him or her from the family system, for all family members are forever a part of the family energy."

There is nothing that a family member can do that would isolate him or her. This startling statement is relatively new in the family, historically and sociologically. Few of us would defend parents today who forced their children into work or marriage against their will, but at one time such parental rights were wholly accepted by society.

In the recent past parents exercised the right to shun or disown children who fought on the wrong side of a movement or war, who married someone of another religious or ethnic group, who divorced and remarried, who refused to enter the family business or who moved across the country against their parents' will.

Shunning still goes on, however, and we may now be facing

the most difficult evolutionary step in the family—that of accepting differing lifestyles, such as surrogate parenting, homosexual relationships, Murphy Browns, and serial or lifelong cohabitation. All these are situations that raise our moral hackles. They render insignificant parents' pain over such things as a child's refusing to continue the family business or moving across the world to take a job.

How far do the rights of the individual extend when they conflict with the moral underpinning of society? How much must parents accept to maintain a loving family relationship? These are tough questions, but ones we cannot duck.

What are we to do? We must distinguish between accepting a person's makeup or orientation and approving a person's behavior. Homosexual orientation doesn't trouble many Christians, but homosexual relationships do. Single parenting doesn't reap censure, but surrogate parenthood might. But Jesus didn't seem to have a problem with this distinction. He accepted and loved the nonconformists in his ministry—and there were many—while making it clear he did not approve of their behavior or lifestyle.

As a parent, a Catholic, and a family-life educator, I see only three realistic responses by parents to nonconformist offspring who disappoint them, defy their moral code or do both. Each of these responses has its advantages and drawbacks.

Let's pretend that my thirty-year-old son informs me that he is homosexual and is entering a relationship with another man, which my church and conscience tell me is immoral. Or that my heterosexual thirty-year-old is entering a cohabiting relationship with a member of the opposite sex. Or that my divorced thirty-year-old is being remarried without an annulment. Or that my married thirty-year-old is using artificial contraception.

All of these are taught as seriously sinful by our church, and I must respond as a parent. Returning again to the example of my thirty-year-old son, what are my choices?

1. I can react with moral judgment, letting my mature child know that I do not approve and do not want to continue our

relationship until he behaves according to the moral code I hold sacred and have taught my children to hold sacred.

In other words, I can throw my child out of the family. The plus is that I am acting on my principles. The disadvantage is that I am sacrificing the relationship. But this is an option, and one that parents have chosen for generations.

2. I can react with moral judgment and a personal effort to change my grown-up child. I may offer to pay for a psychiatrist, lay on the guilt, beg, nag, bribe, threaten and let him know that I am praying daily for his transformation.

   The plus of this choice is that I keep the relationship open while adhering to my principles. The disadvantage is that I am going to drive my child away, from a deep to a superficial relationship. My disapproval clearly tells my child that I don't accept him as he is, and visits home will become fewer and shorter, mere obligations. "It's just so unpleasant, I duck in and out a couple of times a year," one gay man told me at a seminar. "I would love to be close to my family, but they won't allow it."
3. I can clearly state my moral principles but explain that because he is a mature person now, his actions and lifestyle choices are now between him and God. I will not let my child's differentness affect our relationship because I will always love, welcome and support him. The plus side is that I keep the relationship strong. The negative is that I may feel I have failed as a parent.

Of the three choices, I prefer the last. Our children, who are only loaned to us, grow up to be adult persons and as such they are responsible for their choices and behaviors. As the saying goes, "God knows no grandchildren." Each of us has to develop our own relationship with God and family.

Reinhold Niebuhr's "Serenity Prayer" ministers to families struggling with nonconformists in their midst. It is a simple invocation, asking God to help them to accept what they cannot change, to change what they can, and to seek the wisdom to know the difference. Perhaps we need to pray, as families, churches, and society, for that wisdom. Are we wise enough to

Welcoming a Homosexual Child

You don't have to be intimidated by your love for your children. For example, as often happens, suppose a son or daughter decides to take a path different from what the parents hoped for. Do parents have to go along? No, you do not.

Recently a Hispanic couple discovered that their son had moved into the gay scene. They were very upset. The young man was religious, hardworking and diligent. He had struggled with himself before making that unfortunate decision. His parents loved him and wanted to do the right thing. They asked me, "What should we do?" I said, "Well, the first thing is do not reject him."

As a matter of fact, the young man had already come to see me. He had said, "Father, I want you to do me two favors. One, don't reject me. The other is, don't agree with me. If you agree with me, I'll never get out of this."

"Don't worry about it," I said. "I'm not going to agree with you. But I won't reject you either."

His parents did not reject him. But one day they called me with a question. "He's coming home with his friend. Can they stay over?"

"You must decide that question," I replied. "It's your home, not his. He already knows that you do not approve of his lifestyle."

His boyfriend was a nice kid, another Catholic. They went to mass every Sunday. They knew they had a problem, but I think they were trying to solve it the wrong way. I advised the parents, "For heaven's sake, be nice to the other fellow. But you do not have to let them sleep together in your home. If you want to have them over for dinner, of course you can do that."

Now, some people get terribly upset about this, but I think that's good advice. It preserves the relationship while expressing disapproval of sinful behavior. Situations like this are very common. Where I live, possibly 10 percent of the adults are homosexual. Many of these people are extremely discreet, even religious, and some lead chaste lives. If the statistics are accurate, there are 400,000 homosexual adults living in New York City. Sixty thousand of them parade around during gay pride celebrations. (This may mean that 340,000 of them do not at all approve of the demonstration and may wish the others would go home.) And I know saintly people who have homosexual tendencies and who, perhaps, in the past lived in some kind of relationship. But in my experience many come to live chaste lives.

Fr. Benedict Groeschel, C.F.R.

recognize our weeds as simply different kinds of flowers? Wise enough to water and nurture those weeds even if they aren't like us? Wise enough to realize that if we destroy them, they will leave a hole in our hearts, hearths and pews?

For Discussion

1. Why is it important for nonconformists to feel acceptance by their parents and families?
2. What approaches can parents take to nonconformists? Which do you think is the best?

For Reflection

1. Do I have a nonconformist in my family?
2. (If so) How do I and the family relate to the nonconforming member?
3. What can I do to express love for the nonconformist? How can I approve the nonconformist while disapproving his or her behavior?

What You Can Do If Your Kids Leave the Church

Parents should not feel guilty when kids leave the church. They can take some positive steps to help bring them back.

Bert Ghezzi

Kids leaving the church is right up near the top of the list of the leading causes of parental pain. Nowadays it seems to happen to many, if not most, Catholic families. It hits parents with a double whammy of grief and guilt. We feel a deep sense of loss for the child's sake and we think that somehow we are to blame.

Parents also feel helpless to do anything about a child's dropping out. Nothing they try seems to improve the situation. Some tacks, like pleading and arguing, only tend to make matters worse. Is there anything at all parents can do when children leave the church? Can we do anything to get them back?

The answer to these questions is *no* and *yes*. If you are looking for a quick reversal of a young person's decision, I think the answer is almost always *no*. A quick fix cannot undo the years of trouble, boredom or whatever it was that caused a son to drift away; that caused a daughter to make a gutsy announcement one day that she wasn't going to church any more.

But the answer is *yes*, if we can muster enough patience and self-control to take a long-term approach. We can take some steps that will help draw our kids back to the church.

Who's to Blame? Facing a child's dropping out is a little easier when we get the right perspective.

First, parents must stop blaming themselves. "But if I had only done a better job," we say, as we second-guess our best efforts. True, we are responsible to introduce our children to faith in God and to the church. But we are not accountable for our children's decisions. The Lord wants each of our children to choose freely to follow him.

We can drag daughters and sons to places where we think the Holy Spirit might strike, but we cannot climb into their skins and manipulate their wills for them. Our kids' faith decisions are between them and God, so if they drop out, we must not hold ourselves to blame.

Are Dropouts Leaving God? Second, we must understand that kids' leaving the church does not necessarily mean they are leaving God. Sociologists report, for example, that many Catholic dropouts say they love God and spend time praying. Religious educators tell us, too, that on their way to faith young people pass through a healthy, but trying, stage of doubt. They tend to test authorities, challenge traditions and experiment with lifestyles—all as part of sorting out their relationship to God. Many dropouts also return to the church once they slog through their doubts to a faith decision. An estimated 42 percent of Catholics leave the church at some time during their lives, but the majority of them return later on.

For sure, kids' leaving the church does not mean that God leaves them. The Lord is assembling a family of sons and daughters. He wants to include our children. He stays close to them while they seem to drift away from him. He patiently waits for a time when he can draw them back. We can take a dim, incomplete view of our unhappy situation and be desperate. Or we can keep God in the picture and have hope. Faith and common sense both tell us that the latter is our only real choice.

Remove Obstacles. To win kids back to the church, parents may have to work more on their own behavior than they might have expected. Most young Catholic dropouts leave not because of faith problems but because of family relationship problems. A son or daughter does not get along well with Dad, Mom or siblings and religion quickly becomes a weapon in the warfare. Sometimes parents worsen an already bad relationship by overreacting when a child drops out.

Children will find their way back to the church more easily if we remove the obstacles from their path. For many parents, that means working to repair broken relationships with a child who has become alienated from them. There are some unilateral actions parents can take that will build bridges.

- Take responsibility for your own bad behavior. Tell the son or daughter you are sorry and ask them to forgive you. Be specific in detailing your wrongdoings. Don't require them, or even expect them, to reciprocate immediately.
- Behave in ways that they will have to see unmistakably as signs that you love them. This does not mean spoiling them or giving in to them. Ask yourself what now is the loving thing to do for this young person, and do it. For example, the loving thing could mean taking pressure off a teen by lowering expectations about some areas, such as orderliness or dress.
- Make children who have left the church always welcome in your home. Be sure to involve them in family activities. I include here children who are opting for unacceptable lifestyles. You can find a way to make it clear that you love

them, but do not approve of the evil in what they are doing. I think parents who have tried shunning sons or daughters should do everything they can to reverse it. Invite them back home and keep the door open, even if they don't respond at first. Be a Prodigal Father or a Prodigal Mother.

No New Obstacles. Most children who leave the church are absolutely clear on where their parents stand. So we don't need to keep telling them what we think. We may need to say directly that we do not approve, but we should also say that we love them and hope that they will find their way back to the church. But once that is said, we should drop the issue. Here is a short list of don'ts:

- Don't nag them about faith or lifestyle issues.
- Don't put guilt trips on them. ("If you'd start going to mass again, maybe you wouldn't have so many financial problems.")
- Don't meddle in their lives. (For example, no matter how much Grandma wants to see grandchildren baptized, she should not harp on it. She should mightily resist the temptation to baptize them herself in the bathtub. Let God take care of the children.)

Practice biting your tongue when you feel the urge to say anything that might drive the young person farther away. The scar tissue will be worth it.

What If They Join Another Church? Some children who leave become members of other Christian churches. Often they discover a personal relationship with Christ through the ministry of a congregation and decide to join it. I think it is a mistake for parents to view such a decision negatively, or to behave as though the child is lost or has somehow betrayed them. Parents may be sad when young persons do not return to the Catholic church, but we should be happy that they have faith and are living for God.

At the same time, we should try to attract them to the Catholic church. We can tell them that we are glad they love the

Lord and are going to church, but that we also hope they stay open to Catholicism. When appropriate, we can invite these children to accompany us to mass or other parish activities. But we should never be pushy. If they are in a church that is anti-Catholic, you can ask them to discuss issues calmly with you or with a third party.

Faithfulness and Prayer. Our own commitment to the Lord and the church means a lot to our children. If disappointment over a child's dropping out were to cause us to lose faith, our daughter or son would be deeply affected. Remember, keep God in the picture. Remind him regularly in prayer that you are counting on him to bring your child back into his family and home to the Catholic church.

For Discussion

1. Why can it be said that parents are not to blame when a child leaves the church?
2. What can parents do to draw a child back into the Christian community?

For Reflection

1. Have any of your children left the church?
2. If so, what can you do to maintain good relationships with that child?

When You Love an Alcoholic

Take steps to get help for yourself before you try to help a family member who is addicted to alcohol.

Sr. Thérèse Del Genio, S.N.D.

At least one out of ten drinking people is addicted to alcohol, and each alcoholic affects, at minimum, the lives of four people every day. In a parish of three thousand families, approximately one thousand members are alcoholics, who in turn impact four thousand family members, friends, coworkers, neighbors. This means that something like half the parishioners are affected.

For these nonaddicted people, living on the addiction roller coaster can be terrifying. It's no wonder that they often call the rectory in crisis with a tearful appeal: "What can I do to help?" The assistance the caller usually wants is for someone else: an alcoholic or drug addict who may be the caller's parent, spouse, son, daughter or close friend. Yet the person who calls needs help just as desperately.

When dealing with any form of addiction, we cannot expect a magic solution to appear with the wave of a wand. But if someone you love is an alcoholic, take heart. There is hope, for anyone willing to risk and to work. Here are ten suggestions:

1. Stop whatever you're doing and try to name your situation. Chances are that in order to cope, you've been busy picking up the pieces of someone else's life, carrying a double load, becoming emotionally responsible for righting every wrong.

The first thing to do is think about your situation and name it. What was going on during the last period of stress? What prompted you to ask for help? Perhaps assistance was needed before, but somehow you always managed to cover the bases. This last time was different. Why? Did someone you care about get drunk and become physically or emotionally abusive? Were threats of divorce or violence made? Did someone's drinking destroy something precious to you? Until you can name your reality, you can't help an alcoholic to see the impact his or her behavior is having on you and the family.

2. Try to feel whatever it is you're experiencing. Emotions are immediate responses to reality, but sometimes we let our feelings go numb. Family members have too often been told *not* to feel, and then been scolded or punished for what they've felt. Have you ever been told variations of the following? "You shouldn't be mad at your father. He's paying your tuition, isn't he?" "Don't be disappointed in your wife. She's drunk a lot but she's doing the best she can."

And so your feelings get forced below the surface. But they usually pop up in unexpected and unhealthy ways. You may end up eating more, sleeping more, taking prescription drugs to calm your nerves, getting so busy that you don't notice much else—or suddenly unleashing your pent-up emotions on the alcoholic. It's better to find a trusted person and a safe place to deal with ***your*** feelings. No alcoholic will be motivated to change by your negative emotions or remarks.

3. Reach out and ask for help. Perhaps until now fear or shame prevented you from seeking assistance. Your inner critic may have harped: "You should be able to handle this. Others have it a lot worse."

But you don't allow that kind of thinking to dominate other aspects of your life. When your car breaks down, do you take a quick course in auto mechanics to fix it? If you had appendicitis, would you do surgery on yourself?

It's OK—indeed it's a sign of wisdom—for you to seek help for the emotional pain you feel over another's drinking problem. Try Al-Anon, Families Anonymous, Adult Children of Alcoholics, and so on. You might ask a local treatment center for referral to a counselor. Many free or low-cost services are available through agencies or church groups.

4. Learn about alcoholism and what can be done for treatment. There are many well-written, low-cost pamphlets available from Alcoholics Anonymous. You can order them through central offices in your city (found in the Yellow Pages) or purchase them at local Twelve-Step group meetings. The following national offices will send you an order blank of available materials:

Alcoholics Anonymous General Service Office
468 Park Avenue South
New York, NY 10016
212-686-1100

Al-Anon Family Group Headquarters
P.O. Box 182
Madison Square Station
New York, NY 10159-0182
800-356-9996

The following publishers have toll-free numbers to call in order to receive catalogs of valuable reading material for alcohol, drug, and other addictions:

Compcare: 800-328-3330
Hazelden: 800-328-9000
Parkside: 800-221-6364

Almost all local treatment centers offer free lectures to the public on some aspect of addiction and recovery. Their staffs are available for consultations, referral, and reading material.

5. Join a Twelve-Step group. Al-Anon, Families Anonymous, Adult Children of Alcoholics, and Alateen, to name a few, will support you in making the changes you need to feel better about yourself and your living situation. By calling the number in the phone book you will learn where meetings are held not far from where you live. The meetings are free and promise total anonymity and confidentiality. Two members from the group would be willing to meet with you to share their stories, strength and hope. To help an alcoholic, you must first get the help *you* need most.

6. Protect yourself from harm. You may be accepting an abusive situation as normal. But you and your family do not have to endure this behavior any longer. You have a right to respect, security and protection.

Develop a safety plan now while you are not in immediate danger and then share the plan with a friend or relative. It's difficult to think clearly in a crisis.

Mavis, a thirty-year-old mother and wife of an alcoholic, personally contacted the police to learn her rights and how to secure an order of protection. She received full cooperation because she agreed to press charges against her husband, Harry. Countless times before, Mavis had dropped the charges, giving Harry clear permission to intimidate and harm the entire family without consequences.

She also visited a local shelter for battered women and learned how the staff could assist her if and when she called. Mavis came to realize she couldn't help Harry when she lived in fear. When she did pack up and move to the shelter, she left a note for Harry on the kitchen table, giving him the names and phone numbers of three contacts for help. Harry called AA and got sober.

7. Give up your codependent behavior. While trying to cope with active alcoholism, you have probably developed some *enabling* and *codependent* behaviors. That is, doing for the alcoholic what the alcoholic should be doing for himself or herself. Your behavior is codependent if you *depend upon* and support the other's unhealthy patterns of conduct, thus *enabling* the addicted person to continue the same offensive behavior.

Such behaviors might include covering mismanaged finances; paying bail bond; calling in sick for the alcoholic when he or she is unable to go to work; cleaning up messes; picking the alcoholic up off the floor, couch or lawn; and putting him or her to bed.

By becoming less codependent, you allow the alcoholic to face the pain and consequences of addictive behavior. And that pain is often the greatest motivator for change.

8. Remember the three C's. You can't *cause, control* or *cure* addiction. You may, however, be part of the problem and not the solution if your main response is simply to blame, nag or argue. None of these behaviors motivates the alcoholic to get sober, and none of them leaves you feeling good about yourself.

You can't, in the long run, control the progression of alcoholism by hiding the car keys or disposing of the booze, any more than you can control cancer by telling the patient to eat balanced meals. The only one you can control is yourself. At present there is no cure for addiction. Yet there is hope. With treatment, which includes a holistic program of recovery and Twelve-Step meetings, alcoholism can be put into remission. Recovery is a day-by-day process.

9. Be prepared to do "little i" and "big I" interventions. "Little i" interventions occur any time you as an individual confront the disease. You can address the alcoholic clearly, directly and compassionately about the consequences of abuse. For example, "Tom, last night you came home drunk. You tripped over the coffee table and slumped in a heap on the floor. I was afraid you had hurt yourself, but I couldn't waken you. You would have never spent the night sprawled on the floor if you hadn't been drinking. I'm concerned about you and would like to see you get the help you deserve." At the very least, such personal interventions can prompt a loved one to reflect more deeply upon his or her actions—and possibly seek the necessary treatment.

A "big I" intervention is a formal process. It involves preparing and supporting family and friends—as a team—to confront the alcoholic and offer options for recovery. Trained in intervention skills, treatment-center staff as well as outreach teams in some parishes are willing and qualified to help you and the alcoholic about whom you care so much.

10. Pray and hope. In your own way, ask God to be with you. As Mavis discovered, you might find that the nature of your prayer may change from requests like "God, get Harry to stop drinking; let him drive home safely" to "God, please let me know what you desire and give me the ability to deal with each situation. God, grant me the serenity to accept the things I cannot change, the courage to change the things I can, and the wisdom to know the difference."

Many of Jesus' cures involved setting people free of paralysis. This is a good kind of healing for all of us to pray for as we try to overcome our paralysis, and that of our loved ones in the fight against addiction.

Your prayers, at times, may seem awkward, especially if you have been angry with God because of the way your life has been affected by addiction. But your honest expression of anger indicates that you already have a close relationship with God. The important thing is to keep making contact daily and frequently with the Lord, who is with you in all of this and who loves you very much.

No matter how painful your situation is, it has a solid chance of improving as you try these suggestions. You and your family are worth the effort.

For Discussion

1. What do you think is the most important thing you could do for an alcoholic family member?
2. In what ways do relatives and friends engage in behaviors that support the alcoholic's addiction? How can they stop such behaviors?

For Reflection

1. Is someone in my family addicted to alcohol or drugs? If so, how has the person's behavior affected the family?
2. Do I need to make any personal changes in order to help an addicted family member?
3. Have I taken steps to get help for myself?

Prayer Saved My Family

When all seemed lost in this family, the Holy Spirit intervened with a dramatic healing.

Peter Herbeck

Monday night began like so many others during my senior year in high school. Little did I know then that this evening would be the catalyst for my personal faith journey. It was also to be an unforgettable lesson in prayer for my entire family. I was sitting at the dining room table, trying to concentrate on my homework. My father stumbled through the kitchen door. Dad had been out drinking, a habit he had developed in the war, long before I or my six brothers and sisters were born. I braced myself for the verbal abuse that I'd learned to expect.

But this time Dad sat down beside me and began to cry. I saw in his eyes brokenness instead of belligerence. "Peter," he said, "I'm sick and I need help." He rose from the table, called our family physician and committed himself to a six-week in-patient treatment program at St. Mary's Extended Care Center. That night many years ago was the last time I saw my father drunk.

For many years my father and my family had tried unsuccessfully to conquer his alcoholism. On the outside our lives appeared normal, filled with church, sports, school activities and a successful business. But in reality we were a dysfunctional, powerless family. We were unable to escape the huge problem at the center of our lives. By the time I reached my teens it had taken a toll on me. I was confused, occasionally rebellious and deceptive. I often felt directionless and angry. Why was my father finally able to face and overcome his alcoholism? What brought each of my family members into a more faith-filled relationship with Christ?

Above all, prayer was the key that opened the door for healing and conversion. For as long as I can remember, my mother prayed fervently every day for her children and my father. One night I was out late and sneaked upstairs. There as I passed my mother's open door, I saw her interceding for me at her bedside.

Even back then, her faith gripped me and I knew that her quiet inner strength and perseverance were from the Lord. She faithfully interceded, attended mass, prayed the rosary and read the Scriptures. Several months before my father entered treatment, two of my older sisters began to experience a personal renewal of faith. Through their earnest prayer for Dad they became convinced that the Lord wanted to heal him.

After four weeks in the program, Dad's counselor called our family into the treatment center for our first session together. We were excited and hopeful as we traveled to see him. That day Dad was to present to us an honest inventory of his past, to admit his own powerlessness and then move on to the next step of treatment. As he spoke, however, his counselor interrupted him and told him to sit down and shut up. We were stunned and angry. "Your father isn't being fully honest. He's still living a lie," the counselor told us later. "Until he really faces up to his problems, I frankly have no hope for him."

We sat around my father's bed, humbled and despairing with nowhere to turn. Some of us wept openly. It was then, in our weakest moment, that we cried out to God, and his power was "made perfect in our weakness" (see 2 Corinthians 12:9). We joined hands that evening and prayed for Dad's healing and for greater faith for all of us. A few days later the counselor called. "Please come back," he said. "Something's changed in Joe. He can stay and I think he's going to make it."

Although Dad's recovery was dramatic and victorious, it was only the first step in a process of healing that occurred in our family. Shortly after Dad entered treatment we began meeting together regularly as a family—sharing, crying, laughing and oftentimes praying. Our humble surrender to God released a grace in us and we began to change. Some experienced a deepening of their faith. Others, like myself, had an outright conversion of heart. Although some felt more comfortable than others, we all participated. It was a rich time of drawing nearer to God and to one another.

Throughout the years we've learned to face the daily

challenges with prayer and strong family support. My mother has initiated a family phone chain to pray for illnesses, births, travels and other significant needs. Every Christmas we gather together at a lodge to celebrate and thank God for all he has done for us. My parents preside with joy over the festivities of tree trimming, gift giving and a Christmas pageant. After a time of prayer and thanksgiving, we draw together around Mom and Dad—their seven children and spouses, thirty-one grandchildren, and four great-grandchildren—and ask God's blessing on them. As a family and as individuals we are not perfect, yet God has done more in us than we could have imagined. Our testimony to the power of prayer and God's faithfulness continues as the Lord begins to draw our own children nearer to himself.

I pray that my own family's story is a source of hope and encouragement to others. As a teenager, I witnessed the power of prayer to overcome our weaknesses and heal our mistakes. I saw God take an impossible, desperate situation and use it for good. I knew God was real and that he cared for me personally. As parents we can't do everything right to ensure the salvation of our children. But we can pray; God truly hears the cries of the faithful.

Shortly after my own conversion, I attended a conference, hungering for more of God and seeking a deeper confirmation of his presence in my life. After a powerful and life-changing weekend, I returned home late Sunday night. My mother was waiting for me when I walked in the door. Seeing her, I tried to relate my experience but began to cry. My mother embraced me and tenderly said, "I know Peter, I've prayed for this moment all your life."

For Discussion

What seems to have been involved in getting the father in this story free from his addiction?

For Reflection

1. Is there anyone in my family or extended family who suffers from a chemical addiction?

Keep St. Monica Busy

Now, I have a dear old friend who can be a tremendous help to anybody who's suffering because of their relatives. That's St. Monica, the mother of St. Augustine. Over in the old section of Rome, near the Pantheon, is San Augustino Church. Buried on the side, in a rather unobtrusive tomb, is Monica. I think they should have a big highway leading there with candles all over the place. They should be selling holy pictures of St. Monica by the dozens outside. Plaques, vigil lights, the works. If there is any saint that ought to be busy today, it's Monica.

In Manhattan there's a little old church called the Church of the Most Holy Crucifix. It was run at one time by the Augustinian Friars. On one side there's St. Augustine with his miter and crosier, looking very important. And on the other side there's an old lady holding a handkerchief. Guess who? Monica. Sixteen years, give or take a couple of months, she spent praying for the conversion of her son. If you're miserable about your family, get busy praying.

Fr. Benedict Groeschel, C.F.R.

2. What can I and my family do to help another family member who has an addiction?

Think, Pray & Act

Love Costs

When children declare independence and throw up the barricades, parents need a blend of different responses. We need fortitude and kindness. We need firmness and gentleness. And in our pain we pay a price, because love costs. How are you doing with your teens? Do you need to figure out how you are going to respond to a nonconformist? Are you ready for this? Let the questions at the end of the articles in this unit prompt your thoughts. Is there one thing you could do that would make a big difference in your family situation? Consider using the tools at the end of chapter one to help you sort out your action ideas.

Resources

- Stephen Arterburn, *Addicted to "Love"* (Servant Book Express: 313-677-6490).
- Bert Ghezzi, *The Angry Christian* (St. Paul Books & Media: 800-876-4463).
- Bert Ghezzi, *Facing Your Feelings* (St. Paul Books & Media: 800-876-4463).
- Archibald D. Hart, *Healing Life's Hidden Addictions* (Servant Book Express: 313-677-6490).
- David Stoop and James Masteller, *Forgiving Our Parents, Forgiving Ourselves* (Servant Book Express: 313-677-6490).

TEN

Power and Light

The strength and wisdom for guiltless Catholic parenting comes from the Holy Spirit. The more we grow in him, the better the job we'll do raising our kids Catholic.

What It Takes to Be a Catholic Parent

Joy is the secret ingredient that puts zest in Catholic parenting.

Wendy Leifeld

"I've figured out what makes my mother-in-law's chicken soup so great," my friend Suzanne announced with joy. "She adds some of her homemade marinara sauce to it! Only a small amount but it really makes a difference." I would never have thought of adding marinara sauce to chicken soup. My friend's mother-in-law, however, is an extraordinary cook. As extraordinary cooks all know, it's precisely that ability to add the unexpected, to take a risk with a recipe, that makes their cooking superb. The same is true with good parenting and, specifically, Catholic parenting.

Obviously, to make chicken soup you need chicken, noodles and chicken stock. You can't get around that. Then the fun begins. I like to add celery, onions and carrots along with herbs and salt and pepper. I also add a can of mushroom soup—but don't tell anyone. That's what makes my soup different from others, just as Suzanne's mom adds marinara sauce. Now, laying all modesty aside, I have to say that people rave over my soup just as I rave over Suzanne's mom's soup, even though our secret ingredients are different.

With parenting, there are some basics that everyone agrees on: unconditional love, spontaneous and frequent affection, consistency, patience, some basic rules, respect—you know them as well as I do. These qualities form the basis of parenting just like chicken and stock are the basis of chicken soup. Catholic parenting is like making chicken *noodle* soup instead of just chicken soup. We still have to start with the same basics.

If we aren't good parents, then it doesn't matter if we are pagans or exemplary Catholics. In fact, our Catholicism might make it more difficult for our children to believe in God at all, let alone his church. There is no way around it: for our children we are the primary, essential models of God and his church. That is why the church calls a family the "domestic church." To the degree that we model the qualities of love, consistency, respectful discipline and patience, we reveal God as our Father and the church as our mother. We all know people who have had terrible, tragic experiences with fathers or mothers. They often have difficulty believing that God is different from their father or that the church is a place of refuge and healing. Our parenting is the single most important way that we can build a base of faith in our children's lives. I guess in some ways, good parenting is the secret of being a good Catholic parent, as obvious as that may seem.

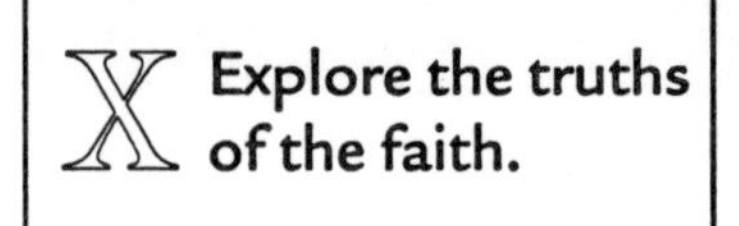

Not that our specifically Catholic faith isn't important. To draw a crude parallel, our faith is like the noodles in the soup. Faith adds a heartiness, a richness to the broth and meat of being a parent. It makes the soup a meal instead of a first course. Our faith illuminates the meaning of being a parent. Just because they are our children, we will strive to raise them well. But because we are children of God the Father, we strive to prepare them to live as his sons and daughters. We know that we are the first to witness the faith to our children. That gives us an additional reason to be good parents.

So, now we have the chicken, stock and noodles. Now the fun begins in parenting—the chance to make your parenting not only unique but even superlative. I can't tell you the definitive secret ingredient because people can have different styles of parenting that may be more to your taste. After fifteen years of parenting four children and after watching hundreds of other parents raise their children, I think I have found the secret ingredient for myself.

Joy. That's it. Joy. Joy in life. Joy in your children. Joy in each other. And if your goal is to raise good Catholics, especially joy in your faith. Joy is like the salt in the soup. Without a pinch or two of salt, soup is fairly tasteless. If we don't have joy, our children will have little hope for their own lives. Joyless parents teach their children without words that life is a grim business, the church is going to ruin, and the world to hell in a hand basket.

I'm not necessarily talking about pleasure, because that is fleeting. I'm not talking about fun, although that will come as we experience joy. I'm talking about that combination of belief that life has meaning and purpose, of trust that God loves us and cares for us, of love for ourselves and others because we are unique and irreplaceable. It's not false hope—that's denial. Joy is one of the eternal realities that helps us to rise beyond our past, to enjoy our present, and to transform our future. It is a fruit of the Spirit, as we were taught, and the power to put our faith to work for us. That is what joy is for me.

With joy, the church becomes more than just a set of rules and practices that must be followed or we go to hell. With joy, God is a loving presence who longs for us to be near him. With joy we stop perceiving him as an exacting tyrant who must be pleased for him to care for us. With joy, we are able to look beyond the present troubles in our lives, difficult phases in our children and troubles in the world and church and find a way to resolve them.

Joyful parents teach their children wordlessly that life is good no matter what our present circumstances are. They teach their children that the church is more than the sum of rules, bickering, struggles and trials that will always be with us as we try to live out our faith. They teach their children that love sees the whole person. The person who lives forever, not just the sins, failings and weaknesses that can irritate or even hurt us today.

Children respond to joy like flowers to the sun. They will open themselves to God and his church. They will be willing to follow your leadership. Be joyful and have faith in God, and his church will be attractive to them. Joy is the power and measure of the truth of your faith, and children sense that at the core of their being.

So being a Catholic parent takes the basics—the plain ingredients of good parenting, a liberal helping of faith, and don't forget to add joy. Simple as it is, just like chicken soup, it can nourish our children for life.

For Discussion

What do you think it takes to be a good Catholic parent?

For Refection

1. Am I the kind of adult Catholic I want my kids to become?
2. Do I find joy in my life, my faith and my parenting?

Filling Your Catholic Gaps

If you feel that you don't know your faith well enough to teach your kids, you can take some steps to catch up.

Bert Ghezzi

Your seven-year-old comes home from religion class with a question. "Dad, how does Jesus get into that little piece of bread?" Or maybe another conversation stopper, like "Tell me, Mom, how can God be three and one at the same time?"

You don't know the answer. Don't panic, you tell yourself. You may find safety in one of several options:

- "Right now I'm watching this important segment of *Home Shopping*. Come back in a few minutes." *Maybe the kid will forget.*

- "You know, your mom is the expert on that one. Go ask her." *Let her deal with it.*
- "Well, what do *you* think about it?" *Perhaps the kid will recall what his teacher said.*

Or you may think of some other creative dodge.

Before you had kids you were probably not aware of the gaps in your Catholic formation. But now your ignorance gets exposed. You feel inadequate to talk to your children about the faith.

What happened to you? Maybe you were bored to death with religion, as your child may also be someday. Maybe all you got out of religion class was warm fuzzies. Or perhaps you became Catholic when you married and didn't learn enough about it. Whatever the cause, now your Catholic gaps are a problem. Your kids know more about being Catholic than you, and it embarrasses you. What can you do about it?

Books and Magazines to Grow On

- *The Catechism of the Catholic Church.* This is not a book you would snuggle up in front of the fireplace to read on a winter's night. But it is the authoritative reference you would consult on the hard questions. How is Jesus present in the host? How do I understand the Trinity? The new *Catechism* is the first place to look.
- Use John Hardon's *The Faith* (Servant Book Express: 313-677-6490) or Alfred McBride's *Essentials of the Faith* (Our Sunday Visitor: 800-348-2440) as a road map to understand and apply the new *Catechism.*
- Explore the mysteries and truths of the faith in Edward J. O'Connor's *The Catholic Vision* (Our Sunday Visitor: 800-348-2440) or Alan Schreck's *Catholic and Christian* (Servant Book Express: 313-677-6490).
- For easy-to-digest-and-apply practical approaches to daily Catholic living, try *50 Ways to Tap the Power of the Sacraments* (Our Sunday Visitor: 800-348-2440) and *Keeping Your Kids Catholic* (Servant Book Express: 313-677-6490), both by yours truly.
- Read magazines like *God's Word Today* (612-962-6725), *Catholic Parent, New Covenant* and *The Catholic Answer* (800-348-2440 for all three).

Bert Ghezzi

You could stonewall it. Pretend that it's not a problem. Many parents do. They insulate themselves behind a wall of silence and let their spouses handle religious formation alone. That's a great pity. It deprives children of one of the most important things a parent can give: a personal witness to Christ and his church.

There's a better approach. Do something to fill your Catholic gaps. You're never too old to learn your faith. It's not too difficult. Just decide to take advantage of the many opportunities available to you. Consider these possibilities:

- Attend your parish's inquiry class to get an overview of Catholic doctrine. Ask the priest or instructor your hard questions. Let the teacher show you how you can find answers on your own. Or participate as a guest in your parish's Rite of Christian Initiation for Adults (RCIA).
- If there is a Catholic university nearby, enroll as a guest in a theology or Scripture class. Take something basic, like Introduction to Church History or How to Read the Bible.
- Take advantage of adult religious education opportunities. Many parishes and dioceses offer mini-courses or sponsor speakers. Check your local Catholic paper for offerings in other parishes.
- Participate in a study group. Join a Catholic family group with your spouse. Or attend a Bible study group in your parish. There you will find friends who are also trying to learn more about their faith and they will be a support to you.
- Study right with your children. Once or twice a week sit down with them and review their religion lessons. Use their books as a guide. Do this especially when the children are preparing to receive first reconciliation, first communion or confirmation. When your parish offers education for parents of kids in sacrament preparation, participate in them to the max.
- Read good books and magazines about the faith. Use your parish or public library. Browse the shelves at a Catholic bookstore. Write Catholic publishers for their catalogs and browse in them, too. Acquire some good books for ready reference at home. (See the box for a few suggestions.)

Remember you are not alone. Everyone must study in order to grow in the faith. You just have some catching up to do. So get busy and do it for your kids.

For Discussion

1. Why do some Catholics have gaps in their understanding and practice of the faith?
2. What do you think they can do about it?

For Reflection

1. Do I have any gaps in my Catholic formation?
2. What can I do to ensure that I am always learning more about my faith?

What Single Parents Can Do

The task is the same, but the job is harder. So look to Christ and the church for support.

Patricia Lorenz

Believe me, dear reader, I am *not* an expert on how single parents can raise their children Catholic. What I am is a product of my own Catholic upbringing, which probably had more to do with how I raised my children than anything I learned or experienced as an adult.

To put it quite simply, I was raised in a loving Catholic family. When I became a single parent struggling to raise four children alone, it was easy to depend on the same Catholic church with its familiar traditions, customs and comforts.

My father was born into a strict German Catholic family. My mother, raised in a Protestant Christian home by a father who was an elder in his church, converted to Catholicism shortly after she married my dad. Mother had us on our knees every day during Mary's months of May and October. We prayed the rosary in front of the Blessed Mother's statue on the marble-top chest in the dining room. We attended mass every Sunday and every holy day of obligation. We marched in every procession that our parish held. We fasted during Lent and feasted at every parish festival. The feasting came, of course, *after* our family worked shifts at the bazaars, bake sales, ice cream socials, spaghetti dinners and anything else our parish did to support itself. We were good, practicing Catholics.

But most importantly we children were sent to Catholic school. I was taught by the wonderful Sisters of Loretto for fourteen years, including my first two years of college.

Years later, in 1975 when my non-Catholic, abusive, alcoholic husband and I divorced, I moved from Missouri to my home state of Illinois the same day. I found myself in a strange new world. Suddenly I was a single parent with three children, ages three, four and six.

The next day I enrolled Jeanne, my oldest, in the Catholic grade school I attended as a child. I found a part-time job and the next year Julia entered kindergarten in the same school. A year later Michael began his Catholic education. The good sisters did the bulk of the work for me. They were raising my children Catholic and all was well.

In 1978, I remarried in the Catholic church, after going through the annulment process. My new husband was a public school principal. A year and a half later when our son Andrew was born we moved to Wisconsin. Even though Harold was Catholic, he wanted our children educated in the public schools. After all, they were paying his salary.

Five years later, when the children were in high school, middle school and grade school, Harold moved out, filed for divorce, married his girlfriend and died two years later. And so, the day our youngest, Andrew, started kindergarten in 1985 I became a single parent again, solely responsible for raising my children as Catholic Christians.

Did I succeed? Well, ten years later, three of my four children are practicing Catholics. My oldest, Jeanne, 26, an artist in California, doesn't practice any religion, yet she is one of the most spiritual persons I know. Even though she's not involved in the church, she loves God and others a great deal, so I'm not worried about her soul.

The other two older children, Julia and Michael, were confirmed as Catholics and are both practicing their religion as adults. They both taught CCD in their college-town parishes during their college years.

Julia, 24, and her husband, Tim, who converted to Catholicism, volunteer in the nursery in their parish. Michael, 23, and his fiancée, Amy, who is also Catholic, plan to be married in a Catholic church. Andrew, my fourth and youngest child, the only one still at home, is taking high-school religion classes at our parish church and attends mass with me every Sunday. When he was fourteen he began volunteering at church as a lector and as a worker at the various parish events.

Did I do anything unusual to draw these children into the Catholic church? Probably nothing more than any other Catholic parent does. It's just that as a single parent I had to be especially firm and consistent during their teenage years. When the children grumbled about attending mass or religion classes I got tough. The rule was mass every Sunday and religion classes through the confirmation series. They were then allowed to make their own decisions as to whether or not to be confirmed.

Jeanne, the oldest, chose not to be confirmed. Julia waited until age twenty-two, when she understood more about the Catholic faith. Michael was confirmed with his class at age seventeen, and Andrew will be making his decision soon.

Besides being firm and consistent, there are a number of other, more tangible things I did over the past ten years that no doubt helped guide my children toward Catholicism.

From the time my children were a year old, bedtime stories were always part of our "good night" routine. When they were preschoolers I made sure two or three of the books that we read were about Jesus or books with prayers they loved to recite from memory.

Andrew often asked me to read from the "picture Bible." I was never sure if he enjoyed following along with the comic-book-like pictures or if the stories intrigued him. But it didn't matter. Either way he wanted to hear the stories of the Hebrew Scriptures read aloud to him.

Bedtime prayers were also a nightly tradition in this single parent's home. We weren't on our knees on the side of the beds very often, however. Instead, after long days at work and then household chores until the late hours, I often collapsed on top of each child's bed with him or her while we prayed simple, heartfelt prayers. Sometimes it was just "Lord, thank you for all our blessings. Help Andrew pass his math test tomorrow. Bless all our friends, relatives and neighbors."

We'd end with an Our Father, Hail Mary or perhaps the Guardian Angel prayer. Knowing we all had guardian angels who watched over us somehow made our single parent home feel more protected.

Right after Andrew's father and I separated when Andrew was five years old, I enrolled him in the "Rainbows for All God's Children" program at our parish. This is a wonderful national support group for children who are living in single parent families because of divorce, separation or death of a parent. If you know someone in this situation, call your archdiocesan office and ask where the nearest Rainbows program is located.

Another thing we've done in our family over the years is turn holidays into holy days. One year we looked up interesting information about St. Valentine before Valentine's Day. On various Memorial Days the children and I visited the cemeteries where their grandmother and great-grandparents are buried. One year we attended a special Memorial Day mass and then marched in procession with the entire parish to the Catholic cemetery for a blessing of the graves. The Memorial holiday of flags, parades and picnics took on a new meaning for us after that day.

Attendance at mass on Thanksgiving and our tradition of going around the table in spontaneous prayer, sharing what each of us is thankful for, before we eat, are two more ways to turn a secular holiday into a special day with religious significance.

Certain feast days have also been special times for us. On the feast of St. Lucy, December thirteenth, we lit candles and talked about St. Lucy's life. She holds a special place in our hearts because my mother, whose name was Lucy, died when I was pregnant with Andrew when she was only fifty-seven years old. Celebrating the feast of St. Lucy helps the children keep their grandmother alive in their thoughts.

Of course, the annual Advent wreath is another way we've helped turn what becomes more and more secular every year into a true celebration of the birth of Christ. The children took turns lighting the Advent wreath candles and reading aloud one of the many Advent prayers I'd gathered over the years.

Part of our Advent routine included giving each child a large plastic bag. Off they'd go to their rooms to gather toys and clothing that they'd outgrown during the previous year to give to Human Concerns, fire victims or out-of-work families. One year we delivered the bags ourselves to an inner city family I'd heard about at the radio station where I worked.

Each year on Christmas Eve we attended early evening mass, went home for oyster stew (a German tradition from my father's family) and then read the Christmas story in the Bible before opening presents. These days the older children still flock home for Christmas. They insist on the same routine, including the oyster stew, even though they all claim not to like it. After all, it's the sameness of those year-after-year experiences that are the very fabric of their tradition: The threads of these year-after-year experiences, woven together, form the rich tapestry of Catholic family life.

Don't Just Stand There—Do Something!

As a single parent there are many things you can do to get help raising your children Catholic. If your parish doesn't have an organization for single parents, start one. Ask your pastor for a list of the single parents who have registered in the past three years. Arrange for a meeting room in the parish hall, then draft a letter to the singles. When you get together and discover your common needs, dreams and problems, you'll be amazed what happens. Single parents of preschoolers can organize a babysitting co-op. Single parents of older children can get together for evenings out together: movies, roller skating, bowling, dancing or dinners. When you socialize with other single parents, you become a support system for each other, an extended family with lots of adults helping with the children.

Ask your pastor for a list of older widows and widowers in your parish so you can start an "Adopt-a-Grandparent" program. The children of single parents often need another adult in their lives. In the "Adopt-a-Grandparent" program, both the youngsters and the oldsters benefit. Who better to mentor your child than an older Catholic with the same set of values as you?

Take an inventory of your home. Is there a crucifix or picture of Christ displayed there as a sign of your devotion to your faith? Do you speak to your children the way you want them to speak to you? Do you say grace before meals? Do you sit down together each evening to share a meal? Are you attending mass regularly? Actively involved in your parish? Do you let someone in your parish know if you're having hard times—financially, spiritually, emotionally?

Catholicism isn't just a religion. It's a way of life. It's faith bound together by family and headed by God the Father. Even if your family is just you and your five-year-old daughter, as a Catholic you are automatically an important part of a huge family that surrounds you with warm, loving arms of care and devotion. Sometimes, besides living a Catholic life at home, we single parents have to ask for help. Believe me, it's there, right inside the doors of your parish church.

For Discussion

Do you think a single parent should do anything differently from a couple to raise children as Catholics? If so, what?

For Reflection

If you are a single parent:

1. What are you doing to pass the faith on to your children?

2. What kind of help do you think you need for the task? Where can you get it?

If you are not a single parent:

Is there something you can do to support single parents in your parish community?

Calling All Catholic Dads

Are you doing enough to help your kids be successful and happy?

Bert Ghezzi

Will you take a few minutes to consider what you are doing to help your children become successful and happy?

You love your children very much. You nearly burst with pride when they were born. Your chest still expands with that feeling each time they accomplish something new. You are working hard to provide for them, making many personal sacrifices. You want the very best for your children because that's what a dad's love is all about.

You want them to be happy and successful human beings, so you prepare them thoroughly in practical affairs. You send them to school and involve them in activities that develop their talents. You regularly help them with homework, enduring even the agony of word problems and science projects, when you could be relaxing. You have spent many hours coaching or watching their sports events. You have dutifully listened to music lessons and attended recitals. You praise them to build self-esteem, counsel them through problems and pick them up when they fall. All these are efforts well spent, valuable investments in your kids' well-being.

But there's no guarantee that education and achievement will make your kids successful. Some of us are already puzzling over the failures of a son or daughter who had every opportunity to succeed. Neither do you have any assurance that education or achievement will cause your kids to be happy. Happiness eludes even the most successful, who are often downright miserable.

Your kids need something more from you for their happiness and success because there's more to them than mere ordinary lives. They were built to last—forever—to enjoy success and happiness with God. They need your help to get ready for their eternal lives.

Recently the national news featured a sixteen-year-old boy who was killed in an auto accident. His parents donated his organs to sick people, a generous act they had encouraged the boy to choose when he got his driver's license. I wondered what other preparations they had helped him make for his death. What had his dad done to help him live his spiritual life? It made me consider what I am doing to help my kids now with the spiritual lives they will live after they die. You should think about your kids, too. What are you doing to prepare your kids for their real futures? For their real success and happiness?

Some dads I know are already taking a concern for their kid's Christian lives. You pray with your children, get them to mass, teach them to love the Lord, to love and forgive others, involve them in serving the poor, and so on. Perhaps there is more you can do. If you don't know what it is, ask your wife. She'll probably have a few ideas.

But many dads let moms handle all spiritual concerns alone. You have your reasons for not getting involved. Perhaps you simply don't know what to do. Maybe you think that religion is not manly or that faith is too private a matter to share even with family. You may feel that somehow you have outgrown your need for the church, its laws restricting you and burdening you with guilt. A priest or other leader may have hurt you seriously and caused you to turn away. Maybe you're just plain angry with God over some tragic loss.

I know your reasons are big and run deep because they cause you to abdicate your fatherly duty to help your children learn to live as Christians. They may even be roadblocks in your own relationship with God. Don't you think it's time you did something about it?

I challenge you to take up your responsibility for your family's spiritual welfare. The place to start is a heart-to-heart talk with the Lord. He is patiently waiting to hear from you. Tell him exactly what's going on. He can handle anything you have to say and he'll do something to help you.

You can't afford to ignore this opportunity. The issue is significant—your kids' eternal success and happiness, your wife's, and your own. When you get right down to it, it's really a matter of life or death.

For Discussion
Why is it important for dads to pay attention to a child's religious formation?

For Reflection
Do I invest as much in my child's preparation for faith as I do in his or her preparation for successful living?

Family Friends for the Journey

Participation in Catholic family groups offers parents everyday wisdom and a supportive social environment for raising their kids in the faith.

Bert Ghezzi

My wife and I grew up amid the movements that surrounded Vatican II. At college we were both active in the liturgical movement. I made a Cursillo just before we were married. Mary Lou attended one shortly after. As newlyweds we participated in the Christian Family Movement at Notre Dame. And we have been involved in the charismatic renewal since its start. All these renewal groups have enriched our lives by helping us focus on Christ.

Involvement with Catholic movements has also strengthened our family. They linked us with other Catholic families whose love has brightened our days over thirty years. We could not have done without their support, nor they without ours. Thus, renewal movements helped Mary Lou and me realize that families are not supposed to go it alone. Families work well only when they are mutually interdependent. God arranged it that way. That's why he put us in his own family of families, the church.

Friendship with other Catholic families is supportive in many ways. But perhaps the most important thing it does is help us

A Pattern for a Catholic Family Group

Use this model "as is" for a local Catholic parents' group or adapt it to fit your circumstances:

- Meet for one and a half hours every two weeks for prayer, study and sharing.
- Invite participants to make a commitment to meet regularly.
- Have the group select material it wants to study.
- Use this sample meeting format:
  -prayer and Scripture (ten minutes)
  -discussion (twenty-five minutes)
  -family life review (twenty-five minutes)
  -closing prayer (five minutes)
  -social time (twenty-five minutes)
- During the family life review, have a parent or couple share on each of the following questions:
  -What is the Lord teaching me about raising my children Catholic?
  -What successes have I had in caring for my family in the past two weeks?
  -What main needs do I see in my family now?
  -What was my action plan for the past two weeks? Was it successful? What is my action plan for the next two weeks?
- Consider this pattern for closing prayer:
  -Each parent or couple states a need.
  -Individuals pray spontaneously, each for one need.
  -Close with the Lord's Prayer.
- Rotate leadership among the couples.
- Try the following schedule of three-month units:
  -September through November
  -December—family Christmas party
  -January through March
  -April through June
  -Summer—family events

Bert Ghezzi

raise our kids in the faith. Mary Lou and I learned this early from our experience with the Christian Family Movement (CFM). Twice a month we spent evenings with Bud and Mary, Jake and Judy, Don and Jackie and others. Together we prayed, studied Scripture and talked about our families. We put our heads together to figure out tough questions one of us faced. Back then we discussed helping a four-year-old who seemed unable to tell the truth. Now we might ask, "How do you deal with teens who held a drinking party when we were gone?"

Catholic family friends are a rich source of everyday wisdom. Equally important, they build a social environment that cultivates our children's faith. Our network of CFM families gathered for many events. We had picnics, birthday parties and baptism celebrations. Since we had a lot of kids, we spent a good deal of time together. We also worked at creating Catholic home lives. Our kids had many Catholic friends who did things just the way we did. That reduced their resistance to Catholic practices and customs. The children never asked, "Why do we have to go to mass?" because all of their pals were right there in the next pew.

Informal family groups have made the job of raising our kids Catholic easier for Mary Lou and me. They can do the same for you. Why not give serious consideration to joining a Catholic family group in your area? Call your parish or diocese office to see what's available. Or why not be gutsy and start your own Catholic family group?

Your Family—The Holy Spirit's Greenhouse

In our family relationships parents and children can acquire the behaviors that make us more like Christ.

Bert Ghezzi

Every summer my Aunt Minnie planted a big garden and enlisted me to help water and weed it. As soon as the ground defrosted in western Pennsylvania, she scattered seeds that would yield beans, lettuce, pumpkins and other vegetables. Later on as summer approached, Aunt Minnie put in her tomatoes, which were my favorite because they were the raw materials for the luscious marinara she served with her homemade ravioli.

To be successful in Pittsburgh's short growing season, tomatoes need a head start. So Aunt Minnie always went to the greenhouse at the nursery nearby and selected hearty seedlings, which she thrust in the ground with a little fertilizer and a lot of care.

The greenhouse had played an important role in preparing those tomato plants for their life's purpose, which included providing the fruit that would become the best spaghetti sauce this side of Naples. The glass walls and roof protected the little plants from the cold and let in the sunlight and kept in the warmth that they needed for growth. Gardeners cared for them, watering them daily and fertilizing them as they needed. The greenhouse gave those tomato plants good beginnings.

Our families are like that. They are the Holy Spirit's greenhouse for us and our children. Family living prepares our kids to fulfill their life's purpose of loving and serving the Lord and his people. With us the children get protection, nourishment for their bodies and souls, and instruction and practice in daily living. In our family relationships they start to acquire the fruit of the Holy Spirit, the behaviors that mark them as followers of Christ.

So our families are spiritual greenhouses that give our kids a good start on the Christian lives they must live in the world. They are also the place where parents continue their own Christian growth by developing the fruit of the Spirit to maturity. In our daily life together we learn love, joy, peace, patience, kindness, goodness, gentleness and self-control (see Galatians 5:22). These are the qualities the Holy Spirit produces in us as he transforms us in Christ's image.

Deciding to take a few deliberate steps to help all family members produce spiritual fruit is a proper goal. But choosing the right approach to cultivating the fruit of the Spirit requires understanding of what they are and how they work. The following four facts about the fruit of the Spirit will clear away some common misconceptions. They will lay the groundwork for your family's Christian growth, just as turning the soil prepared the little hillside plot for my Aunt Minnie's garden.

Fact #1: The fruit of the Spirit are not feelings. Many Christians misinterpret these Christian characteristics. For example, they may mistake attraction for love, pleasure for joy, calmness for peace, and so on. The fruit of the Spirit may involve feelings because they affect our whole being, but that's not what they are mainly about. They are primarily actions, not feelings. We define them and acquire them by what we do, not by how we feel. Sometimes, in fact, our behavior manifests spiritual fruit when we feel quite the opposite.

Once, for example, two of my sons were embroiled in an angry dispute. The younger one, with fists threatening, was ready to settle it with a fight. But the older one stood his ground and, with arms at his side, said, "Go ahead and hit me if you want to. But I am not going to fight with you." He wanted to work things out peaceably, and as a result they did not slug it out.

This is a down-home illustration of the fruit of the Spirit that we call "peace." Peace is not merely a calm feeling or even the cessation of hostilities, which are faint shadows of the reality. Peace is the maintenance and repair of unity in relationships. For example, Paul says that Christ made peace between Jewish and Gentile Christians by breaking down the wall that divided them and uniting them in his person (see Ephesians 2:14-15). My son's actions—his refusal to fight his brother and his insistence on settling things some other way—preserved the peace in our family. Had he followed his feelings there would have been a fight, for he did not feel very peaceful, but angry and afraid.

Fact #2: We do not receive the fruit of the Spirit passively, but acquire them actively. When we notice that we lack a certain Christian quality, we are inclined to pray for it. If we have persistent bouts with anger, we pray for patience. If we wrestle with pesky desires, we pray for self-control. Prayer is the right place to start, but if that's all we do, we'll never produce the spiritual fruit we are seeking.

The problem with this approach is that it does not go far enough. It stops short because it incorrectly assumes that the fruit of the Spirit are qualities that God pins on us like medals on a soldier's breast. But that's not how they work. We don't receive the fruit of the Spirit passively as direct dispensations of grace. We acquire them in the act of performing the behaviors that their names describe. We get patience, for example, by taking steps to control our anger. We get self-control by refusing to take orders from bad desires, and so on.

Fact #3: Each fruit of the Spirit is an antidote for an opposite evil behavior. When Paul first presented the fruit of the Spirit, he contrasted them to the "works of the flesh," evil deeds that are the fruit of self-indulgence (see Galatians 5:19-23). Each Christian mark is the obverse of a wicked one, like opposite sides of a coin. But the fruit of the Spirit are not only opposed to the works of the flesh, they are also antidotes for evil conduct. Love, for example, leaves no room for hatred; kindness is a gentle replacement for meanness; and peace defuses enmity, as it did for my sons when they worked things out without coming to blows.

Fact #4: We acquire the fruit of the Spirit mainly in our relationships. Anyone who has tried consistently to obey Christ's commandment that we love one another has discovered how difficult it is (see John 13:34-35; 15:12-13). Christ's kind of love goes against the grain of our natural tendencies to self-interest and sin. Without the help of the Holy Spirit, we just would not be able to love others selflessly. He makes it possible by disposing us to do the right thing in all of our relationships. When we follow his promptings and conduct ourselves in Christlike ways toward others, we produce the fruit of the Spirit.

Each of these Christian characteristics, even those which seem to be private, shapes the way we relate to others. Patience, for example, may restrain us from angrily lashing out against someone. Faithfulness may seal our determination to keep our commitments to a person who has been disloyal to us. Self-control, which may seem to be a purely personal, internal quality, affects others because it curbs conduct like greed and lust that can destroy relationships.

Because the fruit of the Spirit are behaviors that promote loving relationships, the family is the ideal place to learn them and put them into practice. Here are some steps parents can take to cultivate them in their "Holy Spirit greenhouse":

1. *Pray to the Holy Spirit.* The Holy Spirit dwells in us as a constant source of help for everyday living, and we all could rely on him a great deal more than we do. The whole family will benefit from frequently praying the "Come, Holy Spirit" together at prayer time. And Mom and Dad should invoke the Spirit's intervention in their care for their kids. Recently, for example, I have been asking him to temper my agitation with a strong-willed child, and while I still have miles to go, I have begun to relate to the child more calmly.

2. *Show and tell.* To foster growth of spiritual fruit in their children, parents must first develop it themselves. If we want our children to be generous, for example, we must become models of giving and hospitality. If we want them to be humble, we must show them how to serve others at the expense of their own interests. Parents must also tell their children the reasons for their Christlike behavior. Kids absorb a lot just by being with us. But to ensure their growth in the fruit of the Spirit, they need instruction from parents in basic Christian relationships.

3. *Turn occasions of sin into occasions for growth.* Families have daily opportunities to produce spiritual fruit. Our self-indulgence is rampant. Every day it occasions bad behaviors that require the antidotes of the fruit of the Spirit. Parents must begin with themselves, replacing their evil tendencies

with good actions. And when children do something wrong, parents should teach them the alternative good behavior. Then the next occasion of sin may become an occasion for Christian growth.

4. *Make love your aim.* Scripture says that love covers a multitude of sins, recognizing that human beings require love to heal the hurts that come from living in close relationships (see 1 Peter 4:8). Since each fruit of the Spirit applies love in a particular manner, the best way to cultivate them in our families is to heed Paul's admonition and make love the aim of everything we do (see 1 Corinthians 14:1). Then like the tomato plants in my aunt's garden, we and our children will produce fruit that will be a delight to all.

For Discussion

1. What makes family life a greenhouse for the fruit of the Spirit?
2. What can parents do to cultivate these qualities in their children?

For Reflection

1. Which fruit of the Spirit do I manifest most clearly? How can I help my children acquire it?
2. Which fruit of the Spirit do I most need to develop? What can I do to acquire it?

How Your Children Can Help You Grow in Christ

Your children can cause you to be frustrated, but they can also cause you to be holy.

Paul Thigpen

Dinner had just begun when my four-year-old smeared spaghetti sauce across his grinning face and called it "Indian war paint." I spoke sharply to him when I saw the mess, and soon after we left the table, I was feeling angry at myself for losing patience with him.

"Lord," I said with a sigh, "if you give me any more children, I may *never* get out of purgatory!"

When our kids push us to the limits, we may find ourselves looking wistfully at the local monastery. Wouldn't it be easier to grow in Christ if we didn't have to hassle with temper tantrums and sibling spats, rotten report cards and broken curfews?

According to the fathers of Vatican Council II, this is not the case at all. On the contrary, they insist, "Children contribute in their own way to making their parents holy." What a startling notion: We can strive for holiness, not *despite* our role as parents, but *through* our role as parents.

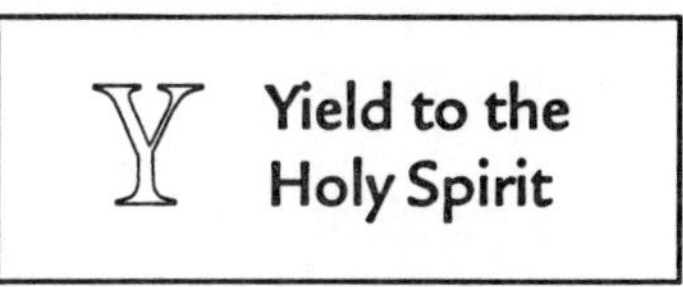

The key lies in recognizing that some of the best opportunities for spiritual growth emerge precisely at those places where we encounter the most difficult challenges of family life. So consider these tips for turning parenthood into a school for sainthood.

1. **Let your children's needs and shortcomings drive you to pray daily.** Get on your knees first thing every morning and ambush the little bandits with prayer before they even get out of bed. Take it *all* to God—not just the big problems. If, as Jesus said, the Lord has the hairs on their heads counted, then he's also concerned about your toddler's toilet training and your teen's crush on the kid with the purple spiked hair.

2. **Search the Scriptures and other sources of parenting help.** Meditate on Ephesians 5:21 to 6:4. Learn from the successes and mistakes of parents in the Bible: Read about Joseph and Mary's care for Jesus (see especially Matthew and Luke); David's conflict with his rebel son, Absalom (2 Samuel 13:1—19:1); Rebekah's deception (Genesis 27—33); and Eli's neglect of his sons' spiritual training (1 Samuel 2:12-17, 22-36; 4:12-18).

   Study the lives of saints who grew in Christ through their

role as parents. Begin with St. Rita of Cascia. She's called "the saint of the impossible." When you find out about her family life, you'll know why. Check out other parenting books by Catholic authors. Try a subscription to *Catholic Parent, The Family,* or another Christian magazine for moms and dads.

3. **Take seriously your children's questions about spiritual and moral issues.** My three-year-old-daughter once asked how Jesus could be both God and God's Son at the same time. My five-year-old son wanted to know why the Lord still lets the devil run free. When I have to answer such difficult queries, I end up growing in my own understanding.

4. **Latch on to a few other parents you can trust for support and advice.** Don't be embarrassed to talk and pray over your parenting problems with other Catholics who are strugglers like you. Look around. Whose children demonstrate the kind of attitudes and behavior you want your own kids to have? Ask their parents how they do it.

   Share your concerns with other members of an adult education class. Older couples with grown children can provide a healthy, long-term perspective. Parents with children the same age as yours may have recent experiences still fresh in their memory. Adults who know your children well may be able to help you see them in a different light.

5. **Gain parenting strength from the sacraments.** The grace we receive in the Eucharist fortifies us for the task of parenting, as it does for every other duty of life. Receive it as often as you can. Meanwhile, recognize that parenthood is one of God's secret strategies for driving us to the confessional. Go regularly to be cleansed of your parenting blunders and refreshed for the next round of challenges.

6. **Let your kids teach you some basics about the spiritual life.** Jesus said that unless we become like our children in

certain ways, we can't enter the kingdom of heaven (see Matthew 18:3). So become a student of your children. What can you learn from their example of simplicity—honesty, zeal, faith? Listen to their insights as well. You may be surprised by an occasional gem of wisdom.

7. **Learn to see the hassles of parenting as scouring pads**—they can either scrape you raw or scrub you clean. If you resent your children's needs, demands and shortcomings, they'll forever be rubbing you the wrong way. But if you embrace the frustration and heartache as part of God's plan to polish you into a saint, in time you'll find yourself shining in ways you've never shone before.

For Discussion
In what ways can children help parents become holy?

For Reflection
1. How have my children helped me grow closer to Christ?
2. Have I ever studied Scripture to learn more about raising my children in the faith?
3. What means do I mainly use to receive God's help for my parenting? Could I make good use of any other means?
4. What one thing could I do to foster my personal Christian growth?

Think, Pray & Act
Becoming Like Christ
When we let the Holy Spirit guide our parenting, we and our families bear good fruit—the fruit of the Spirit, that is, that form us in the likeness of Christ. We want our kids to become adult Catholics marked by qualities like love, joy and peace. So we must grow in Christ ourselves. Are you the kind of Catholic Christian you want your kids to be? How well do you cooperate with the grace of the Holy Spirit? Review the *For Discussion* and *For Reflection* questions at the end of each article. They will help

you evaluate your spiritual condition. They will also prompt action ideas that can foster your Christian growth. And don't forget to ask the Holy Spirit for his suggestions. You may want to use the *Action Idea List, Decision Grid* and *Action Plan* presented in chapter one.

Resources

Catholic Family Groups

- The Christian Family Movement, P.O. Box 272 Aces, IA 50010
- Couples for Christ, 15/F Strata 200 Bldg., Ortigas Center, Pasig, Metro-Manila, Philippines
- Teams of Our Lady, 14704 Pebblestone Drive, Silver Spring, MD 20905

Program

- Rainbows for All God's Children (708-310-1880) is a national support program for children in single parent families. Rainbows National Headquarters, 1111 Tower Road, Schaumburg, IL 60173

Publications

- *God's Word Today* (612-962-6725) is a daily Bible study magazine for Catholics.
- John and Therese Boucher, *Christian Marriage: Sacrament of Abiding Friendship* (Resurrection Press: 516-742-5686).
- Therese Boucher. *Spiritual Grandparenting: Bringing Our Grandchildren to God.* New York, NY: Crossroads, 1991.
- Bert Ghezzi, *50 Ways to Tap the Power of the Sacraments* (Our Sunday Visitor: 1-800-348-2440).
- Bert Ghezzi, *Keeping Your Kids Catholic* (Servant Book Express: 313-677-6490).
- Fr. Benedict Groeschel, C.F.R., *Heaven in Our Hands* (Servant Book Express: 313-677-6490).
- C. S. Lewis, *The Screwtape Letters* (Bantam Books: 312-827-1111).

- Henry Libersat, *Way, Truth and Life: Living With Jesus as Personal Savior* (St. Paul Books & Media: 1-800-876-4463).
- Patricia A. McCarthy, *Parent-S.H.A.R.E.* is a guide for parish-based parent support groups. (537 E. 11th, Casper, WY 82601).
- Susan Muto and Adrian Van Kaam, *Divine Guidance* (Servant Book Express: 313-677-6490).
- Pope John Paul II, *On the Family* (St. Paul Books & Media: 800-876-4463).
- William Rabior and Vicki Wells Bedard, *Handbook for Single Parents* (Liguori Publications: 800-325-9521, ext. 657).

The ABCs of Guiltless Catholic Parenting

How to raise kids Catholic without feeling bad about ourselves.

Bert Ghezzi

A **Always pray confidently.** We can expect the Lord to say *yes* to prayers for our family. He cannot say no to them. His nature is to have a family of sons and daughters. He cannot go against it. He wants our daughters and sons in his family even more than we do. Let's pray daily for our kids, expecting the Lord to intervene in their lives.

B **Be deliberate.** If we don't purposefully influence the way our children turn out, someone else will. Maybe Madonna or Howard Stern, for example. So let's be determined to do a few important things in our family that will have a lasting effect on our children's character.

C **Care for one another.** Wives and husbands should make their own relationship a priority. We should treat each other with kindness, generosity and mutual respect. Our unity lays a foundation of love in the family. It is the cornerstone of all our parenting.

D **Discern good and evil.** We and our families are immersed in a worldly culture. It swirls with many values that are hostile to ours. We must participate in our society wisely, embracing the good and avoiding the evil. And we must teach our kids to do the same.

E **Express affection and forgiveness.** A family that expresses affection and forgiveness becomes resilient. It can rebound from problems and repair brokenness. When a family regularly says, "I love you," "Please forgive me," and "You're forgiven," it can withstand any hurricane or tornado that life sends.

F **Form children fully in the Catholic faith.** We are religious educators by marriage. The church assigns us parents the primary responsibility to raise our kids Catholic. It also gives us plenty of support. But to give our kids a thorough introduction to Catholic doctrine and practice, we must use all available means and seize every opportunity.

G **Get help from friends.** The Lord doesn't want us to raise our kids Catholic all by ourselves. He has given us a local Christian community to collaborate with us and support our efforts. We should become friends with members of our parish. And our kids with their kids, too.

H **Have only a few rules.** We should only set boundaries to guide kids' behavior in areas that are important to us. If we try to control them with many rules, we'll crush them. Or drive them away.

I **Introduce children to God in a personal way.** Our kids need to meet God as a person who loves them. Otherwise he will remain a distant authority figure or an abstract idea. To make the introduction of our kids to the Lord, we first have to get well acquainted with him ourselves.

J **Just do a few important things.** The responsibility of raising our kids Catholic can weigh heavily on us. But to do a good job we only need to do a few significant things consistently. We can work on them one at a time until each is in place.

K **Keep talking with your kids.** Conversations are the main means of communicating faith to our children. Talking with them makes truths explicit and real. It gives the reasons for our behavior. And listening—the other half of conversation—lets us meet our kids right where they are.

L **Laugh a lot.** Family life is full of surprises and unexpected inconveniences. So parents must cultivate a sense of humor. When the gallon of milk spills as you were about to leave for work—laugh. Humor is an expression of joy, a fruit of the Spirit and a boulevard to holiness.

M **Meet regularly to talk about your family.** Moms and dads should take time regularly to discuss family care. Even five minutes a week helps keep family life on track, clarifies expectations and dispels confusion. Single parents also need to review their family life with another single parent or a friend.

N **Never compromise on morality.** Parents must uphold high moral standards and enforce them strictly. We cannot prevent children from committing sins. But when they do, our sanctions will teach them the seriousness of offending God and others.

O **Orient your life on God.** The church gives us saints to demonstrate that ordinary people can live extraordinary lives by putting God first. We do this by subordinating everything in our lives to the Lord—family, work, recreation, service, school, friends, whatever. The ideal of loving God above all will appeal to the natural longing he has placed in our kids.

P **Permit yourself to start over.** Parents are going to make some mistakes and have some false starts. Things may not go the way we planned, circumstances may block our efforts, change may throw things into confusion. But no one is keeping score of our "failures" except us. So when things don't go right, let's give ourselves permission to start again or to do something different.

Q **Quit feeling guilty.** Our kids must make their own faith choices. We cannot choose God and the church for them. That's the way the Lord set it up. He created human beings with wills so that they could freely decide to love him. A parent's role is to point the children in the right direction. We can lead our kids to the water of life, but we cannot *make* them drink.

R **Reach out to others in service.** When Jesus walked the earth he ministered to people through his physical body. Now he ministers through us in the church, the body of Christ. Our families are units in that body. Our call is to use our resources and gifts to serve people. The best way to teach our kids about Christian love is to involve them in some kind of service to others.

S **Show *and* tell kids how to live as Catholics.** We tell our kids everything they need to be successful in their daily lives. Why don't we tell them what they need to be successful in their eternal life? We may feel our good example is enough. But actions do not speak louder than words. More than anything else, our kids need to hear us tell in our own words what the Catholic faith means to us.

T **Take time for family prayer.** A regular family prayer time brings many benefits. Talking with God acknowledges his presence in our home. It shows our children that God is a person who loves them. It engages the Holy Spirit in family life. Prayer time is also a chance for parents to talk to the children about the Lord and the church. And it's the way kids learn to pray.

U **Use the sacraments as a source of strength.** The sacraments bring the Holy Spirit into our daily lives. That means that God himself has made himself our partner for life. So we should participate in the sacraments with awareness and faith. We meet the Lord there and he strengthens us for our days.

V **Value vocations and encourage them.** We should be open to a child's choosing a religious vocation. Sometimes our view of success shuts out this possibility. But the Lord may be inviting one of our kids to be a priest, a sister or a brother. Or to serve him in some other dedicated way. We should encourage our children to consider such service.

W **Witness to your experience of God.** If parents never speak of their experience of God and the church, children can easily mistake the parents' religious behavior as empty formalism. Our kids need to know how we came to meet the living God. That will prepare the way for their entering a personal relationship with him, too. So let's keep talking to our kids about our divine relationship.

X **Explore the truths of the faith.** Study is one of the essential means of Christian growth. God made us to know him, and he has revealed truths about himself as our path to that divine knowledge. We are not looking only for head knowledge, but for life-changing truths. We study not only for our own growth, but to be better prepared to pass on the faith to our children.

Y **Yield to the Holy Spirit.** There are two ways for parents to care for their families. We can try to keep everything under control. This is a willpower approach. It taxes our energy and our nerves. Worse, it hardly ever works. The other way is reliance on the Holy Spirit. Yielding to the Spirit means doing what we can, but prayerfully depending on the Holy Spirit to produce the right outcome. We parents raise the sails. Then we let the breezes of the Spirit fill them and move things ahead.

Of course, there is no **Z** because we don't know everything there is to know about raising our kids Catholic. But let's pool our wisdom and help each other do a better job.

The Best Gift of All

Signs of hope and splashes of humor help defuse the guilt from Catholic parenting.

Bert Ghezzi

Our Christmas Eve party is our family's favorite celebration. Older children come home to Winter Park from their jobs and schools in other parts of Florida. We dress up, eat fancy foods, play Taboo, exchange gifts and head off to midnight mass. Affection flows among the kids, Mary Lou and me. It's a magical time, and it delights me most of all.

At that event several years ago, our second son, Paul, gave

Mary Lou and me a gift we'll never forget. Remembering it has been a source of hope and peace.

On that Christmas Eve, Paul, then age twenty-two, drove home from Tallahassee. He was just finishing his first term as a junior at Florida State University. Paul is our most carefree son. (In an impatient moment I once told him he was as laid-back as a fly on a barroom floor.) But that night his behavior was out of character. His intense interest in moving things ahead caught my attention. He even did something he had never done before. He volunteered to wash the dishes. That cinched it. Something was up.

A little background will help you appreciate the significance of Paul's gift. He was the first child to challenge me, and I didn't like it one bit. At age twelve his strong will began to collide with mine. His teenage declarations of independence infuriated me. I responded by upping the ante. I was constantly on his back. I got after him for his lackadaisical attitude and underachieving behavior. I was critical of his dress, his manners, his room. Everything. For a long time I seethed with anger towards him. When it inevitably exploded, Paul used to say that "Dad blew a hairy."

Gradually I learned to back off some, but our relationship was difficult throughout his teens. My demeanor provoked Paul to take stands I did not like. He was especially resistant to efforts to involve him in church activities. In all, he did not seem to like some things about our family life. But Mary Lou and I always let him know that we loved him. We prayed, too, for my relationship with him to improve.

Now back to that memorable Christmas Eve. When the festivities were over and everything cleaned up, Mary Lou and I retired to our bedroom. There was the surprise Paul could hardly wait for us to find. On a small table covered with an elegant burgundy cloth he had set two long-stemmed, fluted glasses. In the center, on ice in a silver bucket, sat a bottle of Dom Perignon champagne.

I choked up as I read Paul's note. And sometimes when I

think about it I still do. He wrote that having seen all the brokenness in other families, he had really come to appreciate ours. He said the wine expressed his love for us and his thanks for all we had done to make our family happy.

What better gift could a mom and dad ask for than a grown child's appreciation?

I saved the empty Dom Perignon bottle. Now it stands as the centerpiece in our china closet. From my place at the table, I can see it over the heads of my current teens. It's a little beacon of hope for Mary Lou and me. It sparks encouragement in us as we face new challenges with other children.

My story has this footnote. Late that January Paul called me from school. The new term had been in session two weeks, he said, and he did not have enough money to buy his books. He wondered if I could help him out. As I wrote the check for $110, I said to Mary Lou, "You know, I think we are paying for a bottle of Dom Perignon."

But it was worth it.

Copyright Acknowledgements

The editor and publisher wish to express their gratitude to the following for permission to reproduce or adapt material of which they are the authors, publishers, or copyright holders.

Many of Bert Ghezzi's articles originally appeared in *Catholic Parent* or *The Catholic Transcript*. He is a regular columnist in both publications. They are reprinted with the author's permission.

ONE / "What Do Catholic Kids Need?" *Catholic Digest* (Aug 1992), ©1992, Ron Keller; reprinted with the author's permission.

TWO / "The Family That Dines Together, Binds Together," *Catholic Parent* (Jan/Feb 1995), ©1995, Paul Thigpen; reprinted with the author's permission; "The Fish Story," *The Family* (Jan 1994), ©1994, Mary Bahr Fritts; reprinted with the author's permission; "Is Your Home Teenager Friendly?" *Catholic Parent* (Sep/Oct 1993), ©1993, Neta Jackson; reprinted with the author's permission; "25 Ways to Strengthen Family Ties," adapted from "31 Ways to Strengthen Family Ties," *St. Anthony Messenger* (July 1992), ©1992, Patricia L. Fry; reprinted with the author's permission.

FOUR / "Six Reasons to Cultivate Family Customs," *Catholic Parent* (Nov/Dec 1993), ©1993, Paul Thigpen; reprinted with the author's permission; "How to Encourage Vocations," adapted from "No Greater Love," *Catholic Parent* (Jan/Feb 1995), ©1995, Fr. Edward Buelt; reprinted with the author's permission.

SIX / "Teaching Your Kids," from *Bringing Christ's Presence into Your Home* (Nashville: Thomas Nelson), ©1992, Keith Fournier; reprinted with the author's permission.

SEVEN / "Discipline Without Feeling Guilty," from "Why Discipline?" *The Family* (Jan 1994), ©1994, Raymond N. Guarendi; reprinted with the author's permission.

EIGHT / "Must We Rock Around the Clock?" adapted from "Is Your Home Built on Rock?" *The Family* (Apr 1993), ©1993, Angela Elwell Hunt; reprinted with the author's permission; "'C' Is for Chastity (Not Condoms)" is adapted from the pamphlet, "Mixed Messages," ©1994, Molly Kelly; reprinted with the permission of the author; "The Parent-to-Parent Covenant," from "Parent Peer Pressure: Help Needed," *Momentum* (Feb/Mar 1993) ©1993, Sr. Ann Regan; reprinted with the author's permission; "Ending the Tyranny of too Much TV," *Catholic Parent* (Jul/Aug 1993), ©1993, Michael Medved; reprinted with the author's permission.

NINE / "Love—No Matter What," from "What Can Parents Do to Help Hard-to-Reach Kids?" *Catholic Parent* (Jan/Feb 1994), © 1994, Bert Ghezzi and Meg Raul; reprinted with the authors' permission; "Family Nonconformists," *U.S. Catholic* (July 1993), ©1993, Dolores Curran; reprinted with the author's permission; "Welcoming a Homosexual Child" and "Keep St. Monica Busy," adapted from "Finding Peace in a Troubled Family," *The Family* (Nov 1994), ©1994, Fr. Benedict Groeschel, C.F.R.; reprinted with the author's permission; "When You Love an Alcoholic," adapted in *Catholic Digest* (Dec 1991) from *Catholic Update* (Sep 1991), ©1991, Sr.Thérèse Del Genio, S.N.D.; reprinted with the author's permission.

RAISING KIDS CATHOLIC WORKSHOPS

Presented by Bert Ghezzi

- ***The Keeping Your Kids Catholic Workshop*** gives people a vision and an easy-to-apply strategy for introducing Catholic truths and practices in the home.

- ***Tapping the Power of the Sacraments*** is a workshop that teaches parents practical ways to help every family member apply sacramental graces in their lives.

- ***Help and Hope for Catholic Families*** is a workshop for diocesan and parish leaders, teachers and interested parents. It focuses on how to equip parents to assume confidently their role in passing on the faith to their children.

Each workshop provides a vision and practical approaches for raising Catholic families. Participants are led to select and to plan the implementation of actions that are both important and easy to accomplish.

Participants enjoy talks, small group discussions, personal reflections, questions and answers, role plays, activities, action plans, worship and fellowship.

For more information write to: